i

Building a Brand That Matters:

*Helping Colleges and Universities Capitalize on
the Four Essential Elements of a Block-Buster Brand*

Robert A. Sevier, Ph.D.

Strategy Publishing

■ ■ ■ ■ ■

Other Books by Bob Sevier

From Strategy Publishing

Thinking Outside the Box: Some (fairly) Radical Thoughts on How Colleges and Universities Should Think, Act, and Communicate in a Very Busy Marketplace - 2001. See final page of this book for more information.

From CASE Books

Strategic Planning for Colleges and Universities: Theory and Practice - 2000.

Integrated Marketing Communication: A Practical Guide to Developing Comprehensive Communication Strategies (co-edited with Bob Johnson) - 1999.

Integrated Marketing for Colleges, Universities, and Schools: A Step-by-Step Planning Guide - 1998.

■ ■ ■ ■ ■

How to Order

To order one or more copies of *Building a Brand that Matters* <u>or</u> *Thinking Outside the Box*, please contact us through our Web site: www.strategypublishing.com or write, Strategy Publishing, P.O. Box 186, Hiawatha, Iowa 52233.

Acknowledgements

I would like to thank a number of people for their help with this book and for the contributions they have made to my thinking about branding and marketing. First, the many clients I worked with during the year it took me to write this. They often served as initial sounding boards for new ideas and new ways to present old ideas. Their insights and generous spirits are appreciated.

Second, my colleagues at Stamats. In the day-to-day rush of just getting things done, I sometimes forget how fortunate I am to work at one of the best higher education consulting companies in the country. The people I work with are pros. They care deeply about the work they do for our clients and I am fortunate to count many of them as friends. In particular, I think of Guy Wendler, Peter S. Stamats, Bill Stamats, Dick Damrow, Marcy Bader, and Pat Odegard. Of course, I can't forget Suzanne Schloss, Toni LeVasseur, and the woman who keeps me pointed in the right direction; my extremely able (and patient) administrative assistant, Jenny Olson. There are others: Jeremy Crawford for keeping my computer working and keeping me connected. I am thankful for his professionalism and good humor; Becky Morehouse for being a trusted colleague, but more importantly, for being a good friend; Eric Sickler for telling me to relax; and Lorna Whalen, who always believes it can be better.

While dozens of non-Stamats colleagues helped me with this book, three in particular deserve special recognition: Mike Norris, Tom Torello, and Martha Harris. Writing the three case studies was one of my favorite parts of this project and as I interviewed these people and reviewed the materials they provided, I was amazed at their accomplishments. I was thrilled by Mike's work at Centre, totally captivated by Tom's work at RPI, and inspired by Martha's work at the University of Southern California. I am heartened by their stories.

Finally, I would like to thank my wife and son. Pat is my best friend and my wisest advisor. I am thankful that she is also my wife. And then there is Andy. When I wrote my first book he was 12 and thoughts of college were far away. Now he is 16, and thoughts of college are nearly every day. He's my walking, talking focus group and his insights are extraordinarily helpful. Plus, he's just a good kid and we are so proud of him.

■ ■ ■ ■ ■

Forward

Ours *is* a world of brands. They are everywhere. But behind the simple graphic swoosh of Nike or the script of Coca-Cola, lies the most important part of an enduring brand: the valued promise it makes to its most important target audiences.

It is this aspect of branding—the brand as a promise—that I find so fascinating.

I have long wanted to write a book on branding, but I have never been particularly interested in an orientation toward branding that focused on the 3 Ls: look, letterhead, and logo. Somehow, in the grand scheme of things, the graphic elements of a brand seemed relatively inconsequential.

I knew there had to be more to branding than a well-executed logo and I began to get a glimmer of the possibilities of branding when I read the works of such branding pioneers as Aaker, Frankel, Ries and Ries, and Trout. The more I read, and the more I talked to colleagues and clients, the more things began to coalesce around the central tenant of a successful brand: the promise that it makes.

It stands to reason that a successful brand promise has many outcomes. One is the creation of brand equity. Another is the improvement of your competitive position. A third is the possibility of both qualitative and numeric growth. Finally, a successful brand promise differentiates you from your competitors in ways that matter.

While these outcomes are all worthwhile and achievable, there is one other brand outcome that is perhaps even more important: a successful brand promise captures the heart of your institution even as it meets the heartfelt needs of your target audiences.

It is this part of branding—the creation of a brand promise that prospective students will pay for, donors will support, and faculty and staff will live out—that is so important. It is this part of branding that fires imaginations and broadens horizons. It is this part of branding that is daunting on the one hand and daring on the other. It is this kind of branding that is alive, and that gives an organization life.

If you are interested in this kind of branding, then read on. I think you will enjoy what these pages have to offer.

Bob Sevier

Cedar Rapids, Iowa
July 5th, 2002

■■■■■

Table of Contents

Table of Contents - *continued*

■ ■ ■ ■ ■

Test Your Branding IQ[1]

Have a handle on branding? Then take a few minutes to complete this branding IQ test. If you answer eight or more of the following questions correctly, then you've got it nailed.

1. The best definition of a good brand is:
    a. An easily identifiable logo
    b. A great tagline
    c. Being perceived as the only solution to a problem someone has
    d. Why your college is the best in its class

2. A brand is focused around:
    a. Your logo
    b. Your look
    c. Your mission
    d. A valued promise you make to your target audiences

3. Your brand strategy should be led by:
    a. The people in your bookstore
    b. Your president
    c. Your athletic department
    d. Your graphic design department

4. Branding and advertising are:
    a. Synonyms
    b. Antonyms
    c. Distant but related cousins
    d. Two different approaches to the same problem

5. Branding is:
    a. 100 percent emotional
    b. 100 percent irrational
    c. 50 percent rational and 50 percent emotional
    d. 100 percent rational

6. The truest test of a brand is:
    a. People remember it
    b. People like it
    c. People seek it out, will support it, and will pay more for it
    d. None of the above

7. The value of a brand is proven when:
    a. Your endowment takes a downturn
    b. The marketplace becomes even more competitive
    c. You decide to open a branch campus
    d. All of the above

8. A brand must appear:
    a. On your letterhead
    b. On your Web site
    c. On your printed material
    d. In every aspect of your institution

9. Branding is:
    a. A fad that will likely pass
    b. Long-term and enduring
    c. Something you only do in a crisis
    d. Something that will go away as the Web becomes the dominant marketing tool

10. The creation of an effective brand:
    a. Is tactical, chances are your public relations office can handle it
    b. Is tactical, if your public relations office can't handle it then you should hire a good consultant
    c. Is strategic, it begins with your mission and is proven in the marketplace
    d. Is strategic, it begins with the quality of your academic programming

The answers can be found in **Appendix A.**

■ ■ ■ ■ ■

Section One
It's All About Brands

In today's marketplace there is little that your competitors–be they colleges or corporations–cannot duplicate in a matter of weeks or months.

If you have a great idea for a new program, a great new facility, or a successful marketing initiative, you can be certain that somebody will begin to copy it the moment it becomes public. Not only will your competitors follow your lead, but some may also be able to do a better job.

The question then becomes, "What competitive edge do I have that cannot be copied by anyone else?"

The answer? Your brand.

■■■■■

Chapter 1
The Idea of Branding[2]

"I didn't even think of going there."

In a nutshell, this statement from a prospective student summarizes the importance of branding.

If students (or donors or media reps) don't know you–and don't know what you are all about–you will not be included in their choice set.

In their minds, you are not a brand. Either you are totally unknown, or you are a commodity.

If you are a commodity, your target audiences will differentiate you from other commodities on two variables: price and convenience.

Instead of Sunkist, a trusted brand able to charge a higher price, you are, as someone once said, just another orange.

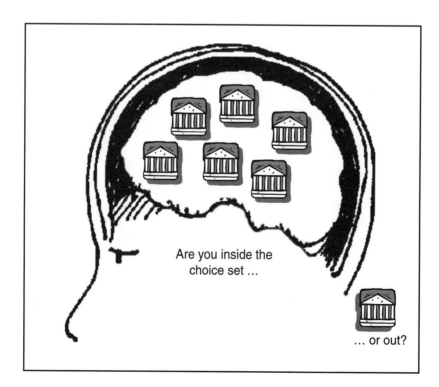

Are you inside the choice set ...

... or out?

Our infatuation with brands

We are infatuated with brands.

We don't buy tennis shoes. We buy Nikes.

We don't buy jeans. We buy Old Navy or Levis or Tommy.

We don't buy computers. We buy iMacs. Or Dell.

And we don't go to (or give to) colleges. We go to Samford. Or Beloit. Or Harvey Mudd.

We seldom buy a thing. Instead, we buy a name and all the associations that go with that name. In other words, we buy a brand.

Still not convinced? Let's take a look at some anecdotes that might help highlight the importance of branding.

3,600 colleges and universities

There are 3,600 two- and four-year colleges in the United States. Even as a member of the academy, how many can you name? How many can your prospective students name? Or prospective donors? Can they name yours? Will they?

Among this list, there are:

- More than 35 schools with "central" as part of their name (and that's just in the United States)
- More than 25 schools with "northwestern" as part of their name
- Nine Concordias
- Three Xaviers
- Four Loyolas
- Fifteen schools with "Mary" as part of their name

Having trouble keeping them straight? So does your marketplace.

Like a needle in a haystack

Students of talent … or means … will be recruited by hundreds and hundreds of colleges and universities. They will receive thousands of letters, publications, telephone calls, and e-mails.

In this avalanche of messages, did they even notice your search piece? And if they did, did they respond?

The average family in America is contacted by mail and telephone more than 300 times a year to give money to organizations, causes, and events.

Did they notice your annual fund brochure … or telephone call? Did they respond?

An emerging typology

For years we have relied on the Carnegie typology for the classification of colleges and universities. Of late, however, another typology has emerged that seems to be slightly more market-oriented. This new typology, developed by William Massey of Stanford University, organizes colleges and universities into three broad categories:

- **Convenience institutions.** Highly user-friendly, focused on job-minded students, more likely to be adult; both for-profit and not-for-profit institutions operated like a business. This group is comprised of such institutions as the University of Phoenix, Yakima Valley Community College, and Motorola University.
- **Mass providers.** Mix of traditional and professional degrees, more part-time students, slightly more selective and more status than convenience institutions. This group includes such institutions as Bradley University and the University of Portland.
- **Brand-name.** Selective, high status, affluent; cater to traditional full-time students who have traditional academic values. Duke and Kenyon are members of this group.

The Chivas Regal effect

One of the more interesting marketing trends of late is the number of colleges and universities that seek to heighten prestige with the understanding that families will pay more to attend a school that is more well known and highly regarded. Bruce Hammond, writing in *Discounts and Deals at the Nation's 360 Best Colleges: The Parent Soup Financial Aid and College Guide*, calls this the *Chivas Regal effect*.

Hammond, and others who consciously or unconsciously subscribe to this theory, believe that well-known institutions are able to charge more, in part, because they are more well-known. Interestingly, in a sort of upward spiral, they subscribe to the belief that if you charge more, you will become better known, and if you are better known you must be worth more.

Winner-take-all

In a past issue of *studentpoll*, Richard Hesel mentioned *The Winner-Take-All Society*, by economists Philip J. Cook and Robert H. Frank. In a chapter on college choice, the authors postulate that students and their parents are increasingly inclined to choose colleges that society identifies as "winners," those with high status and affirmed prestige. Cook and Frank define the decision as a "positional choice" and that this association with a winning institution positions the student and family as winners.

"Such behavior," the economists argue, "almost pervasively characterizes American culture, from the decisions people make about careers to the growing disparities between the salaries paid to ordinary performers and superstars in professional sports, business, and even the academy. And it explains our society's increasing obsession with rankings that identify winning institutions, whether they be hospitals and universities or five-star restaurants and hotels."

The idea of reputational capital

In 1996, Charles Fombrun, in *Reputation: Realizing Value from the Corporate Image*, introduced the notion of *reputational capital*–a form of intangible wealth that is closely related to what accountants call "good will" and marketers term "brand equity." He noted that a college or university with a large stock of reputational capital actually gains a competitive advantage against rivals because its reputation enables it to charge premium prices for its products.

Fombrun goes on to say that "questions of reputation are of particular concern to knowledge-based institutions like … universities because their most valuable assets–the services they provide–are largely intangible. Economists call the services of these groups 'credence goods'–goods that are bought on faith, that is to say, on reputation."

Yale is Yale

A number of years ago I had a conversation with a student interested in attending Yale. As you might know, Yale is located in a sometimes tough city–New Haven. The student, and her parents, were very much aware of Yale's location. When asked if they were concerned about the city, they said, "yes." But they also said while it was a concern, it wouldn't affect their final decision because, they said, "Yale is Yale." In other words, the brand that is Yale–that of a top-flight academic institution–is more important to this student and these parents than other, perhaps negative, variables.

Cost-benefit analyses

People seldom make decisions in a vacuum. Rather, they weigh perceived benefits against perceived costs. The relationship between costs and benefits is something we call value. Let's look at how this relationship between costs and benefits affects how we make decisions. People, including students, add up the perceived dollar and non-dollar costs of doing something, then add up the perceived benefits. If the costs outweigh the benefits, they don't choose it because they believe they <u>are not</u> getting a good deal. But if the benefits outweigh the costs, they choose it because they believe they <u>are</u> getting a good deal. When students say, "You cost too much," what they are sometimes saying is that you are not worth the cost–the value isn't there; they do not perceive enough benefits for the costs they must incur.

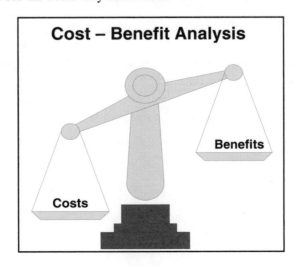

7

Donors also understand the relationship between costs and benefits. When they decide not to donate, it is seldom simply a dollar concern. More likely, they are concerned about non-dollar issues; about being identified with a particular campaign or institution, about a drain on their time, or about being inconvenienced. However, if the benefit of donating is significantly large, the cost/benefit scale will swing in favor of a donation because perspective donors will find value in their relationship with the institution.

Study after study indicates that having a "reputation" for something is one of the most powerful of all benefits and can have an incredible effect on the cost/benefit balance. Reputation is a benefit that affirms a decision to oneself and to one's peers. It is a benefit that makes a promise. And it is a benefit that, by your association with it, enhances your personal marketability; it even helps build your personal brand.

Hopefully by now you have begun to get a sense of just how important branding is and how valuable a strong brand can be.

A borrowed conversation[3]

I was working on this manuscript while waiting for a flight at O'Hare. A young man noticed me marking up some copy and asked, "What are you working on?"

I replied, "A book on branding."

"I'm not into brands," he said. "I think brands are superficial.

"Oh," I responded, "aren't those Nikes you're wearing?"

"Yes," he said, "but I wear them for the fit, not the label."

"I understand," I replied, "Nikes are good shoes. But what about that shirt? Isn't it a Tommy?"

"I didn't buy it because it was a Tommy," he said, "I bought it because it made me feel good. I buy things because of how they make me feel."

I pointed to his garment bag. "Isn't that a Tumi?"

"Yes," he said, "it is. But I didn't buy it because it was a Tumi. It does a great job protecting my clothes."

As we sat, the young man pulled out a CD-player. It was a Sony. He checked his messages on a Sprint cell phone and updated his appointments on his Palm VII.

He said he wasn't into brands. But his actions told a different story.

■■■■

Chapter 2
What Is a Brand?

Before we go too much further, we need to ask and answer an important question: what is a brand?

Let's begin with a little history. As you may know, the term *brand* once referred to what a rancher did to his cattle. To keep his cattle from being confused with other cattle on the range, the rancher would sear a cow's hide with red-hot irons that left distinctive marks, or brands.

It is from this use–and definition–of branding that we get a host of branding derivatives including:

- Names
- Marks and trademarks
- Symbols
- Looks
- Icons

Like brands from the old West, the purpose of today's "mark" is to identify goods and services with their owner or producer, and most importantly, distinguish these goods and services from others in the marketplace.[4]

Of course, this still very popular definition of branding focuses almost exclusively on a brand's visual interpretation–look and logo–in the marketplace. While this is an important part of branding, it is not the whole of branding and it does not even begin to touch what branding has to offer.

A little broader understanding of branding

Al Ries and Laura Ries, in *The 22 Immutable Laws of Branding: How to Build a Product or Service into a World-Class Brand,* reached an important conclusion about brands. They remind us that more than a look, a brand is a trustmark, a warrant, a promise. This idea of *promise* is critical to the understanding of brands and branding, and we will return to this idea again and again throughout this book.

Alan Bergstrom, president of the Brand Consultancy, notes that to be successful, a brand must consistently provide quality and satisfaction; it must meaningfully distinguish itself from the competition to create customer preference; it must be relevant; and it must appeal to individual lifestyles, attitudes, and beliefs.[5]

Daryl Travis, writing in *Emotional Branding*, suggests that the heart of branding can be found by asking this question: how does the product or service make you feel? He goes on, "...the most powerful brands engender powerful emotions. They go way beyond the confines of their own product dimensions. They create their own mind space. They give you not just a physical product or service, but an experience that engages your imagination."

Are we getting closer? Let's take a final run at it.

Travis notes that your brand exists at the intersection between your core institutional strengths–what you do well– and what customers value and are willing to pay for.

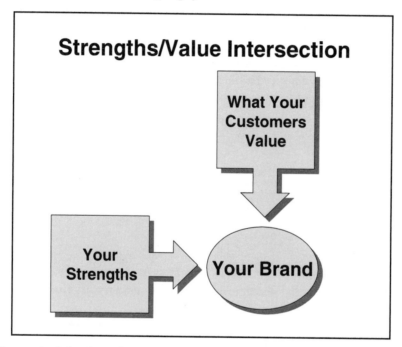

Strengths/Value Intersection

What Your Customers Value

Your Strengths

Your Brand

Finally, Rob Frankel remarked that branding is not about getting your targets to choose you over your competition. Rather, branding is about getting your prospects to see you as the only solution to their problem.[6]

─────────────**Sidebar**─────────────

A bit more from Frankel

Frankel goes on to write about branding in the fourth dimension. He says that branding in the First Dimension tells people who you are. Branding in the Second Dimension tells people what you do. Branding's Third Dimension communicates how you do what you do. Finally, he says, we get to the Fourth Dimension. He says that this Fourth Dimension is his favorite because it is where "the gravitational pull of market forces stretch and shape your brand, producing a relevance your prospects find intriguing. It can be a quality claim. A product attribute. But whatever you choose, it has to be memorable, compelling and powerful enough to grab your prospects by the lapels, lift them off the floor and tell them they'd be complete dolts for choosing anyone other than you for whatever it is you're selling."

Branding and marketing

Finally, I want to briefly explore the all-important relationship between branding and marketing. Al Ries and Laura Ries, writing in *The 22 Immutable Laws of Branding*, mention that the purpose of marketing is to build a brand in the mind of a prospect. Understanding that marketing has a significant relationship to the larger goal of creating a strong brand helps clarify the relationship between the two.

The two essential elements of an effective brand

Before we go on, I want to present a new way of looking at brands that will help serve as a guidepost for the upcoming discussion.

To be successful, I believe that brands must have two critical components: awareness and relevance.

First, there is the <u>awareness</u> component. In other words, among the 3,000 or so other messages they will receive this day, did your audience members notice yours? Did your message stand out from the background clutter? Did your target audience sense that it was important, and did they know how and when to respond?

Second, there is the <u>relevance</u> component. After the message was noticed, did members of your audience begin to sense how the message–and you–might begin to fill a need they had? Was the message relevant to them? Did it build on previous messages? Did it lay the groundwork for future messages? Did it help create a relationship?

These two ingredients, awareness and relevance, are essential components of an effective brand. If people are not aware of your brand, you will never have a chance to be relevant. This is much like the great academic program that no one ever hears about. The quality may be there, but if the marketplace is not aware of it, the quality is for naught.

At the same time, if the brand is noticed, but the relevance is not there, the target audience will respond with, "so what?" Maybe your target audience notices your program in geology but they are interested in English literature. They were aware of your program, but it was not relevant to them.

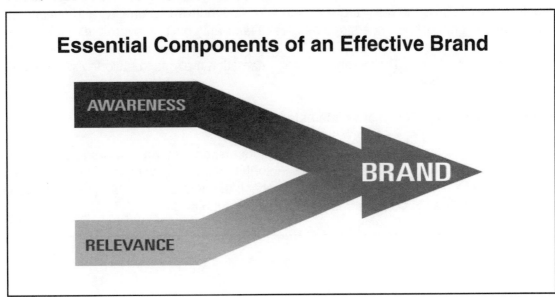

Essential Components of an Effective Brand

AWARENESS

BRAND

RELEVANCE

Who's on first?

If you think about it for a minute, effective brands must successfully accommodate two different perspectives. From the institutional perspective, a branding strategy must first seek to create relevance and then build awareness. However, from a marketplace perspective, the branding strategy must first focus on creating awareness in the minds of your target audience and then establishing relevance.

──────────Sidebar──────────
The idea of trust

Central to the idea of a successful brand is the notion of establishing and sustaining trust. Interestingly, the more blurred our society becomes, the more important trust is to people. In 2000, David Maister and a couple of colleagues noticed this phenomenon and wrote *The Trusted Advisor,* a masterful work on how consultants can establish close, even trustworthy, relationships with their clients. What is particularly interesting is how Maister's formula for creating trusting relationships can apply directly to branding. He calls his formula the *trust equation* and it works like this:

$$T = \frac{C + R + I}{S}$$

Where:

      T = Trust
      C = Credibility
      R = Reliability
      I = Intimacy
      S = Self-orientation

To bring the trust equation to life we need to understand the following:

- **Credibility** is content expertise and presence (how we look, act, react, and talk about our content). Credibility depends not only on our experience, but also on the experience of the person doing the perceiving.
- **Reliability** is about whether customers (students and donors) think you are dependable and can be trusted to behave in consistent ways. Reliability links words and deeds, intention and action. Reliability is the repeated experience of links between promises and action.
- **Intimacy** might best be understood as careful familiarity built up over time.
- **Self-orientation** is the degree to which we appear to be more interested in ourselves than in the client or customer. The greater the self-orientation the <u>less</u> trustworthy we will appear in the eyes of the client.

So what does this mean for those of us interested in branding?

If we consistently make promises of interest to our students, donors, and others (credibility), deliver on these promises (reliability) and establish a meaningful relationship with our key audiences over time (intimacy), and keep our own self interests in check as much as possible (self-orientation), then we have come a long way to building trust, and a successful brand.

────────────────────────

Personal involvement with brands

In *Strategic Marketing for Educational Institutions*, Philip Kotler and Karen Fox note that people often develop a high level of personal involvement with their favorite brands. While Kotler and Fox cite a handful of "laws" to support this conclusion, two are particularly relevant to our conversation. They are:

- The cost to carry out the buy decision involves major personal or economic sacrifices
- There's considerable group pressure to make a particular choice or to act in a particular way, and the customer is strongly motivated to meet the expectations of these peer and reference groups

This personal involvement with brands is borne out in the graphic presented below. As you can see, brands become personal after a number of critical stages are achieved. First, beginning at the bottom of the pyramid, there is awareness. At this point the customer says, "I am aware of the brand." Then there is preference. And then loyalty. And finally, there is a sharing of goals at which point the customer notes that his or her goals are consistent with the goals of the brand.

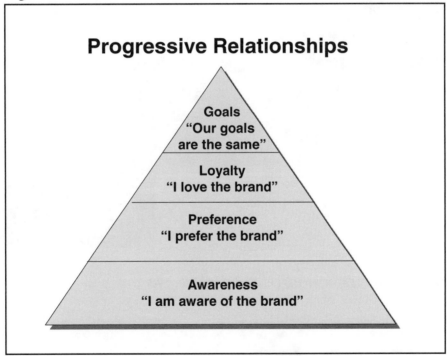

In a presentation on branding, Curtis Cichowski, Associate Dean for Administration for Valparaiso University School of Law, offers these four examples, drawn from companies with which we are all familiar, of how brands can become personal:

- Starbucks is not in the business of selling coffee, they are in the business of developing a "third place"– a place of refuge from both the home and the office
- The Ritz does not rent rooms, it provides an experience that "enlivens the senses, instills well being, and fulfills even the unexpressed wishes and needs of our guests"
- What Harley-Davidson sells is the ability for a 43-year-old accountant to dress in black leather, ride through small towns, and have the townspeople fear him

- Intel Inside is a monster brand. Customers lust for the product even though they can't, and probably never will, see it and have no basis to compare it to competing products. It even trumps the brand on the computer

Of course, you should be asking yourself this question: can colleges and universities achieve the same high level of "personalness" as Harley Davidson and Starbucks? I think they can. Consider:

- The almost pathological devotion that Texas A&M students ... and alumni ... have for their institution
- The life-changing qualities of the personal relationship that students have with Berea
- Or consider the incredible emotional energy that is recognized by the trio of bumper stickers presented below:

Not marketplaces, but minds, hearts, ... and pocketbooks

By now you should begin to sense that brands do not exist in marketplaces, but in the minds of your target audiences.

We call this *positioning*. A critical part of branding, then, is owning a position in the minds of prospective students, donors, and other key target audiences.

Scott Bedbury, of Nike and Starbucks fame, recently wrote *A New Brand World* in which he noted that a brand is not a product, it is not something you drive, and it is not something you drink. He says, "These are all products. A brand is the sum total of everything an organization does–the good, the bad and even the off strategy–that creates a large context or an identity in the customer's mind. As a result, brands are visceral. They reside in people's hearts and heads."

Essential qualities of good brands

Before we move on, I want to spend just a little more time with Rob Frankel. It was Frankel, you will remember, who described a brand as the only alternative to a problem that a customer has.

Frankel's forthright common sense is again evident when he describes the six characteristics of good brands. From his perspective, and in his words, a good brand:[7]

- **Delivers the message clearly.** I don't know if it's our university system, but someone out there is teaching people that if you use enough syllables, you'll eventually impress–or bore–your audience enough to the point that they really won't care about what you're saying. Alternatively, our politically correct culture dictates that taking a stand on just about anything guarantees that somebody, somewhere will take offense to it, spawning an entire industry that specializes in saying nothing with as many words as possible.

  The best brands go against the cultural grain and make clear, concise statements. You don't have to be a creative genius to make these kinds of statements, either. Having contempt for lawyers certainly helps. But in any event, simply stating something clearly in a society weaned on weak generalities is the first step toward creating a solid brand.

- **Communicates quickly.** In the age of the quick cut music video, where scenes seldom last more than a fraction of a second, an entire generation has grown up believing that if they don't dig it in a second, it's time to change the channel. This has never been truer than it is on the Web, where your home page does it all. If your brand doesn't get them the second after they've hit you, they're back to the search engine's listing of everyone else in your category–and you're dust.

- **Projects credibility.** Sometimes it seems that everyone's been trying to sell me something since the day I was born. I don't mind that so much, except that somewhere along the way, their claims, language and promises became so ridiculously inflated that they actually mutated from non-believable to laughable.

- **Strikes an emotional chord.** No matter where I travel or who I meet, the reaction is always the same: everyone concentrates on technology products–everything but the people who do the purchasing. Even on the Web, programmers push pounds of technology across the wires, promoting its efficiency, all the while forgetting that technology ain't doing the buying. The technology is there for one reason: to put people in touch with other people.

- **Motivates the respondent.** A Big Time Brand will motivate the respondent to cross the psychological barrier that sometimes separates desire from action. A Big Time Brand not only presents itself as the solution, but it draws in customers, as well.

- **Creates a strong user loyalty.** Out of all of them, this is the one for which branding is most widely known. Yet it's just as misunderstood as the rest because it's almost always wrongly attributed to any number of causes. The very best brands are a mix of rational differentiation and compelling personality; two powerful ingredients that cause end users to invest their emotions–along with their wallets– into your brand.

All of which brings us to Frankel's *Third Law of Branding*:

Advertising grabs their minds. Branding gets their hearts.

Frankel concludes, "First you create the brand, then you raise the awareness of the brand. As you can see, doing it the other way around makes absolutely no sense at all, yet that's exactly what most of mainstream America does every day of the year. Bad news for them. Good news for you."

Sidebar
A long-look at the history of branding

We learn from the BrandConsulting Web page that the first known use of branding dates back to the ancient Egyptians where craftsman placed a unique mark on bricks they produced to identify the authenticity of their products. This usage came to signify product quality and origin. There are also documented accounts of trademarks appearing on Greek and Roman lamps, Chinese porcelain, and marks being used in India as early as 1300 B.C.

Branding was applied extensively throughout the Middle Ages when guildsmen signified the unique qualities of their products by stamping them with a special name. This became necessary as the population grew and more than one blacksmith, mason, shoemaker, or carpenter began to live and work in the same community.

Encarta offers a somewhat more brutal definition of branding as the searing of flesh with a hot iron to produce a scar with an easily recognizable pattern for identification or other purposes. Branding was once used on human beings, but the practice is now limited to identifying animals. Branding today is often done with chemicals, tattooing, paint, tagging, or ear-notching.

The practice of branding horses and cattle was brought to North America in the 16th century by the Spanish conqueror Hernán Cortés. Used at first as proof of ownership, branding is done to keep records on quality. In most cattle states, registration of brands is required by law, and altering a brand is a criminal offense.

Integrated marketing, integrated marketing communications, and branding

Five years ago, I wrote a book on integrated marketing for colleges, universities, and schools. At that time, I defined integrated marketing as a listening-first, database-dependent, approach to marketing that includes a willingness to segment and coordinate such strategic assets as product, price, and place, and to develop effective promotion strategies for key target audiences.

Of course, the 4 Ps have been augmented by the 4 Cs. Instead of product, we have customer. Instead of price, we have cost. Instead of place, we have convenience. And instead of promotion, we have communication.

Integrated marketing communications, as we know, is a subset of integrated marketing. It focuses more completely on the promotion and communication aspects of integrated marketing and is defined as a comprehensive, coordinated, institution-wide effort to communicate mission-critical values and messages in ways that target audiences notice, understand, and respond to. IMC stresses data-driven segmentation, message integration, and evaluation.

To help clarify a couple of key issues, we need to take this definition of integrated marketing communications a bit further. As you can see from the diagram below, integrated marketing communications actually comprises three distinct elements: brand marketing, direct marketing, and customer relationship management. As we have been discussing, brand marketing is all about creating awareness in the minds of your most important audiences. Direct marketing, on the other hand, is about initiating action. Customer relationship management is all about building loyalty by providing exceptional service.

If I might use an analogy, brand marketing is Ford telling people that "Quality Is Job One!" Direct marketing is all about selling a Taurus. The third element, customer relationship marketing, is asking the customer, "Based on your experience with the Taurus, can I interest you in a Lincoln?"

Ideally, any discussion of branding and brand marketing must also include a discussion of direct marketing and even customer relationship management because these three undertakings are so closely related.

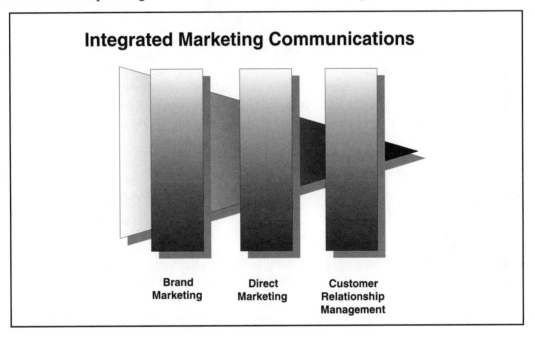

Integrated Marketing Communications

Brand Marketing Direct Marketing Customer Relationship Management

From interruption marketing to permission marketing

Perhaps one of the most important outcomes of a successful branding strategy that builds a strong personal relationship with its target audiences is the movement away from interruption marketing to permission marketing. Notes Seth Godin in *Permission Marketing*, with interruption marketing, you literally butt your way into the minds of your target audience. You send message after message. Your strategy is inundation rather than segmentation. And because you are not relevant, your only option is *more*. More messages. More ads. More direct mail. Witness, for example, the college in Pennsylvania that sends out 220,000 search pieces for a freshman class of 500. They had to spend so much more on their direct marketing strategy because their brand was ineffectual.

With permission marketing, however, you have done the research, segmented the audiences, refined the offer, and used careful messaging to build a relationship over time. You have become a partner. Colleges and universities that field an aggressive array of summer camps and educational experiences for middle schoolers, for example, are well on their way to becoming first-choice institutions for this same group of students a few years down the road.

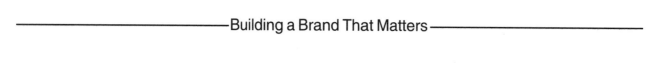

Branding Bullet

Branding in the marketplace is similar to branding on a cattle ranch. The purpose of a branding program is to differentiate your cow from the other cattle on the range.

With interruption marketing you are rebuffed, scorned, or ignored. With permission marketing you are invited in.

Let me illustrate the possibilities of permission marketing with the amazing story of scottslawn.com.

Scottslawn.com

My romance with Scotts Lawn began when I discovered that my lawn had grubs. I have to tell you that the idea of those little buggers chewing the roots off my sod drove me to distraction. At least it did until I discovered scottslawn.com. Scottslawn.com is perhaps the coolest Web site on the planet. Here's why. When you log on to Scottslawn.com, it asks you for your zip code. It then uses your zip code as a geographical reference point to calculate what you need to apply to your lawn … and when. And to top it off, it sends you little e-mails when its time to spray this or cultivate that.

One fall, I received the e-mail I had been waiting for and dutifully went to my local Scotts dealer to load up on Grub-Ex (even the name sounds powerful). I then spent one very satisfying Saturday, fully garbed in my Haz-Mat suit, waging war on my grubs with the full confidence I was being guided by the world's experts on lawns–the folks at Scotts.

Scotts may not have realized it, but they were practicing permission marketing. They had built a relationship with me over a period of time. And because their products–and accompanying advice–worked so well, I trusted them. I gave them a little info about me (my zip code and e-mail address) and they used that information to help me solve a problem. In other words, I gave them permission to enter into a relationship with me.

I have given similar permission to Amazon.com.

And alibris.com. And Nordstrom. And Specialized.

Interestingly, I have only given my permission to companies that want to sell me something because I completely understand their motivation. I know they are in business to make money. And they understand that if they keep me happy and don't betray my trust, they will keep me coming back again and again.

Can colleges and universities practice permission marketing? Absolutely.

Must colleges and universities practice permission marketing? Without a doubt.

(Some of the) 22 immutable laws of branding

In 1998, Al Ries and his daughter, Laura, wrote *The 22 Immutable Laws of Branding*. Some of my favorite "laws" are presented below:

- **The Law of the Word.** A brand should strive to own a word in the mind of the customer. When you think of engineering, what school do you think of?

- **The Law of Quality.** Quality is important, but brands are not built by quality alone. You must be known for quality. And remember, the definition of quality resides in the minds of your target audience, not just you.

- **The Law of Consistency.** A brand is not built overnight. Success is measured in decades, not years.

- **The Law of Contraction.** A brand becomes stronger when you narrow its focus.

- **The Law of Change.** Brands can be changed, but only infrequently and only very carefully.

What great brands do

Merging some comments and insights from Scott Bedbury and Alan Bergstrom, we discover that great brands accomplish a number of very important things. We know for example, that:

- **Great brands are in it for the long haul.** In an age of accelerating product (and service) proliferation, enormous customer choice, and growing clutter and clamor in the marketplace, a great brand is a necessity, not a luxury.

- **A great brand knows itself.** Anyone who wants to build a great brand must first understand who they are. The real starting point is to go out to customers and find out what they like or dislike about the brand and what they associate as the very core of the brand concept. Now that's a fairly conventional formula–and it does have a risk; if you follow that approach all the way, you'll end up with a narrowly focused brand. To keep a brand alive over the long haul, to keep it vital, you've got to do something new, something unexpected. It has to be related to the brand's core position. But every once in a while you have to strike out in a new direction, surprise the buyer, add a new dimension to the brand, and reenergize it.

  Of course, the other side of the coin is true as well: a great brand that knows itself also uses that knowledge to decide what <u>not</u> to do.

- **A great brand invents or reinvents an entire category.** The common ground that you find among brands like Disney, Apple, Nike, and Starbucks is that these companies made it an explicit goal to be the protagonists for each of their entire categories. Disney is the protagonist for family entertainment and family values. Not Touchstone Pictures, but Disney. Apple wasn't just a protagonist for the computer revolution. Apple was a protagonist for the individual; anyone could be more productive, informed, and contemporary.

- **Brands have a personality and a style, and are expressed through emotional attributes.** The common ground among companies that have built great brands is not just performance. They recognize that customers live in an emotional world. Emotions drive most, if not all, of our decisions. A brand reaches out with that kind of powerful connecting experience. It's an emotional connection point that transcends the product. And transcending the product is the brand.

- **A great brand is a story that's never completely told. The brand and the story are timeless.** A brand is a metaphorical story that's evolving all the time. This connects with something very deep–a fundamental human appreciation of mythology. People have always needed to make sense of things at a higher level. We all want to think that we're a piece of something bigger than ourselves. Companies that manifest that sensibility in their employees and consumers invoke something very powerful.

- **A great brand is relevant.** Brands are about meaningful and valued relationships with customers. They convey strong images and expectations. A lot of brands are trying to position themselves as "cool." More often than not, brands that try to be cool will fail. They're trying to find a way to throw off the right cues–they know the current vernacular, they know the current music. But very quickly they find themselves in trouble. It's dangerous if your only goal is to be cool. There's not enough there to sustain a brand.

- **Brands are experienced by customers through many different encounters.** Each represents an opportunity to influence and shape the overall brand image.

- **Brands are everybody's business.** They can be the glue that ties the organization together toward a common identity and purpose.

- **Brands rarely succeed when they try to be everything to everyone**. Focus is everything.

————————Branding Bullet————————
The stronger your brand, the less you will spend to
recruit students and raise dollars.

Can every college be "branded?"

So the question becomes, then, if we can brand bananas, can we brand colleges? The answer to that question is "yes." The key is setting the proper context for your brand and executing your brand strategy.

David Hoover, Senior Director of University Marketing Communications at The Ohio State University, makes this point succinctly when he notes that OSU's uniqueness can come only from the "whole" rather than the individual parts. He goes on, "We must define all of our attributes, that can, in combination, serve to distinguish us. For example, at Ohio State, none of our core attributes (large size, academic excellence, diversity, located in a capital city, Midwestern values, football strength, high admission standards, land-grant heritage, etc.) are that distinctive on their own, but in combination, we are finding that we can define a university that is different from all others."

Why it's sometimes so difficult to build strong brands

David Aaker notes that it is not always easy to build a brand in today's environment. The brand builder who attempts to develop a strong brand is like a golfer playing on a course with heavy roughs, deep sand traps, sharp doglegs, and vast water barriers. It is difficult to score well in such conditions. In the same manner, the brand builder can be inhibited by substantial pressures and barriers, both internal and external. Some of the pressures that hinder brand development include:

- Pressure to compete on price
- Proliferation of competitors
- Fragmenting markets and media
- Complex brand strategies and relationships
- Bias toward changing strategies
- Bias against innovation
- Pressure to invest elsewhere
- Short-term pressures

Of these eight pressures, seven have direct impact on higher education. **First, pressure to compete on price**. Few colleges or universities in the U.S. are comfortable with the tags of either "most expensive" or "least expensive." Rather, there is ongoing pressure to be positioned as the value alternative in the particular cohort. Amid discussions of financial aid and tuition discounting, most colleges would prefer to have a price position in the top of the middle third of their cohort.

Second, the proliferation of competitors. There are 3,600 colleges and universities in the United States. There are another 7,000 technical schools. And there are thousands of proprietary schools. And these are just the bricks. There are also hundreds of clicks jockeying for your students.

Third, complex brand strategies. The push to segmentation–the breaking of large populations into smaller homogenous subsets–makes establishing a brand across the universe very difficult. In addition, colleges and universities that have undergraduate programs, foundations, graduate schools, continuing education, athletic teams, and even the odd hospital or performing arts center often spend a great deal of time sniping at each other about who owns what look.

Fourth, bias toward changing strategies. If senior administrators think your brand is just your look, then you will constantly be under pressure to change it. Miss a class? Time for a new logo. Have a new president? Time for a new logo? Interested in marketing? Time for a new logo.

Fifth, bias against innovation. Fat and happy is a dangerous market position. Unfortunately, many colleges believe things are OK because they meet their class each fall. What they failed to realize is that while enrollment may be up, tuition revenue is often down. There are also other market forces nipping at their heels: unparalleled competition for residential students. Competition for donated dollars. The Net. Aging faculty and aging facilities.

Sixth, pressure to invest elsewhere. Dollars are tight and if you pit the need to manage your brand against the need to remodel your science program, you will likely opt for Bunsen burners and beakers.

And finally, short-term pressures. A desire for short-term results can undermine long-term investments in brands. American businesses have long emphasized short-term revenue profits at the expense of long-term investments and there is little reason to believe that our colleges and universities think any more strategically. The pressure to get this class or land that gift can sometimes distract us from strategic branding.

Two myths of branding

In the September 20, 1999, issue of *Brandweek*, Agnieszka M. Winkler presented a number of myths about branding. Two of the myths discussed by Winkler are especially appropriate for higher education.

Myth 1: A brand is built over a long time

Says Winkler, "It is written in stone that it takes a long time, years in fact, to establish a brand in the national psyche. I've even included this truth in lectures to business schools around the country. What kind of time? Ivory Soap is 125 years old; Tide, 50; Crest, 40. Apple is only a little more than 20 years old, a mere child in the brand sandbox, but it certainly has developed a fanatical following. The important thing, however, is that Steve Jobs and company accomplished that feat within Apple's first few years, when they introduced the Macintosh computer in 1984. America Online, with awareness in American households as high as 80 percent, and Yahoo! are still very young companies, strong as they already are, and their brands were built in a handful of years. Then, of course, there are Amazon.com, and the Palm computer, both of which became sensations almost overnight.

"With the advent of new communications technologies, it is now possible to spread the word, like a village drumbeat, to all corners of the world in months, weeks, or even days. The drumbeat is often carried by the users themselves—a more believable source of information in our jaded, skeptical society."

Myth 2: Advertising is the major creator of a brand

P&G, Colgate, GM, Ford, and Chrysler spent vast amounts on advertising because it was the key way to assure brand contact with their customer.

Today, advertising dollars are not as important as they used to be. In fact, significant brands have been built with no advertising dollars at all. Amazon.com became a household word in the rapidly growing world of Internet users without spending a penny in traditional media, as did Netscape and Yahoo! They relied on word of mouth, on creating buzz in the market, and on the opinions of influential market gurus and analysts. They paid significant sums to link to sites on the Web, and they paid for banners. Perhaps most importantly, they relied on the actual experience of customers who tried their product or service, and became loyal, repeat customers.

Note: As illustrations for this point, take a quick look at the USC and Centre branding case studies on pages 123 and 150, respectively.

Some reasonable benefits of branding

Before we move on to talk about brand identity in the next chapter, I want to spend just a minute highlighting some benefits that the well-branded college or university might accrue. Based on both empirical and anecdotal evidence, it is reasonable to expect that the well-branded institution can count on:

- Messages that cut through the clutter of the marketplace
- An ability to charge—and have students pay—more for their products and services, thereby increasing cash flow and reducing dependence on tuition discounting
- An ability to attract and retain better faculty and administrators
- Higher retention rates
- Greater loyalty among stakeholders
- A higher level of alumni satisfaction that translates into alumni participation in alumni events, audiences, and relationship-building
- Greater success raising money

Interested in these outcomes? Then consider the creation of a comprehensive branding strategy.

■ ■ ■ ■

Chapter 3
Brand as Identity — Brand as Position

In this chapter we will explore two important aspects of branding. First, brand identity. And second, brand as position.

Brand identity

A brand, like a person, has a personality. It projects qualities, characteristics, and associations that differentiate it from others. According to Curtis Cichowski, brand identity includes the emotional benefits people associate with your brand as well as its attributes, personality, and symbols. Further, says Cichowski, institutions with a strong brand identity carry a halo of positive assumptions that build trust and confidence and lead us to positive outcomes.

Consider the brand identity for UNLV. What teenager, for instance, could resist the tagline, "Be a Rebel"?

Consider the brand identity of Harvard; the almost royal crimson that permeates so many aspects of the campus, the Harvard Yard, the highly symbolic yet wholly historic "H."

Or consider the Razorback, that pugnacious, aggressive, and ever-ready-for-a-fight mascot for the University of Arkansas. Their athletic Web site, for example, is an inspired hogwired.com.

The symbols, emotions, culture, and personalities that make up your brand identity are an extremely important part of a successful brand.

Two elements of brand identity

For our discussion, we will focus on two key components of a brand identity:

- Brand image
- Brand loyalty

Brand image

Brand image describes the desire of students, donors, and others to use brands as signs of status and success. An excellent example is the well-displayed college bumper sticker. When my older brother went to Stanford, my dad immediately applied a Stanford bumper sticker to the back of our '65 Chevy wagon.

A year later, when my sister went to a public college, no bumper sticker was applied.

Brand image has another dimension: licensed apparel. Licensed apparel is big business in the United States. In fact, total sales of licensed college apparel for 2001 approached half a billion dollars. Of course, some schools sell much more licensed apparel than others. Take a look at the list below and see if you can figure out why these schools—the 10 colleges and universities that sell more branded college apparel than any others—sell so much?

- Notre Dame
- Michigan
- North Carolina
- Kentucky
- Tennessee
- Penn State
- Nebraska
- Florida
- Florida State
- Alabama

Figure it out? It's the allure of big time college sports, especially football.

—————Branding Bullet—————
One of the most important elements of a successful brand is a consistent look, sound, and feel.

Conveying brand image

As you can see from the diagram on the following page, brand image is conveyed through a number of channels. The key is to create synergy among all these different media so the brand image is consistent and coordinated.

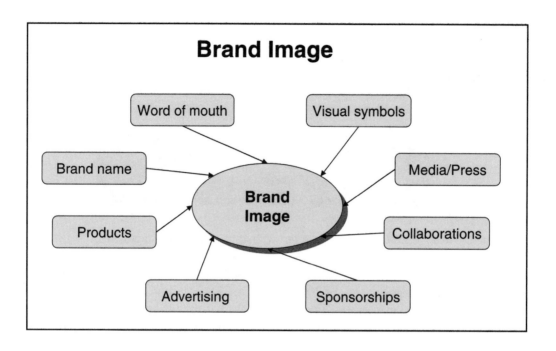

Measuring brand image

A cohesive brand image is actually comprised of a number of different components. Because of this, the "sum is greater than the parts" aspect of brand image, evaluating your image can be a very complex undertaking that might involve measuring such qualities and characteristics as:

- **Awareness.** Strength of presence in the target audience's mind including top of mind, unaided recall, aided recognition
- **Familiarity.** Recognition gained from past exposure; determining how much customers feel they know about the brand
- **Favorability.** Overall affinity for the brand; how well they like the brand
- **Image perceptions.** Association of product and image dimensions. For example, good value, academic reputation, quality of education, convenient location, safety, etc.
- **Personality perceptions.** Association of personality characteristics with brand. For example, friendly, innovative, smart, energetic, sophisticated, traditional, etc.

Brand loyalty

Now that we have a basic understanding of brand image, let's take a look at the second component of brand identity, **brand loyalty.** Brand loyalty means the degree to which people seek out and even take comfort in your brand amidst all the other brands that are in the marketplace. Brand loyalty is also concerned with how often a customer returns to a single brand again and again, and how well a person supports the brand over their lifetime.

The alum who insists that his daughter or son attends the University of Southern California is evidencing brand loyalty.

The young woman who earns a B.A. and later a M.S. from Yale is showing brand loyalty.

The newly minted graduate who strives to contribute to the annual fund even as she balances a new job with paying off her student loans is showing brand loyalty.

The older donor who gives to three successive capital campaigns is also showing brand loyalty.

The importance of the familiar

A couple of years ago I completed a consulting project for the University of the West Indies in Trinidad. One evening I went to a local market for something to drink. Amidst all the unfamiliar labels was the red and white Coke logo. Confronted with all the unfamiliar messages and brands, I went for something I knew; something I could trust.

I am no different than prospective students or donors in my affection for the familiar. When prospective students are contacted by hundreds and hundreds of schools, which envelopes do they open? To which e-mails do they respond? Chances are high they open the envelopes and e-mails from those schools with whom they are already familiar, the brand-name institutions.

The sometimes high cost of loyalty

Brand loyalty is especially impressive when being loyal comes at a cost to the individual. In some cases, that brand loyalty is as simple, and important, as continued financial support in a down market.

One emotionally-charged example of brand loyalty is evidenced by John Comstock, a student from Texas A&M. What makes Comstock's brand loyalty so impressive is that he was one of the students injured in the bonfire collapse three years ago. Some 12 Aggies died in that accident. Comstock was partially paralyzed and lost his left leg below the knee. Not only does Comstock believe that the bonfire tradition should be retained, but he wants to light the next fire.

—————————————**Sidebar**—————————————
Five branding cues

Creating brand image and brand identity depend, in part, on the establishment of five sensory cues in the mind and heart of the target audience.[9] These five include:

- **Tangibles.** The appearance of your physical facilities and printed materials; quality of your equipment, landscaping, the whole idea of "first impressions."
- **Reliability.** Do you perform as promised? Do you live up to expectations? And when things go wrong, do you fix them quickly?
- **Responsiveness.** Are you willing to help? Are you courteous? Are you convenient? Are you reasonable?
- **Competence.** Are your employees knowledgeable? Do they know what they are doing? And do they do it in a timely and accurate fashion?
- **Empathy.** Are your employees, and your institution, caring?

Your ability to field a consistent brand promise rests in no small part on your ability to manage these five sensory cues. ————————————————————————————

Brand identity traps

As we think about the importance of brand identity, we need to be aware of three potential brand traps. First outlined by Aaker in *Building Strong Brands*, these traps represent approaches to creating an identity that can have unintended consequences. The three brand identity traps are:

- Brand image trap
- The external perspective trap
- The product attribute fixation trap

The brand image trap

The brand image trap occurs when the entire branding effort focuses almost exclusively on the tactical side of branding; on the creation of a consistent image. In the brand image trap, the patience, resources, or expertise to go beyond the brand image are lacking, and the brand image becomes the entire brand identity. There is no promise; no desire to meet or exceed the needs of your target audience. In other words, the brand is all flash and no substance.

Colleges and universities that are stuck in the brand image trap spend a great deal of time, effort, and money on logos and looks. They have, as we will talk about later, a brand management and not a brand leadership orientation.

The external perspective trap

The external perspective trap occurs when a college or university fails to realize the role that a brand identity can play in helping it understand its basic values and purpose. Because an effective identity is based in part on a disciplined effort to specify the strengths, values, and vision of the brand, it can provide a vehicle to communicate to faculty, staff, and administrators what the brand is about. It is hard to expect internal audiences to make a vision happen if they do not understand and buy into that vision.

The product-attribute fixation trap

The most common brand identity trap–and the trap that applies to most colleges and universities–is the product-attribute fixation trap. In this trap, the strategic and tactical management of the brand is focused solely on product attributes; in our case, curriculum and programs.

Because this trap is based on the sometimes erroneous assumption that product attributes are the major college choice variables, the product-attribute fixation trap usually leads to less optimal brand strategies and sometimes to damaging blunders.

Limitations of product-attribute-based identities

David Aaker presents some insights into why product-attribute-based identities are problematic. Because these traps are so common in higher education, I want to quote from his *Strong Brands* at length. I will also add some commentary to help clarify their importance for colleges and universities. These traps include:

- **Fail to differentiate.** A product attribute can be extremely important to customers, but if all brands are perceived to be adequate on this dimension, it does not differentiate the brand.

  For example, if you offer the same basic classes as your competitors and teach them in the same basic fashion, then you will likely not be able to differentiate yourself from your competitors on this dimension.

- **Are easy to copy.** Attribute-oriented benefits are relatively easy to copy. A brand that relies only on the superior performance of a key attribute will eventually get beaten on that attribute because the attribute is a fixed target for competitors. In the words of Regis McKenna, writing in *Real Time: Preparing for the Age of the Never Satisfied Customer,* you will eventually get "out-spec'd."

  Most recently, colleges and universities seem to be spending a disproportionate amount of time … and money … on wellness centers. The rationale for building many of these complexes has a certain "we need to keep up with the Joneses" quality to it.

- **The rational customer.** The rational customer model suggests that customers collect information about product attributes, adjust the information to reflect the relative importance of the attributes, and then make a reasoned judgment.

  The fact is, however, that many customers are quite schizophrenic in their decision-making. They experience mistrust, confusion, brand distemper, or impatience. In addition, many customers do not care as much about function as they do about style, status, reassurance, and other less functional benefits.

  Earlier we talked about the emotional aspects of branding. We have all experienced emotional responses to a brand that are not rational and might even be considered irrational.

- **Reduce strategic flexibility.** Finally, product-attribute associations reduce a brand's ability to respond to changing markets. If a brand becomes associated with a single product attribute, the ability of that brand to adjust when the attribute's relevance declines is inhibited. If you are known for "what happens in the classroom" you may find your future in question as more and more students seek out an education that includes a Web-based delivery option.

  If you are known as a commuter institution, the decision to build dorms with an eye toward increasing your residential population may prove challenging.

Now that we have a more complete understanding of brand identity, it's time to discuss brand as position.

Brand as position

Yours is a very competitive marketplace. You compete for every student you recruit. You compete for their time. You compete for their abilities. And you compete for the dollars they may bring to your institution. But before any of this can happen, you must successfully compete for a position in their minds. In fact, the ultimate goal of branding is to own a position inside the mind of your target audience.

Let's imagine, for a minute, what's going on inside the mind of a prospective student as she decides which college to attend. Like the rest of us, our student categorizes and labels the world around her. She has begun to organize colleges into groups. Maybe some of her groups include:

- Big school
- Party school
- Prestigious school
- Liberal arts
- Rural school
- Tough school
- Easy school
- Friendly school
- Engineering school
- Safe school

As she moves through the selection process, four things occur. First, she decides that some positions are more important than others. Maybe she begins to focus on schools that have a reputation for a specific major. Or maybe she is interested in an urban campus.

Second, she begins to merge categories that are important to her. Instead of "big" and "safe" as separate categories, she might create a new position, "big safe schools," or perhaps "Christian liberal arts colleges."

Third, she will give more attention to colleges and universities that hold "top of mind" positions, institutions with which she is already familiar (or thought she was) prior to beginning the college choice process.

And finally, she begins to prioritize schools within categories. Which is the biggest and safest, which has the best engineering program, which is the toughest? Generally, but not always, one or two schools assume dominant positions in each category. Other schools are relegated to a lesser status.

Our young woman is positioning colleges and universities in her mind. And later, when it comes time to choose a college, she will evaluate these positions again. She will compare schools with one another. And finally, she will act. She will choose the school that occupies the dominant position in the categories she deems most important.

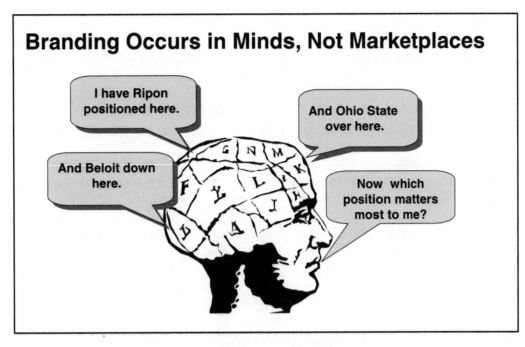

Branding Bullet
Mindshare matters most.

But what does this mean?

Is the above depiction overly simplified? Certainly. But it clearly illustrates two important concepts.

First, your success depends on your ability to create mindshare because without mindshare, you will never have marketshare. If you are not in their mind–if they don't recognize you as the solution to a problem that they have–they will never be in your classes or in your residence halls.

The second concept is equally important. To survive, much less flourish, you need to know a great deal more about your target audiences and your marketplace. In today's marketing environment, you cannot make tactical, must less strategic, marketing decisions without knowing:

- What positions your target audiences value most
- What position you hold in the minds of students
- What positions your competition hold in the minds of students

Synonyms

As you might suspect, branding and positioning are closely related. In fact, in some respects they are wholly identical. The essence of both can be understood by answering this question: when people hear your name, what do they think? They might respond with "liberal arts college" or "jobs." These are the positions that you own in the mind of that person. However, if they respond with "what?" or "where?", then you don't own any position; you are not top of mind.

It's all in the mind

Perry Forster, a friend and branding expert, pulled together some definitions of positioning from different sources:

- Kotler in *Marketing Management*: The act of designing the company's product/service and marketing mix to fit a given place in the consumer's mind.

- Trout and Ries in *Positioning: The Battle for Your Mind*: Positioning starts with a product/service, but positioning is not what you do to a product/service. Positioning is what you do the mind of the prospect. That is, you position the product in the mind of the prospect.

- Peter and Olson in *Consumer Behavior*: The key objective of positioning is to form a particular brand image in consumers' minds.

- Berkowitz, Kerwin and Rudelius in *Marketing: Positioning* refers to the place an offering occupies in consumer's minds on important attributes relative to competing offerings.

And the common denominator in all these definitions: positioning occurs in minds, not marketplaces

Finding out the benefits and attributes that matter most

Typically, colleges and universities describe themselves from their perspective and focus on telling students, donors, and others what they want them to know. However, successful branding requires that you determine which of your benefits and attributes students, donors, and other target audiences value most. In other words, you begin building your brand by focusing on your audiences, not yourself.

As simple as it sounds, the best way to find out what audiences value is to ask them. Called promise testing or benefit testing, this literally involves asking prospective target audiences, "What matters most?" For example, we recently asked prospective engineering students to identify the six benefits they valued most as they considered which school they wanted to attend. We then plotted where these students positioned the client college on a perceptual map built on these six benefits. Perceptual maps are extremely helpful because not only do they help you determine your position, but the positions of your competitors as well.

——————Branding Bullet——————
Ultimately, your brand is what your customers say you are.

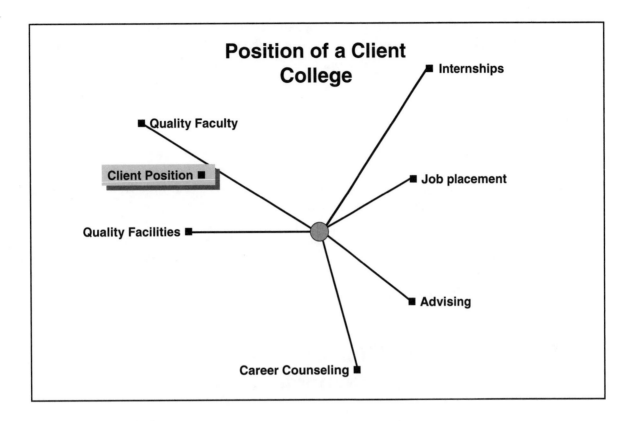

Position of a Client College

- Internships
- Quality Faculty
- Client Position
- Job placement
- Quality Facilities
- Advising
- Career Counseling

Basic rules of positioning

Like any endeavor, positioning is governed, or at least guided, by a handful of rules. First, as stated previously, positioning occurs in the minds of your target audiences. Your ultimate goal is mindshare because mindshare governs marketshare.

Second, positioning and competitive positioning are overt acts. They involve desire, research, planning, resource allocation, and execution. Like the quality of your institutional image, they should not be left to chance.

Third, positioning is heavily dependent on perception. How you are perceived by your target audiences often counts more than how you really are. If you believe you are one thing, and students or donors perceive you as another, they will act on their perception, and not your reality.

Fourth, positioning is competitive and comparative. Students will compare you with other institutions on the positions that they value. Students choose between Beloit and Kenyon. Donors choose between Beloit and the American Cancer Society. Colleges and universities seldom find themselves in a non-competitive position.

At the same time, it is important to realize that your institution will occupy different positions in the minds of people in different geographies. Students close to you will perceive and position you differently than students farther away. Finally, students of higher academic ability will position you differently than students with less ability.

Fifth, directly confronting an entrenched competitor is a blueprint for failure. It is very difficult to dislodge a competitor from a position, and it is equally challenging for two institutions to occupy the dominant position in the same marketplace.

Finally, the success of your positioning strategy will be determined by how students act or don't act, as a consequence of the position they have awarded you. Motivating the student to act is a necessary outcome of positioning.

Competitive positioning

For the purposes of our discussion, positioning is the act of placing a college or a college attribute or characteristic in the mind of a prospective student. Competitive positioning, a more aggressive form of positioning, involves <u>differentiating your institution from competing institutions</u> in ways that prospective students, donors, and other audiences find meaningful, attractive, and noteworthy.

Competitive positioning recognizes that students and donors don't say, "If I can't go (or give) to Grove City College, I won't go (give) at all." We know that the student considering Grove City might well be considering some of the nation's other best Christian colleges. In this way, Grove City College competes head-to-head for students, donated dollars, media attention, and other resources.

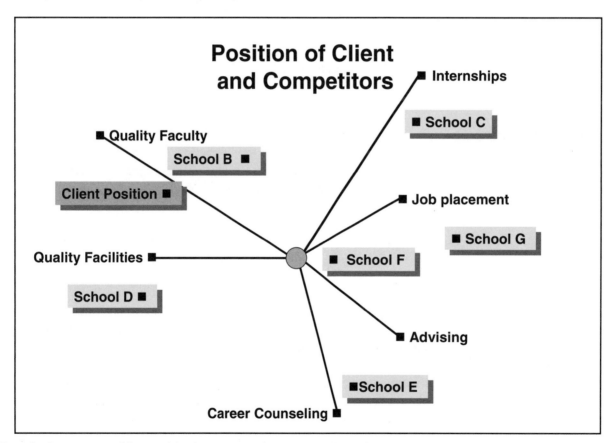

Developing a competitive positioning strategy is not easy. Not only must you gather data that shows how students, donors, and others position you, but you must gather these same data on your competitors. In addition, you must have a willingness to use data to not only sell your institution, but to sell against your competitors.

As you can see from the graphic on the previous page, the client college (upper left quadrant) finds that it is closely compared with School B. Interestingly, before the research was completed, the client perceived itself as most like School G. Competitive positioning data not only tells you where your target audiences have positioned you, but also how they compare you with your competitors.

Alternative positioning strategies

According to Aaker, in *Building Strong Brands*, there are eight brand position options. The following seven apply to higher education:

- Quality position
- Value position
- Feature-driven position
- Relational position
- Aspiration position
- Problem-solving position
- Rivalry-based position

Quality position. The perception of quality is probably one of the most important elements for a brand. It is important to remember, though, that the definition of quality lies in the mind of the buyer and not the seller and that this definition is in a state of flux.

- Discussion: Colleges and universities are very comfortable with the quality position. However, they must keep in mind that the marketplace is changing its definition of quality. While colleges and universities are fixated on issues related to seat time and student-faculty ratios, more and more students in the marketplace are interested in speed, access, and opportunities upon graduation.

Value position. At one time, items that were considered to be a good "value" meant that they were inexpensive, even cheap. However, that stigma has fallen by the wayside. Today, brands that are considered a value are rising in popularity among consumers.

- Discussion: Historically, a college or university did not want to be perceived as the least expensive school in its cohort. However, we also know that there is usually little real benefit in being perceived as the most expensive, either. This is especially true if you are a relatively unknown institution. All things considered, the best cost position appears to be at the top of the middle third of your cohort group.

Feature-driven position. More marketers rely on service and features to differentiate their brands than any other method. The advantage of a feature-driven position is obvious: your messages are straightforward and the positioning will be credible if you stick to the facts about the product. Unfortunately, feature-orientated stances are often rendered useless if the competition comes out with a faster or more advanced model.

- Discussion: Colleges and universities find the feature-driven position very attractive. They universally describe their great faculty and facilities. What they fail to realize is that all colleges and universities describe the same basic features. It is much like a car company differentiating itself from another by describing how many tires they have on their vehicles.

  A feature-driven position must go beyond a simple listing of features. It should seek to translate those features into benefits that the target audiences will value and outcomes they will pay for.

  Interestingly, one of the most popular features of late appears to be technology. We have "Think Pad" colleges, wireless colleges, colleges that are completely wired (see the Yahoo! 100), and everything in between. Unfortunately, technology has no loyalty and anyone who can spend the money can usurp this position. Furthermore, the marketplace increasingly expects certain levels of technology, and rather than being rewarded for having it, you are punished if you do not.

Relational position. One of the most effective ways to create interest in a brand is to send out a relational positioning prompt that resonates well with potential buyers.

- Discussion: This is a very important position for church-related colleges in general and Christian and Catholic colleges in particular. For these institutions, the "sell" includes not only education, but the value system upon which that education is built. Relational prompts are also at the heart of co-branding opportunities. This is one reason why colleges so quickly remind people when they are "ranked" by *U.S. News & World Report.*

Aspiration position. These are positioning prompts that offer a prospective student a place they might like to go, or a person they might like to be, or a state of mind they might like to achieve. Aspiration positions are the heart and soul of many college brands, especially those directed at nontraditional students.

- Discussion: "Start here," many colleges seem to be saying, and "go far." The aspiration position is extremely important for all colleges. Nontraditional students aspire to improve their lives. Traditional-age students hope for bright futures. Aspiration, as long as the college delivers, can be an important position.

Problem-solving position. As the name implies, problem/solution prompts show the consumer how a sticky situation can be relieved quickly and easily with the brand or service. What problem/solution campaigns lack in imagination, they usually make up for in directness and credibility.

- Discussion: At first blush, this position might seem to have little affinity for higher education. Don't forget, however, the adult student who needs that credential for a promotion at work or the young woman who is looking for a law degree so she can address a societal issue with clout.

Rivalry-based position. By definition, positioning deals with how one brand is thought of compared to its obvious competitors. Therefore, the idea of a rivalry-based position might seem redundant, yet many campaigns take this approach.

- Discussion: Think of the bumper sticker that proudly declares, "I'm for OSU and whoever's playing Michigan." Need we say more?

Brand marketing and direct marketing

At this point you might be a little confused about the difference between brand marketing (branding) and direct marketing. I briefly touched on this issue earlier, but it is so important that I want to touch on it again. At its most basic, it works like this. Brand marketing is about establishing a position in the mind of a prospect. Direct marketing is about getting the prospect to respond. A colleague, Dick Damrow, says that brand marketing is all about positioning and creating awareness. It is future-oriented and is about "us," the organization.

Direct marketing, on the other hand, is all about action. It is about generating a response from the prospect. Direct marketing is concerned with the here and now and focuses on the customer.

If you remember our example from Ford, brand marketing is about reminding potential car buyers (and others) that "Quality is Job One!" Direct marketing is all about getting the prospect to buy a Taurus.

A couple of insights might be helpful. First, many of the tools of brand marketing are also used in direct marketing. In the above example, Ford uses advertising for both its brand and direct marketing efforts. Second, institutions need both brand marketing and direct marketing. Direct marketing without supporting brand marketing will likely fail because it will fall on deaf ears or blind eyes.

For our discussion, we are most interested in brand marketing. But remember, brand marketing is setting up the ask. But if you are not willing to pop the question with direct marketing, then you have wasted your time.

Brand Marketing	Direct Marketing
Attitude (perception)	Action (behavior)
Positioning	Prospecting/promo
Awareness	Response
Impart information	Offer information
Future	Now
About us	About you

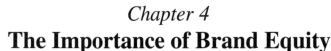

Chapter 4
The Importance of Brand Equity

One of the most important of all branding concepts is the idea of brand equity. And while there are many definitions of brand equity, Lance Leuthesser uses a definition that is especially helpful for higher education. He says that "brand equity represents the value (to a customer) of a product (or service), above that which would result for an otherwise identical product without the brand's name. In other words, brand equity represents the amount of value which a brand, its name and promise, alone contributes to the offering (again, from the perspective of the customer)."

Consider two bags of cashew nuts. The quality of the cashews in each bag is virtually identical.

One bag is labeled, "Planters."

Another bag is labeled, "Sam's Choice," the house brand for Wal-Mart.

Which bag is able to charge a premium price?

The idea of brand equity is critically important because it means that institutions–like cashew producers–with stronger brands can charge more for their product.

Let's try another approach.

Imagine that Coca-Cola fired of all of its employees, sold of all its buildings and equipment, got rid of its inventory. What would be left? If you added up the value of Coke's fixed assets they would be worth something like $7 billion dollars. But the company is worth some $69 billion. The value of the company less its fixed assets is its brand equity. In other words, Coke's brand equity is worth about $62 billion.

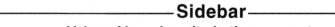

Sidebar
Value of brand equity in the corporate world

According to the Interbrand's 2000 Annual Brand Equity Survey, as reported in the August 6, 2001, *Business Week*, the 10 most valuable brands in the world are:

- ◆ Coca-Cola ($68.9 billion)
- ◆ Microsoft ($65.1 billion)
- ◆ IBM ($52.8 billion)
- ◆ General Electric ($42.4 billion)
- ◆ Nokia ($35 billion)
- ◆ Intel ($34.7 billion)

- Disney ($32.6 billion)
- Ford ($30.1 billion)
- McDonald's ($25.3 billion)
- AT&T ($22.5 billion)

Economists who calculate brand equity remind us that most of the value of these companies is not in such tangibles as manufacturing facilities or even their product line. Rather, most of their value rests in their name … or brand.

It is interesting to note that recent troubles at Ford and Microsoft have negatively impacted their brand equity to a slightly larger degree than the overall decline in the stock market. For example, the value of the Ford brand has declined 17 percent over the last year. This decline has occurred, in large part, because of the possible liability involved with the problems with Firestone tires on some of their SUVs.

The brand pyramid

As you can see from the pyramid below, brand equity depends on a number of important brand qualities. Some of these qualities and characteristics have been discussed previously and while all are not necessary for complete brand equity, the more of these qualities that you can build in the mind and heart of your target audience the more equity–or value–your brand will have.[10]

Brand Pyramid

Brand Equity
Brand Loyalty
Brand Preference
Brand Position
Brand Image
Brand Personality
Brand Identity
Brand Attitudes
Brand Familiarity
Brand Associations
Brand Awareness

David Aaker, in *Building Strong Brands*, has collapsed the brand equity pyramid into four foundation stones:

- Brand awareness
- Perceived quality
- Brand associations
- Brand loyalty

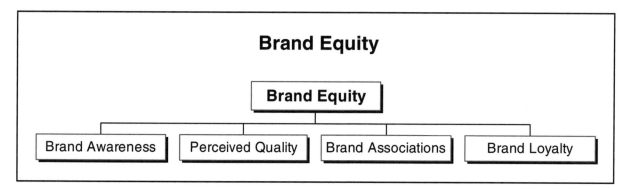

Brand awareness refers to the strength of a brand's presence in the consumer's mind. Awareness is measured by the different ways in which consumers remember a brand, ranging from *recognition* to *top of mind*. All things considered, the more top of mind awareness you have, the better.

Each year Stamats does a study of more than 1,000 college-bound high school students. As part of the survey we ask students to name the first college or university that comes to mind. For the last two years, the most often named college was the University of North Carolina. UNC has significant top of mind recognition among college-bound high school students in the country.

Perceived quality is important because it influences brand associations in many contexts. It is highly personal. Highly relational. And often highly symbolic. One reason the Ivy League schools can charge so much for the education they offer is because the perceived quality is so high. In fact, perceived quality can sometimes be much higher than actual quality.

Brand associations can be anything that connects the customer to the brand. It can include user imagery, product benefits and attributes, situations in which the brand is used, organizational associations, brand personality, and symbols. Much of brand management involves determining what associations to develop and then creating programs that will link the associations to the brand.

OSU's "Block O" is the recognized symbol of Ohio State's extremely powerful brand though some factions on campus, particularly faculty, just can't admit it.

Brand loyalty is at the heart of any brand's value. As noted in the previous chapter, the goal of branding is to build loyalty among key audiences. A brand with a small but intensely loyal customer base can have significant equity.

Centre College enjoys an enviable relationship with its alumni. Not only do alumni financially support Centre to a much higher degree than almost any other college or university in the country, but they are also quite willing to send their sons and daughters to Centre as well.

From awareness to bonding

The discussion of brand awareness from *recognition* to *top of mind* is borne out in the pyramid presented below. At the bottom, there is the awareness issue at which point the individual asks, "Have I heard of the brand?" to the top of the pyramid where bonding occurs, where the person states, "I can't imagine being without the brand." There are two other insights offered by this pyramid. First, notice how each of these tiers builds on one another. And second, remember how these tiers are both logical and emotional.

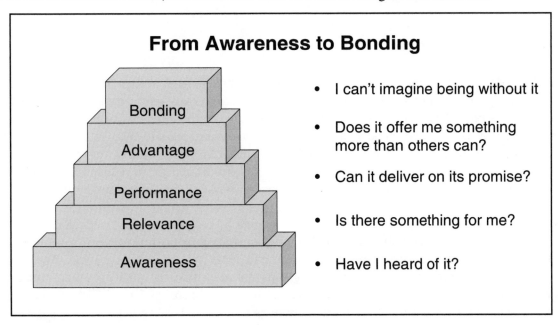

From Awareness to Bonding

Bonding
Advantage
Performance
Relevance
Awareness

- I can't imagine being without it

- Does it offer me something more than others can?

- Can it deliver on its promise?

- Is there something for me?

- Have I heard of it?

Envisioning brand equity for colleges and universities

As we noted earlier, while there are accepted formulae for calculating the brand equity of corporations, there appears to be no comparable formulae for calculating the brand equity of colleges and universities. However, while we may not be able to calculate brand equity for colleges and universities in exact dollars and cents, it might be helpful to consider the following.

Let's assume we have two institutions with similar academic programs, academic quality, and academic facilities. For our discussion, the quality of the education that a student will receive at either institution–by any reasonable measure and institutional ego aside–is largely identical.

One institution is a member of the Ivy League. The other is a regional liberal arts college. Both are located in the Boston-Cambridge area.

Tuition, room, and board at the Ivy League school is $35,000.

Tuition, room, and board at the liberal arts college is $18,000.

It is the Ivy League school's ability to charge $17,000 per year more for the same basic education that suggests the power of brand equity.

While the two institutions may offer largely identical programs with identical faculty and facilities, the Ivy League school is able to charge premium dollars because of the prestige factor. You might remember from our earlier discussion that Charles Fombrun calls this prestige factor "reputational capital." Bruce Hammond calls it "the Chivas Regal effect."

In this way, brand equity represents two important qualities:

- The premium price that the brand can support
- The positive impact of the brand on customer preferences

Another perspective on brand equity

Mark Lindemood, Vice President for University Relations and Development at Kent State University, says that many people in higher education believe that any discussion of brand equity represents the "corporatization of colleges." He goes on, "These people enter their careers with a motivation to avoid such market forces and discussions." However, says Lindemood, colleges and universities must learn to measure brand equity. He says, "Brand equity can be measured by services offered, demand for those services, and creating a scorecard for the individual institution. Brand equity indicators could come from applicant to yield ratios in admissions, percentage of alumni giving, community perceptions of quality and other similar data sets."

Lindemood continues, "Brand equity scorecards need to be built by each institution. American higher education tends to be valued by history and tradition or number of national merit finalists. However, a true measurement of brand equity begins to break down some of those more traditional ways of looking at equity. The question of how the Carnegie classifications or other accrediting groups look at institutional quality also impacts the ability to define and measure brand equity. The fact that students with ACT scores of 20 and GPAs of 3.5 are enrolling in remedial math courses make such conversations necessary. Brand equity can be measured for community colleges, for liberal arts colleges, for regional public universities, and for large research universities. Who should be interested in measuring brand equity? We all should be."

Characteristics of institutions with great brand equity

Institutions with great brand equity generally have a number of the following six characteristics. First, selectivity. Harvard may never consistently field a number one football team, but it can consistently field the best students in the country. This is evidenced by the hundreds, even thousands, of applications it receives and rejects each year.

Second, faculty research. This is measured in terms of quality of research and quantity of research. Third, large endowments. Of course, the question must be asked: does endowment lead brand or brand lead endowment. Fourth, big-time sports. If you think back to the colleges and universities that sell the most branded apparel, you will notice that all of them are either football or basketball powerhouses.

Fifth, image-building. Institutions that work hard to build a strong local, regional, and even national image will build brand equity. TCU, for example, has taken this approach to building brand equity.

And finally, co-branding, the marrying of your brand with another, perhaps more prestigious brand, or a brand of particular interest to a target audience. We will look at how co-branding might help you build brand equity in Chapter 15.

Leveraging your brand equity

An interesting perspective on leveraging brand equity is presented by Anne Heilemann, assistant director of annual giving programs at the University of Iowa.

Writing in *Currents*, Heilemann notes that "When the American Red Cross responds to a disaster, its volunteers and staff face many urgent tasks: distributing supplies, providing shelter, aiding victims, and more. But one of the first things the organization does may seem less than essential. It puts up highly visible Red Cross signage. Why does the Red Cross take the time to display its signs? Because its logo of a red cross on a white background is widely known to mean unconditional help in disaster situations. The signs help ensure that people continue to associate the organization with the vital services it provides. The organization is using its brand equity–the set of assets and liabilities linked to a brand that add to or subtract from its value–to communicate the importance of the aid it provides to disaster victims."

She goes on, "Development officers can and should follow the Red Cross's example, however, and use their institutions' brand equity to make a campaign consistent with the qualities people associate with the institution. Unfortunately, capitalizing on brand equity is not always as easy as posting some signs."

Heilemann then presents five steps that institutions can take to leverage their brand equity for a successful capital campaign:

1. **Tie the campaign's identity to the institution's identity (that is, its brand).**

    Heilemann quotes consultant Robert Moore, "The campaign's identity has to serve the institution's brand as a whole. To do that, however, you must first understand the campus's existing brand and brand equity. If you're all over the map with discordant messages about what your institution represents, how does the consumer of the message understand what you are?" he asks.

2. **Have the campaign embrace the mission, vision, and values that are at the heart of the institution's brand.**

    These elements differentiate one institution from another, and they need to underlie every campus initiative. "If you have a vision of something specific, donors can understand that and help you accomplish your goals," explains fundraising communications consultant Kristin V. Rehder. "You can use a campaign to fund your vision, but without vision, you're asking donors to pony up without giving them anything to hang their hats on."

3. **Use all communications and actions to build brand equity and thus further the campaign.**

    Because each institutional stakeholder usually has multiple points of contact with the campus, campaign messages must be consistent and strategic across the institution and over the course of the campaign. "Otherwise, donors say, 'The institution contacts me so many times, I'm not sure what it wants me to do. I'm not sure what's the most important thing,' " explains Bob Alsobrook, Vice President for Institutional Advancement at Union University.

4. **Ensure that top administrators are brand champions.**

The campus CEO, trustees, and chief academic officers are the embodiments of the institution's brand, and as such, the voices that alumni, major donors, and other influential stakeholders trust most. These voices must champion the institution–and the campaign that supports it–in a more coordinated fashion.

They can spread the institution's brand messages to the campus's top stakeholders directly by creating personal relationships with them, says consultant Keith Rehder. This task is manageable because fewer than 10 percent of donors give more than 90 percent of the campaign dollars. That 10 percent "doesn't make decisions based on anything you hand them,' she says. "They make decisions based on how close they feel to an institution–to the president or to a trustee."

5. **Cultivate further stakeholder receptivity through positive experiences.**

"If we are serious about building awareness of a new vision, increasing participation, and developing a volunteer infrastructure for the future, then we must communicate with students, faculty, staff, parents, and everyone else who is a stakeholder, not just major donors," explains Lisa Swanson of Northwestern. The university broadened the content of its campaign newsletter and development annual report to appeal to a wider audience and mailed them to nearly everyone in its database, despite the substantial additional cost.

Measuring and building

I want to close this chapter by returning to some insights offered by David Shore. He notes, first, that institutions ... including colleges and universities ... can <u>measure their brand equity</u> by focusing on three key issues.

First, do customers ask for your brand by name? Do students self-refer? Do they originate the contact rather than respond to yours?

Second, do customers see a difference between your brand and a competitive brand? Can they describe the difference between you and Denison or you and the University of California, Irvine?

And third, are customers willing to purchase your brand? An important distinction on this third point is whose money is used to make the purchase. If you are discounting tuition and students are effectively using your money to purchase your product, you can make the case that you do not have much brand equity. However, if a student and family are willing to incur significant personal debt to finance an education, or if a student and family begin an aggressive "work and saving" program while the student is still in middle school, then you can make the case you have greater brand equity.

Measuring these three metrics–asking for you by name, differentiated brand, and willingness to purchase–should provide ample insights into the value and currency of your brand equity. At the same time, Shore notes that building brand equity involves managing a fairly simple equation:

$$\textbf{Brand equity = SA + PQ + SD}$$

SA = **Strategic awareness.** Your marketplace is aware of you. You have top-of-mind.

PQ = **Perceived quality.** Your marketplace values the contribution you make or might make to their lives.

SD = **Singular distinction.** You are unique and easily differentiated from your marketplace.

Building SA, delivering PQ, and positioning for SD will help assure the creation of brand equity.

■■■■■

Chapter 5
Brand Management vs. Brand Leadership

Because of the two different orientations toward brands, brands as looks and brands as promise, it is not surprising that there are two different approaches to brand development. These two approaches, brand management and brand leadership, are codified by David Aaker and differ in the following ways:

- <u>Brand management</u> focuses on the short-term. Its primary tool is promotion.
- <u>Brand leadership</u> is based on the premise that brand building not only creates brand equity, but is necessary for institutional success. With brand leadership, the institution's most senior leaders recognize that building the brand will result in a competitive advantage that will pay off financially.

Based on these two approaches, we can posit that:

- Brand management is tactical while brand leadership is strategic
- Brand management is visual while brand leadership is visionary
- Brand management is icon-driven while brand leadership is promise-driven
- Brand management stresses what the institution does in the marketplace while brand leadership focuses on how students, donors, and others interact with the brand
- Brand management is interested in brand image while brand leadership is interested in brand equity

Tactical and reactive vs. strategic and visionary

Brand management has no long-term focus. Every new idea is a good idea and must be pursued. Projects are continually delayed, sidetracked, and changed.

Brand leadership, however, is visionary. As such, it is focused and deliberate. And while it is always open to new opportunities, it stresses sticking to the plan.

Less experienced and less power vs. higher in the organization

Under brand management, the 20-something marketing director will seldom have the power or authority to provide true brand direction. Instead, she or he will be perceived as little more than a coordinator; someone who will spend all of their time trying to scrape together an ad budget.

The brand leader, however, is a senior player who sits on the president's cabinet. Working well beyond the arena of promotion, the brand leader is interested in the institution's most strategic issues, issues often derived directly from the 4 Ps and 4 Cs.

	Brand Management	Brand Leadership
Perspective	Tactical and reactive	Strategic and visionary
Brand manager status	Less experienced; less power	Higher in the organization; more power
Conceptual model	Brand image	Brand equity
Focus	Short-term	Long-term
Brand manager's communication role	Coordinator with limited options	Team leader with multiple communication options

Brand image vs. brand equity

Brand image, while not visionary, seems preoccupied with the visual. Its domain is the 3 Ls of branding: look, letterhead, and logo. A brand leadership position, on the other hand, concentrates on building brand value; value that will be translated into students and donated dollars. Metrics are in place to measure progress. The goal is brand equity.

Short-term vs. long-term

Brand managers never have enough money and seldom have true control over the dollars they do have. A brand leader, however, understands that building brand equity takes time, money, and talent. Brand leaders know a successful brand is not built in one budget year or in the week between Christmas and New Year's.

Coordinator with limited options vs. team leader with multiple communication options

Brand coordinators measure effectiveness by how many column inches they generated or how much media they purchased. In the mind of the brand leader, collaborations and sponsorships are more important than column inches. They understand that successful brands require a rich array of media options, not just print. Certainly not radio. And never just billboards.

The president's role in brand leadership

Because creating and consistently delivering a brand experience involves the entire organization, senior administrators–especially the president–must lead the effort. The inspiration and vision for branding must come from the top. Leadership cannot be delegated.

Let's look at how the president and senior administrators must support brand building.

First, the president and senior administrators need to fully grasp the possibilities that branding has for their institution. At this early "what if" stage it is important to think broadly and boldly. At the same time, the president must factor in the mission, vision, and strategic plan.

Second, you must be honest. The bold thinking suggested in the above paragraph must be tempered by a dose of reality.

Third, the president must declare a direction. Center to this declaration must be the idea of "focus." Strong brands are built around the idea of doing less, but doing what you decide to do exceptionally well. The idea of institutional focus will be addressed again in Chapter 7.

Fourth, the president must be willing to deal with the political fallout. Declaring a direction is much like drawing a line in the sand. Deciding to go one way means you are not going to go another, and those who want to go in that other direction will be riled.

Fifth, the president must commit the necessary resources. In other words, real dollars,

And finally, the president must put his or her brand strategies in the hands of a single, seasoned, administrator who has the experience, the money, the power, and the desire to serve as the brand champion. Having one person in charge of your brand, just as you have one person in charge of your finances, gives your efforts focus, legitimacy, and accountability.

Dr. Michael Ferrari, Chancellor of Texas Christian University, feels that the best way to get everyone on the same page with respect to branding is to create a university-wide task force and make it a project of the Chancellor's office. The first task is to clarify through participatory discussion all of the elements that add substance and emotion to the institution's brand identity— a simple description of the institution's competitive advantage (capturing the essence of its mission and vision), a list of its core values, a powerful logo, word marks, and other institutional defining elements of color and design. The ultimate objective of the group is to recommend strategies for each of the institution's market segments where each time the university's name is seen or heard, a special type or character of institution is perceived, along with deep positive emotions and a feeling of trust."

In the same manner, Dr. Judith K. Broida, Associate Provost at the University of Maryland, suggests that, "It is a huge leap of conscience for the academic community to see itself as a business and an even greater hurdle to act like one. Activities like branding are tainted by their association with corporate strategy yet essential to the understanding of how students, parents, and the public view colleges or universities. Presidents, who are leaders, see the connection and introduce the campus to the new reality."

Broida explains, that the new college president is a CEO managing not only the traditional aspects of the university, but the new realities: marketing and branding, for-profit corporations, competition, investment portfolios–aciivities usually reserved for the business world. More presidents now realize they live in a world where images drive "buyer decisions " and managing these perceptions is now part of the "business of academia."

Dr. Lee Pelton, President of Willamette University in Salem, Oregon offers a slightly different perspective. He says, "We are seeking the best and brightest students and the most talented teachers in the country. In what has become an increasingly competitive environment, we are challenged to provide a clear and compelling picture of who we are, what we do, and what makes us different from other institutions. Some may call it branding; we think it is simply understanding the true essence of our school and communicating it effectively."

The idea of a chief reputation officer

Charles Fombrun, introduced earlier as the author of *Reputation: Realizing Value from the Corporate Image*, suggests the creation of a chief reputation officer to help oversee an organization's brand plan. Fombrun believes that to focus attention on sustaining reputation, an empowered CRO would ensure that the following questions are addressed systematically:

- What are we doing to maintain healthy relationships with our key constituents?
- How well do we monitor our images with each of our different audiences?
- Could we improve our reputation by developing better, more consistent images?
- What kinds of activities should we engage in to sustain our reputation?
- Do our employees understand and appreciate the importance of our reputation? Do our customers, suppliers, and rivals? The local government and community? The public at large?
- How can we obtain favorable media exposure?
- How can we improve our relationships with those organizations which monitor social responsiveness?

While Fomburn is concerned with only one dimension of branding–reputation–his holistic approach is philosophically consistent with that of a brand leader.

More than dollars ... will!

It is hardly surprising that many college and university administrators believe that the biggest requirement for a successful branding strategy is cash. However, while you will likely spend dollars, there is another currency that is even more important than dollars. That currency is institutional will.

For a branding strategy to be successful, you must have the institutional will to conduct the research and respond strategically. A critical element of branding, therefore, is the decision to focus outward rather than inward; the decision to first understand and then respond to customers. A key to this reorientation is the need to plan and evaluate your brand and brand message from the perspective of the receivers, not the sender. For colleges and universities that have long focused on internal stakeholders, looking outward will be a challenge. It will take courage ... and will ... to stay the course.

Corralling the dollars

Even if you have institutional will and focus your brand, you will spend dollars, often very significant dollars. And while there is no way to predict with certainty how much it will cost to establish a brand, there are some variables that will impact that amount.

These variables, as identified in the graphic below, include:

- Number of target audiences
- Size of the target geography
- Whether or not the brand position is contested
- Whether or not the brand position is complex

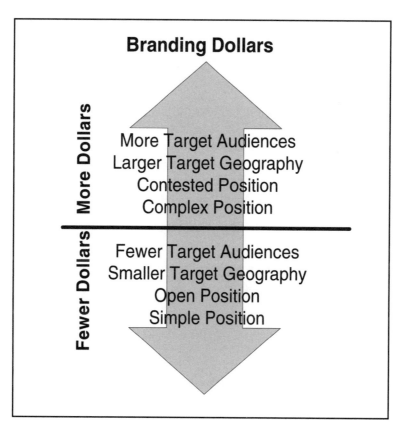

Number of target audiences

Simple mathematics tell us that the more audiences with which you try to establish your brand, the more money it will take. It also stands to reason that it will take more money to establish brands in the minds of larger audiences than smaller. And finally, if your target audience is actually comprised of identifiable segments, it will take more money to establish your brand than if the target audience is homogenous.

Size of the target geography

The odds are high that establishing a brand in one state will be less expensive than a region. By the same measure, establishing a regional brand will be less expensive than establishing a brand that is national or even international in scope.

Whether or not the brand position is contested

If the brand position is "open" then it will be less expensive than if the brand position you desire is already "owned" by another college or university. In fact, it is generally so expensive and time consuming to challenge a contested position that most branding veterans recommend against it.

Whether or not the brand position is complex

Finally, if the brand position you hope to establish is complex, then it will take more money and time to establish than a brand or position that is simple. For example, it would be easier to establish yourself as the "technology university" than the "university of the liberal arts." Most people understand, at least at one level, what technology is all about. However, a position like "liberal arts" is a bit more nebulous and subject to multiple interpretations.

One final word about dollars. You will spend dollars to create and maintain a brand. However, more than new dollars, you will likely spend <u>coordinated dollars,</u> dollars already being spent but now coordinated–and maximized–under one overarching brand leadership strategy.

Five outcomes of brand leadership

Martin Lloyd, as part of an ongoing discussion in a branding chat room, offers five brand leadership benchmarks.[11] As you look at these five brand stages, note how they are tiered. You need to firmly establish one before you can go on to the next. The five benchmarks include:

- **Your brand is the sum of the experiences** that your customers have whenever they are exposed to your product or message. It is this breadth across all college and university offices and functions that gives a brand depth and endurance.

- **You control your brand** if these experiences are planned and conform to your vision. At this level, branding is strategic, not tactical.

- **Your brand is consistent** if these experiences all say the same thing to your audiences. Do customers in financial aid and housing and the student union all feel that they are valued and cared for? Do donors, small and large, understand their worth to the institution? If they do, your brand is consistent across all venues and will experience great synergy.

- **Your brand is working** if these experiences create the desired impression in the minds, hearts, and pocketbooks of your target audiences. And remember, the impression you want to own is one of relevance.

- **Your brand is successful** if the perception you have created makes people act in the right way. In other words, do people follow through? Do they enroll? Do they give money? Do they commit? Or better yet, do they talk you up? Do you get buzz?

Brand leadership

Brand management and brand leadership represent two ends of a vast continuum. For many, brand leadership might be initially out of reach and their quickest gains might actually be generated by a consistent brand management strategy. However, regardless of where you are on the continuum, you should have as your goal the movement of your institution's understanding of branding from that of brand management to brand leadership. In this manner you will begin to build a brand promise that your audiences value and thereby build brand equity as well.

■■■■■

Section Two
Developing an Effective Brand Promise

■ ■ ■ ■

Chapter 6
A Brand as a Promise

Earlier we introduced the idea of a brand as more than a look. In fact, we called a brand a trustmark, a warrant, and a promise. It is this last idea, the idea of brand as promise, that is most important. I want to spend a few minutes exploring brand as promise and then introduce the four essential elements of an effective brand promise.

By way of review, we know that a brand is the promise that the organization makes to its target audiences. Generally this promise involves a commitment by the organization to do something *for* the target audience, something the target audience values.

Like everyone else, I count on a number of important brand promises in my life:

- Scotts Lawn promises to rid my lawn of grubs
- Wal-Mart promises me the lowest prices
- My Volvo promises me safety
- Alibris.com promises to find me any book ever published
- Garrett-Wade not only promises the best hand and power tools, but it also promises to show me how to use them without hurting myself

These promises are important to me. I rely on them. And I am willing to pay more for them.

College and university brand promises

Can colleges and universities make similar brand promises? I believe they can. Consider the following brand promises:

- Wheaton College (Illinois) promises a world-class Christian education
- MIT promises the best technological educational in the world
- Yeshiva University promises to be the most comprehensive Jewish educational institution in the United States

Keep in mind, however, that some promises are more narrowly niched:

- Heritage University in Washington State promises to serve the educational and social needs of the Native Americans who live in the Yakima Valley
- Berea College promises to entwine education with work and service
- Appalachian State University promises to serve the students and communities of Appalachia
- The University of Phoenix promises to help busy adults earn a degree
- Concord Law School promises to help students earn a law degree over the Net

Characteristics of brand promises

As you think about these promises made by colleges, universities, and schools you should begin to notice some similar characteristics. For example, we discover that brand promises:

- Are singular; it is very difficult to promise more than one thing
- Are either focused on specific people, a specific thing, or a specific geography. Some of the best brands are focused on all three
- Are often very personal
- Generate genuine enthusiasm among internal stakeholders such as faculty, staff, and administrators
- Are of value to the marketplace (remember, someone has to pay for the promise)

Four elements of a brand promise

Now that we have firmly established the idea of brands as promises, I want to present the four elements of an effective and meaningful brand promise. These elements, in sequential order, include:

- Make a promise that matters
- Communicate your promise
- Live your promise[12]
- Strengthen your promise

We will spend the balance of this chapter discussing–at the strategic level–how these four essential elements of an effective brand promise fit together. The following chapters will then explore these four elements at greater length.

A Brand Leadership Strategy

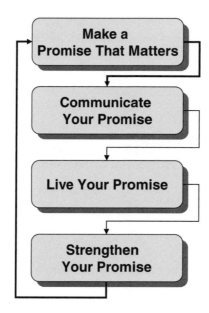

Let's work through the four essential elements of an effective brand promise.

First, you must make a promise that matters. The key is to develop a promise that your internal stakeholders will support and external target audiences will recognize, value, and show a willingness to pay for. Establishing a brand promise typically begins with an evaluation of your own mission and vision, an understanding of the promises of your competitors, and an awareness of the needs and expectations of the target audiences that you value most. Chapter 8 will help you develop a brand promise.

Second, you must communicate your promise to your target audiences. This involves creating segmented messages that your target audiences notice, find relevant, and respond to. In many cases, these messages are "projected" through an enriched media mix. Communicating your promise also involves issues related to look, logo, and graphic identity system. We will explore options for communicating your brand in Chapter 9.

Third, you must live your promise. At its most basic, this means delivering on, or keeping, the promise you made and communicated. Chapter 10 will discuss strategies for living your brand promise.

Finally, your must strengthen your promise. This involves asking both satisfied and unsatisfied customers, "How'd we do? Did we live up to our promises? Did our messages make sense?" Strengthening your promise involves using outcomes research to modify the original brand promise, thereby keeping it vibrant, current, and focused. Chapter 11 will examine strengthening your brand.

Strategic and tactical

As you can see from the diagram below, the four essential brand promises are both strategic and tactical.

Brand Leadership – Strategic and Tactical

The strategic and tactical dimensions of your brand promise

Decisions that relate to making a promise are strategic. They flow from your mission, vision, your core values and an understanding of the needs of your target audience(s) and an appraisal of your competitors. Making a promise involves a careful sifting of the first three Ps and Cs: product/customer, price/cost, and place/convenience.

Communicating the brand promise is tactical. It depends on developing an enriched media mix. From a marketing perspective, this aspect of branding involves the 4th P, promotion, or the 4th C, communication.

Living your brand promise is strategic. It involves delivering on the promise you made to your target audiences earlier. Again, using marketing terminology, this involves the first three Ps: product, price, and place, or the first three Cs: customer, cost, and convenience. Of course, issues of performance (another P) and people (yet another) and policies (yet another) also come into play.

From "a" promise to "your" promise

I suspect that you noticed a slight transition as we moved from making "a" promise to communicating, living, and strengthening "your" promise. This transition is very deliberate and signals that you, your organization and its stakeholders, and your target audiences must be able to claim this promise as their own. If these constituencies cannot or will not, then it is likely that your brand promise will fail.

But what happened to relevance and awareness?

In Chapter 2, I introduced the two essential components of a brand: relevance and awareness. As you can see, those two concepts fit neatly into our four-step promise process.

Making a promise that matters to prospective students, donors, or other key audiences is a relevance issue. Communicating that promise effectively helps build awareness.

Living your promise is all about being relevant. And finally, to stay relevant, you must continually strengthen your promise.

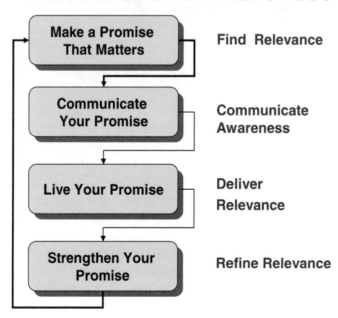

**Brand Leadership –
Relevance and Awareness**

How important are these four elements?

As I worked through these essential elements of a brand promise, I began to wonder what would happen if you failed to take one of the steps. In other words, if you fail to:

- **Make a promise that matters.** You will likely lose any opportunity for significant branding because you have failed to differentiate yourself in any meaningful way. In fact, you may become a commodity in the marketplace, chosen basically on price and/or convenience.

- **Communicate your promise.** If students and donors aren't aware of you, then they will never choose you. You may remain a best-kept secret. Unfortunately, in today's marketplace, there is nothing to be gained by being a secret.

- **Live your promise.** If you fail to live the promise you made and communicated, you have deceived the marketplace and the marketplace will turn against you.

- **Strengthen your promise.** If you don't continually work to strengthen your promise, you will likely become outmoded as the marketplace continues to seek–and find–alternatives.

When You Break Your Promises ...

- **With prospective students:**
  - Rise in nonmatriculants
  - Negative word of mouth

- **With current students:**
  - Increased number of withdrawing students
  - Loss of potential alumni support
  - Negative word of mouth

- **With alumni:**
  - Decline in participation in alumni events
  - Decline in participation in annual fund
  - Loss of future gifts

- **With donors:**
  - Increased number of non-repeat donors
  - Decline in gift opportunities

- **With community residents:**
  - Loss of community support

These four essential elements–making a promise that matters, communicating your promise, living your promise, and strengthening your promise–are like the four legs on a stool. Without all four, you will likely topple.

Now let's move on to a critical issue: the need for focus. We will be exploring the need for focus in the next chapter.

The real and perceived benefits of the brand promise

Before we conclude this chapter I want to emphasize that your most important target audiences must see the obvious benefits of your brand promise; they must see how these benefits directly relate to their hopes and needs. If they don't, your promise will not be successful. We will be exploring the importance of brand benefits in Chapter 8.

Branding and Maslow

I am a great fan of sociologist and psychologist Abraham Maslow. It is Maslow, you will remember, who in the 1960s, developed the Hierarchy of Needs.

Because Maslow's work so clearly understands and anticipates the human psyche, it is not surprising that he has something to offer those of us who are interested in branding. When you think about it for a second, this understanding is both obvious on the one hand, and elusive on the other. While branding is all about making a promise that matters to prospective students, donors, and others, it is critical to recognize that this promise is hierarchical in nature.

At Maslow's lowest tier we find those institutions that are not brands, but commodities. Their promise is directed at people who are keenly interested, because of life's circumstance, in cost and convenience. Their motivation for going to college is almost solely economic; they are trying to build a better life for themselves or their families. These people typically can't imagine attending a Kenyon. In fact, many of them may not know that places like Kenyon exist.

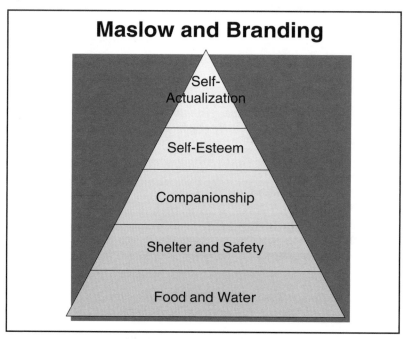

This is not to say that these people are not important. In fact, they and their goals are most important. But they will likely be served by commodity institutions (remember the insights offered by William Massey earlier in this book?) rather than those institutions that are brands. For them, cost and convenience will be the prime determinants. We know, too, that the students who attend these institutions generally do not evidence a great deal of brand loyalty. In their minds there is little difference between one college and another aside from cost and convenience issues.

As target audiences–and their motivations–move up from the bottom tier, they are more likely to be interested in, and even seek out, brand promises that are directed more at self-esteem (image) and self-actualization (fulfillment). They are going to college not so much to get a better job but because they cannot imagine not going to college. They are not concerned about a better job. Their eye is on the best job or some other self-actualizing goal.

To use Maslow to guide your branding efforts you must remember this: you cannot move your audiences up Maslow's hierarchy. Rather, you must determine where on the hierarchy your target audiences already are and then meet them there. Make sure your programs are relevant for their needs and make sure that you communicate this relevance in ways and terms that they will understand.

Just One Thing

A conversation between Jack Palance (Curly) and Billy Crystal (Mitch) in *City Slickers*.

Curly: Do you know what the secret of life is?

Mitch: No, what is the secret of life?

Curly: This! (holds up index finger)

Mitch: Your finger?

Curly: (Looks exasperated at Mitch) One thing, just one thing. You stick to that and everything else don't mean ——.

Mitch: That's great, but what's the one thing?

Curly: That's what you've got to find out.

■■■■■

Chapter 7
Three Critical Questions
(the importance of focus)

Colleges and universities have a tough time focusing their energies, efforts, and resources. It seems, sometimes, as if they believe that the surest path to institutional safety involves offering a little something to everyone. Rather than depth, they have sought breadth. One administrator said it best when he said that most colleges and universities think that the words *planning* and *more* are synonyms. Unfortunately, in an era of scarce resources, most colleges and universities find that offering more majors and programs means, despite the hype to the contrary, razor-thin margins and sometimes marginal quality.

The expansionist approach to strategic thinking

David Leslie and E. K. Fretwell, writing in *Wise Moves in Hard Times,* remind us that strategy, strategic thinking, and even planning have been used by colleges and universities as "euphemisms for indiscriminate expansiveness."

The result of this expansionism on most campuses, they say, is a sometimes unsustainable polyglot of marginal to average programs, expensive facilities, and large faculties. There is no synergy. No momentum. No focus.

The need for focus

If your branding efforts are to be successful, you must rail against this expansionist mandate. Instead of being everything to everyone, you must elect to be something very special to a select few. Instead of broad and often vague promises and messages (we will be "the best," we will be "nationally known,") your promises and messages must be focused. Like turning the lens on a Maglite®, you must focus your efforts to more effectively illumine your path.

Three critical questions

To help focus your brand promise, you must ask and answer three important questions at the very earliest stages of your branding efforts:

- Who do we want to be?
- Who are the target audiences that matter most?
- What is our target geography?

You can't be everything. And while almost every institution in the land is describing itself as a "university" and is seeking to broaden its scope, most simply cannot afford both breadth <u>and</u> depth. Rather than being focused, they are diffused and more often than not sound too much like their competitors.

Second, rather than trying to develop and maintain relevance with every target audience you can imagine, you must focus on a handful, even just two or three, of the target audiences that absolutely matter most.

And finally, instead of seeking to build your brand across the whole United States, or even the world, you must target the typically much smaller geographies that generate most of your students and where most of your alumni and donors live.

Who do you want to be–strategic focus

Not too long ago I sat for an hour and listened to a college president talk about the academic quality at his institution. It was clear that he was enthusiastic and well-intentioned, but he was having a difficult time reigning in the hyperbole. When he paused for a breath I asked two questions. First, how many faculty members he had. He replied, "42." I then asked how many majors he had. He replied, "39." Of course, that faculty-to-major ratio suggested that the institution did not have a great deal of academic quality. And while this is an extreme example, most would agree that many colleges and universities sometimes have a difficult time delivering the academic "walk" that must follow the academic "talk." And to make matters worse, even tighter budgets and under-performing endowments will make the quality crunch even more pervasive.

Of course, the question emerges: if you can't afford quality through and through should you:

1. Settle for less quality … or
2. Offer fewer programs of higher quality

Of the two, from a strategic marketing and branding perspective, the second alternative is much preferred. Narrowing your array of majors will allow you to focus critical resources. It will also allow you to more clearly identify your target audiences. And finally, it will allow you to more consistently target your messages.

The importance of programmatic focus

Al Ries, in his insightful book, *Focus*, makes the case for narrowing your academic focus. He writes, education, "next to health care, is one of the biggest businesses in America. With annual expenditures in the neighborhood of $270 billion, education alone accounts for four percent of the gross domestic product. In the educational arena, you find few specialists. Virtually everybody is a generalist. Many college presidents, for example, can't wait to become chancellors by turning their institutions into universities. Yet a better direction might be to focus on a single field of study. Only a handful of undergraduate institutions have specialized; notably Juilliard School in Music, Rhode Island School of Design in design, Fashion Institute of Technology in fashion, and Babson College in entrepreneurship. Some have achieved a specialist reputation almost by accident, notably The Johns Hopkins University in medicine.

"Some graduate schools have also achieved world-class reputations as specialists; for example, Wharton in finance and Kellogg in marketing. What would work better, however, is for an educational institution to deliberately focus on a single field of study and then make an effort to achieve a world-class reputation. The spectacular success of INSEAD in Fontainebleau, France, is a good example of what can be achieved. A 35-year-old graduate school that focuses on turning out global business managers, INSEAD (European Institute of Business Administration) has a sterling reputation. It's the school most targeted by international corporate recruiters. Nearly 200 visit the school annually, offering starting salaries averaging $75,000.

"Here in the United States, the American Graduate School of International Management in Glendale, Arizona, is mining the same area. Known as "Thunderbird," the nonprofit school has enjoyed a 900 percent growth in revenues in the past five years. Yet few American educational institutions specialize. Almost all of America's more than 2000 four-year colleges are generalists. So far, they have benefited from a steadily expanding market for their services. But there's a limit. As the percentage of high school students going on to college levels off, the competition is going to get more intense." Concludes Ries, "What you are likely to see is a shift toward educational specialization, which is exactly what has happened in the market for goods and services."

Fortunately, some colleges and universities are beginning to specialize and focus. For example, the University of Phoenix only serves adults.

A client that is a two-year institution is laying out a plan to become an institution that specializes in three-year B.A.s. Suddenly, in our rush-to-get-it-done society, it will be impossible to compare this institution with any other on a dimension that students value.

The decision of Trenton State to downsize its enrollment by one-third, and eliminate many graduate programs so it could focus on undergraduate education, has already had enormous strategic benefits.

Audience focus

One of the most important outcomes of strategic focus is a narrowing of the number of audiences with which you must interact. For example, the decision by the University of Phoenix to focus on adults means that they can immediately turn their attention away from middle school and high school students. MIT is most interested in students who seek and value an education that emphasizes technology. MIT will not pursue the student who is interested solely in the liberal arts. St. Johns, on the other hand, is keenly interested in those students who are looking for a truly classical approach to the liberal arts.

By definition, when you narrow your strategic focus, you narrow the number and kinds of people who are interested in your programs. Some people are frightened by this exclusionary outcome. However, by declaring and announcing a specific direction, students, donors, and others who are interested in your mission will actually begin to seek you out. Instead of communicating vague messages to too many different audiences, you are now able to communicate more precise messages to more narrowly defined audiences.

Serving and communicating to more narrowly defined audiences will pay enormous dividends because it allows you to be a more effective steward of your resources, to segment benefits, and to tailor messages as you seek to communicate more effectively with, and deliver programs to, fewer but more highly focused audiences.

Geographical focus

Almost every week I hear or read about a college that wants to be "nationally known." And when I poke around this aspiration, I generally find tremendous institutional ego (after all, we have students from 35 states) masking a complete misunderstanding of what it takes and what it costs to build a national brand. While most colleges get students from many different states, most also get the majority of their students from a much smaller region, typically a state or two. And while everyone (especially those schools in the north) feel they must go to Orlando to recruit (usually during February), the fact is, it is typically much easier to recruit students closer to home than farther away.

Building a national brand is a truly Herculean undertaking that is simply beyond the reach of most institutions and attempting to do so will rob you of the resources you need to communicate your promise to the primary markets that might literally be right across the street.

While it may not be sexy, it is almost always more effective to "think small" when it comes to defining your geographic focus. Pinpointing a smaller target geography allows you to bring a critical mass of resources–media work, advertising, alumni programming, high school visitation, special events … even where the president speaks–to bear. Widening this geography will diffuse and blunt the impact of those resources.

The power of focus

Let me give you an example that will help explain the importance of focus. Years ago, Volvo decided to hang its hat on the promise of safety. It's tagline, "Drive Safely," reinforced this promise. In fact, almost everything about Volvo reinforced this promise. Dr. David Shore, from Harvard, writes, "Volvo's singular distinction is that they build a very safe car. Everything they do reinforces that image. The boxy design makes the car look like a tank. The paper used in their brochures is thicker to reinforce their sturdy image. When Volvo introduced a convertible last year, the C70, the tag for that car was 'Tan Safely."

Now here is the best part. Because Volvo focuses almost exclusively on safety and because Volvo owns the safety position in the minds of American drivers (and drivers in other countries as well), people who are interested in buying a safe car cannot help but look at Volvo. In their minds Volvo and safety are synonyms.

Shore goes on to describe a conversation he had with a student: "We own two cars," said the student, "When my wife drives one car, she drives like a race car driver. When she drives our Volvo, she stays 100 feet back from the next car, she uses turn signals, and she drives defensively." Says Shore, "She seems to drive under the influence of the car's brand image."

To sum

In an era of tight resources, a marketplace that is inundated with thousands of colleges and universities describing themselves in largely similar ways to audiences that are increasingly distracted, your best bet is to focus. Your brand will prosper when you declare a singular direction. Identify five or six "signature" majors of particular value to your marketplace, define your target audience carefully, and focus on a tight geography. Remember, effectiveness is not an issue of effort, but focus.

"I always wanted to be somebody,
but I guess I better be more specific."–**Lily Tomlin.**

If you don't stand for something, you will fall for everything.

■■■■■

Chapter 8
Making a Promise That Matters

The first of the four steps for creating an effective brand is to make a promise that your most important target audiences find meaningful. It must be a promise that will engage faculty, staff, and administrators and that external audiences such as prospective students, alumni, and donors will notice, value, and support with either tuition or donated dollars.

Essential Brand Promise Step #1

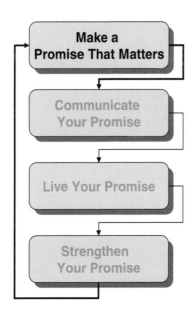

Revisiting familiar ground

As you think about the steps needed to establish a meaningful brand promise–clarifying your mission and vision, conducting research to determine the needs and interests of your target audiences, and evaluating the positions and promises of your competitors–you likely realized that this is familiar ground to anyone involved in strategic planning.[13]

This shouldn't be too surprising because the creation of a valued brand promise is itself strategic. It must flow from your core values and be directly related to your vision. If it doesn't, then the promise will neither be strategic nor of value to the marketplace or institutional stakeholders. It will, instead, be seen as just another marketing fad offering a little flash but not real substance.

Before you begin, a gut check

The creation of a new brand promise, or even the careful refining of a current brand promise, has the power to change an institution. For this reason, the process should not be entered into lightly. It requires clarity of vision and purpose. It requires a willingness to undertake fundamental research and to act on the data. It requires the ability to make tough decisions. And it requires an emotional, political, and budgetary commitment. Before you start, you must ask yourself: are you ready?

A change in perspective

Back in Chapter 2, I introduced the strengths/value intersection and indicated that a successful brand arises from the intersection of your institutional strengths and what your customers value. In other words, it is not an either/or proposition. Successful brands are a melding of the two.

In the past, institutions believed that brands were built on their strengths alone, and that just being good was good enough. From this perspective, brands were not so much a promise as a symbol. The focus was on look, letterhead, and logo. As we continue to shift from a provider-driven model of higher education to a consumer-driven model, we recognize that our customers–prospective students, donors, even faculty and staff–ultimately decide whether or not a brand has value and whether or not they will participate.

The brand team

You begin the brand creation process by assembling a brand development team. Much like you would assemble a team to guide your strategic or integrated marketing planning efforts, a brand team is used to help frame and complete the brand creation process. At the very least, the responsibilities of the team include:

- Oversee the strategic brand audit including interfacing with internal stakeholders and external target audiences
- Spread internal ownership of the planning process
- Synthesize data
- Oversee promise testing
- Guide the creation of the brand marketing plan
- Establish and oversee the brand budget and calendar
- Provide guidance as the brand promise is implemented
- Assist in strengthening the brand promise
- Oversee the brand stewardship program

Guidelines for assembling the brand team

While there are no hard and fast rules about who should be on the brand team, some general guidelines may provide insight and direction.

First, keep in mind that this is a team, a group of individuals who are working toward a common, often heart-felt, goal. At this point it is important to state something that might not be so obvious: everyone on the team should be committed to the idea of building a more effective brand. The team should never include someone who does not believe in the idea of building brand equity. Sometimes presidents believe that a person who hasn't bought into the premise provides a valuable counterbalance. In our experience, this person becomes a tremendous drag on the planning process and, more often than not, poisons the interaction of the team members and the relationship between the team and the larger campus community.

Second, the team should include at least some of the individuals who are most likely to be charged with implementing the brand marketing plan. This will serve two purposes. First, it will increase ownership of the plan. And second, it will help keep the goals of the plan more realistic if some of the people responsible for writing the plan know they will be involved in its implementation.

Third, because the brand team is very likely to be cross-functional, great effort must be expended in developing a work climate that recognizes the need to integrate disparate team members who often have different backgrounds, expectations, and goals–and who may have never worked with one another–into a truly effective team.

Sidebar

Windshields and rearview mirrors

In a recent book, *Thinking Outside the Box*, I wrote about the difference between windshields and rear view mirrors. Let me explain. As I work with colleges and universities I noticed a curious phenomenon. Senior administrators or faculty who are within hailing distance of retirement are often very reluctant to entertain the notion of significant change; especially change that might upset their personal and professional paradigms. It is almost as if they are saying, "I don't have to change. Retirement is just around the corner. I can ride this one out."

For these people, the majority of their professional career is in the past. Their long view is a rear view. Rather than thinking about where they are going, they are content to think about where they have been.

At the same time, younger administrators and faculty (and older administrators and faculty who are young at heart) are looking ahead. They recognize and understand the obstacles and opportunities that are before them and realize that these issues must to be dealt with on their watch. As a result, they are much more likely to accommodate and support real change. These people are saying, "Wow, we better deal with this or we might not have a future." Or even, "If we deal with this, our future will be even better."

Rather than looking through rearview mirrors, their long view is before them. They are looking out through their windshields.

Of course, I am over-generalizing here.

There are many senior administrators and faculty who are change-willing. At the same time, some young administrators and faculty seem overly bound by traditions and traditional paradigms. Change-willingness is not solely a function or age or time in career. It is an attitude. Change-willing people think about, anticipate, and even relish the future. They see a strong link between institutional success and professional success.

As you think about your future and the kind of institution you want to be and begin to assemble your strategic team, make sure you include as many windshield people as possible.

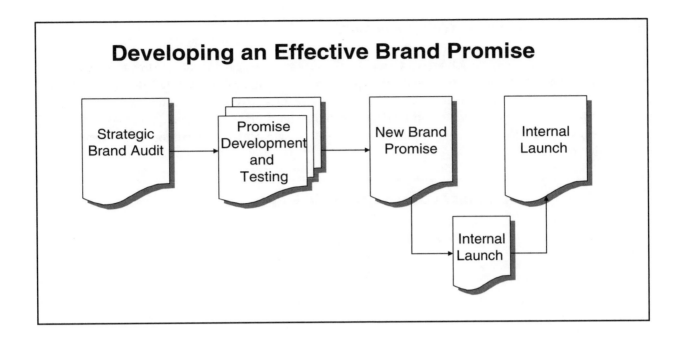

Our goal

Before we progress too much further, I want to reiterate our goal: the creation of a brand promise that your students, donors, and other audiences will value to the degree that they will pay for it. Additionally, your brand promise should be of such importance that internal audiences such as faculty, staff, and administrators will support it and will allow themselves to be guided by it.

By way of review, remember that Ries and Ries suggest that a brand is more than a word or a mark. Rather, a brand is a promise that you make to your target audiences. Frankel reminds us that branding is not about getting your targets to choose you over your competition. Rather, branding is about getting your audiences to see you as the only solution to their problem. Ries and Ries also note that the purpose of marketing is to build a brand in the mind of a prospect. With this quick review in mind, let's take a look at the first step in creating a meaningful and valued brand promise.

Creating an effective brand promise

This chapter will outline the three basic steps for creating a meaningful brand promise:

- Undertake a strategic brand audit
- Develop a new (or refined) brand promise
- Conduct promise testing

The balance of this chapter will cover all three steps in some detail. If you do not have a brand that is valued, these steps will help you develop value. If you have a brand that is valued, then these steps should help you develop even more brand equity as you fine-tune your brand promise.

The three domains of the strategic brand audit

Effective brand promises require solid research and synthesis. Thinking again about the strengths/value intersection, we know that much of the brand development research will be directed internally, at the institution itself and its stakeholders, and externally, at such customers as prospective students and donors. However, there is another research goal as well: your marketplace and competitors. These three domains–your external target audiences, your stakeholders and institution, and your marketplace and competitors–are at the center of the strategic brand audit.

Elements of the Strategic Brand Audit

Outside in

As we think about the strategic brand audit, it is important to take a look at our orientation. Colleges and universities have a long history of looking inside before looking outside. Our dedication to SWOT, for example, emphasizes this orientation when we declare that we will evaluate our strengths and weaknesses (which tend to be internal) before we evaluate our opportunities (which tend to be external).

This inside-out orientation reflects a sort of educational ethnocentrism: we will decide who and what we will do before we talk to the marketplace. Unfortunately, this orientation can be fatal to the development of a meaningful brand promise.

Instead, you must first look outside–at students, donors, and others–to determine their needs and expectations. This change in orientation reflects a major paradigm shift as colleges and universities struggle with the some-times troubling reality that the market place is no longer solely provider-driven, but increasingly consumer-driven.[14]

Not only is there a change in orientation here, but there is also an issue of thoroughness. David Rhodes of the Boston Consulting Group suggests that experienced branders don't just get close to their customers, they try to get inside their customers' experiences and seek to identify deep-seated needs and dissatisfactions, and then translate that knowledge into a brand promise.[15]

External target audience audit

The strategic brand audit begins with an examination of your most important external target audiences such as the following:

- Prospective students
- Donors including foundations
- Parents
- High school influencers
- Media
- Community residents
- Government and political leaders
- Church, synagogue, and religious leaders
- Business and opinion leaders

You can use focus groups, personal interviews, mail, telephone, and Web surveys to help answer such questions as:[16]

- How do these audiences currently perceive and position us?
- What brand promise do these audiences believe we are already making?
- Why do they support ... or not support ... our brand promise?
- How are our target audiences solving their problems without us?
- What are the unmet, even unknown, needs of our target audiences?
- What do our audiences want from us that they are not getting?
- Do our target audiences feel we are keeping our promise?
- Is there a brand promise they would rather have us make, a promise they might value more?
- Can our audiences consistently cite examples of when we failed to complete our promise?
- Do our target audiences feel our brand promise is unique and valuable? How do we know?
- What intangible benefits of our brand do these audiences value?
- How do the people who influence our most important audiences perceive us?
- How do our graduates feel when they say they attended our institution?
- How satisfied are our graduates with their experience at our institution?
- How do our target audiences compare our promise with the promises made by our competitors?
- What do our look, logo, letterhead, and other visual manifestations of our brand "say" to our target audiences?
- What words and phrases do our target audiences use to describe us? Our competitors?
- What words and phrases do we want them to use to describe us?
- What are the media habits of our target audiences?
- How have the media positioned us?

As you can see, these questions cover a great deal of territory. They examine perceptions and misperceptions, attitudes that are obvious and latent, met and unmet needs, and even hopes and dreams.

With this kind of breadth, the likelihood is high that the research will present you with insights you have never had before, insights that might cause you to rethink your mission, vision, and strategic direction. This kind of insight should be expected and welcome.

Exploring unarticulated needs

Daryl Travis describes the extremes to which Maytag will go to listen to its customers. In fact, he says, Maytag researchers actually go into the homes of real people to "sit in the corner like a little mouse" and observe how families interact with each other and their appliances.

Travis says this is part of a developing science called "ethnography." Maytag researchers observe people using appliances in real time and look for an "unarticulated" need. What they're trying to do is find the need that hasn't yet been expressed, and then meet that need so that when people see Maytag's products, they go: "Why hasn't anybody ever thought of that before?'"

We call these "ah ha" moments.

The first time someone decided to allow students to charge their tuition to their VISA card was probably one of those "ah ha" moments.

Another was when a college began renting textbooks so students wouldn't have to buy them.

Someone went "ah ha" when someone imagined the first distance learning program.

Or the first three-year B.A.

Chances are these "ah ha" moments began with research that explored the unarticulated needs of prospective students, donors, and other audiences.

Marketplace and competitor audit

The second step in the strategic brand audit is a look at your marketplace and your major competitors: The institutions you compete with most for prospective students, donated dollars, and media and public attention.

As part of the marketplace and competitor audit, answer such questions as:

- Who do we compete with for:
  - Prospective students?
  - Donated dollars?
  - Media attention?
  - Quality faculty and administrators?
  - Other key resources?
- What promises are our competitors already making in the marketplace?
- What brand promises are already owned by our competitors?
- What promises are unclaimed by our competitors?
- Are our competitors communicating their promise more effectively than we are?
- How effectively are our competitors living their brand promise?
- Are there examples of consistent promise failures by our competitors?
- In what ways are our competitors vulnerable?

Gathering marketplace and competitor data will involve a balance of primary research (asking people) and secondary research (reviewing the marketing, promotional, and fundraising material of your competitors). While anecdotes are illustrative and revealing, they seldom tell the whole story. Get good data.

The stakeholder/institution audit

The final element of the strategic brand audit is the stakeholder/institution audit. It is at this point that you turn inside and interview current students, faculty, staff, administrators, and trustees and evaluate your mission, vision, and strategic plan. Your goal is to answer such questions as:

- Is there a sense among internal stakeholders that our brand is important? Believable? Interesting? Unique?
- Is our brand promise consistent with our mission and vision?
- What target audiences do we most want to serve?
- What essential need do we fill for these audiences? Do we fill this need better than anyone?
- How well is our brand "lived" on campus?
- Is our brand well-supported, marginally supported, or ignored?
- What person, policy, or activity "personifies" our brand?
- How has our brand promise responded to changes in our marketing environment and competitor set?
- How does our promise differentiate us from our competitors in ways that are meaningful to our target audiences?
- Is our brand promise sustainable?
- How effective are our communication efforts in conveying our brand promise to our target audiences?
- What visual imagery does the brand evoke?
- What words and phrases do we use to describe ourselves?
- Does our brand promise present us with some interesting and even unique brand communication opportunities?
- What influencers exist that might be interested in communicating our promise and how can we reach them?
- Where are we consistently doing a good job keeping our brand promise? Why?
- Where are we consistently failing to keep our brand promise? Why?
- Can employees point to how our brand promise has changed how they do their job? If not, why?
- What options do we have for strengthening our brand promise?
- Are we consistently gathering and using data on how well we are communicating and keeping our brand promise?

The role of research

As you begin to work through these questions you are quickly confronted by a likely, "we don't know the answer." Of course, this suggests, as noted earlier, that a serious research effort might be undertaken to help you clarify the issues and opportunities surrounding the creation of your initial brand promise. In fact, there is a significant relationship between the quality of the research used at the brand promise creation stage and the quality of the overall brand promise. Skimping on research early on will likely to lead to trouble later on.

Three kinds of research

As you can see from the diagram below, brand research can be divided into three categories. First, there is generative research. The purpose of the strategic brand audit is to help you generate potential brand promises to be tested. The second stage, evaluative, involves promise testing. It is at this stage that you evaluate potential brand promises on three measures. Is the promise important? Is it believable? And is it unique? The goal of evaluative research is to help you choose a singular brand promise. And finally, there is auditive research. This last stage involves evaluating, or auditing, the success of your brand rollout and campaign.

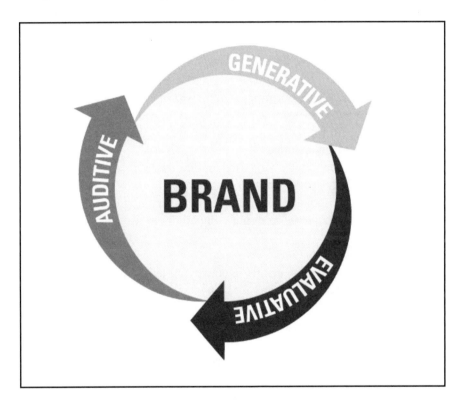

We will explore promise testing at length later in this chapter. We will also discuss other types of research that can be used to help you develop and test your brand in Chapters 17 and 18.

Insight and ownership

Remember that the stakeholder/institution audit is more than an opportunity to just collect information and insights. It is also a powerful opportunity to increase ownership of the branding process. Keeping the process open to everyone and being respectful of all opinions will go a long way toward spreading ownership and increasing buy-in.

Clearly defined or misaligned?

The data you collect as part of the brand audit should allow you to "plot" how different audiences perceive and value your current brand and its major benefits. Let's imagine, for example, that you survey four key audiences to learn how they position you on two key benefits: academic quality and supportive environment. In the first example, presented below, the four audiences have a generally consistent perception of you. In this case, our brand might need a little tweaking but overall it is clearly defined and perceived.

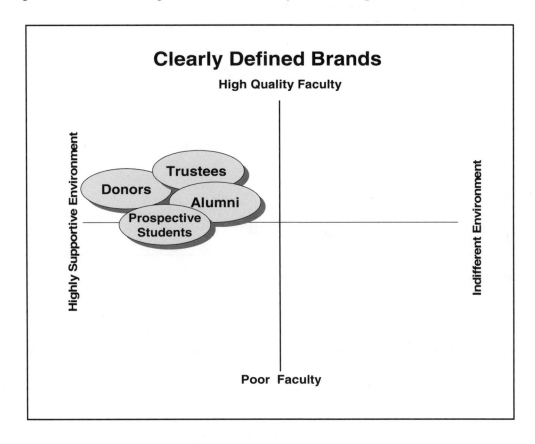

In the example on the next page, the four key audiences have very different perceptions of you. Your brand is misaligned. It is clear that a major revision of your brand is in order.

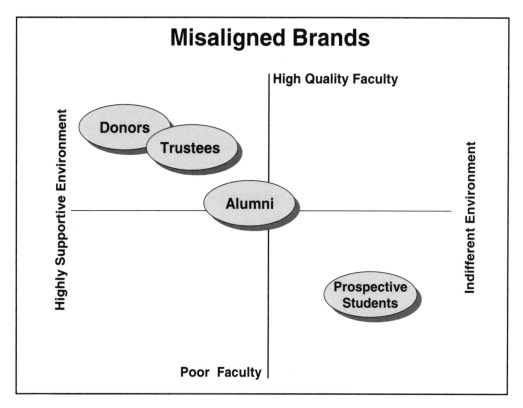

Developing a new or refined brand promise

The second step in the creation (or refining) of a meaningful brand promise–a brand promise that will help build equity–is synthesis. At this point in the process the branding team must gather the insights and conclusions from the strategic branding audit. Somewhere amidst these data and anecdotes is your brand essence and within that essence, in a yet undistilled form, is your brand promise. A solid synthesis requires that you begin to draw some initial insights about potential brand promises and that you test these insights against your institutional mission, vision, and strategic plan.

Essentially, the synthesis is designed to help you answer the following questions:

- Are we on the right track?
- Are the data providing the direction we need?
- Is there congruence between what these data are showing us and our institutional mission, vision, and strategic plan?
- Do we have some preliminary insights on potential new brand promises?

The role of promise testing

Promise testing involves using research to choose one "best" promise from an array of potential promises. This type of evaluative research balances speed and confidence. It is designed to help you develop a position that will stand over time. Before you can test your promises, however, you must first develop some initial promise statements.

Clarifying direction for Wellspring University

Let's say, for example, that you have been asked to help develop a brand for fictitious Wellspring University. As part of your research, you tested 40 different brand benefits; attributes that students, faculty, donors, and others described to you during on-campus focus groups and interviews. Some of these 40 brand benefits include:

- Friendly
- High academic quality
- Outstanding faculty
- Careers
- Great financial aid
- Access to faculty
- Safe campus
- Internship opportunities
- Residential-based
- Full-time faculty
- Commitment to diversity

After a round of evaluative research, you discovered that of these 40 benefits, prospective students, faculty, and donors consistently mentioned five as critical:

- High academic quality
- Great financial aid
- Residential-based
- Full-time faculty
- Careers

It is within or among the constellation of these five benefits that your brand promise will likely rest. These benefits are consistent with your mission, vision, and strategic plan. They represent core values. And based on your research, they are of value to your external target audiences and your internal stakeholders.

Seldom, however, do things work out as neatly as the above example might suggest. Students, for example, might value convenience and the ability to work while attending classes. Faculty might look at these two benefits that students value as an anathema to their understanding of academic quality. Or students might be increasingly interested in late afternoon and early evening classes while faculty prefer to teach in the day time.

Addressing and reconciling these sometimes disparate perceptions on brand opportunities is an important part of the synthesis stage.

Synthesizing some initial brand promises

Drawing again from the example presented on the previous page, we remember that your external target audiences and internal stakeholders particularly valued five institutional benefits: high academic quality, great financial aid, residential-based, full-time faculty, and careers.

From these five benefits, we derive a handful of prospective brand promise statements. Where possible, these promise statements should capture as many different brand benefits as possible so that the promises are somewhat different. However, while the promise statements are different, they must all fall within the institution's mission. They must all be "doable" by the institution. These potential brand promises include:

- Wellspring University is committed to preparing students for extraordinary lives
- Wellspring University is committed to the success of all its students
- Wellspring University will provide an extraordinary education in a residential environment
- Wellspring University offers students a complete college experience
- Wellspring University will be a partner in the lives of our students, our alumni, and our community

Promise testing

A promise test involves literally asking Wellspring University students, donors, faculty, staff, and others four key questions about each prospective brand promise:

- Is the promise important?
- Is the promise believable?
- Is the promise interesting?
- Is the promise unique in ways that matter to our most important audiences?

These four qualities–important, believable, intgeresting, and unique–represent a sort of brand grand slam. Important and believable are essential. Interesting makes telling the story so much easier. True uniqueness is a grand slam; difficult to achieve, but if it occurs, it opens the door for a potentially powerful brand experience.

As you test your promises, remember that the goal is not to find a promise that is popular. It is about being important, believable, interesting, and unique. Popularity is too susceptible to fad and fashion. Being important and believable are intrinsic. Finally, you want to ask one other question that will prove extremely helpful in the next step in the branding process: do your target audiences have any insights into how this brand promise might be illustrated and communicated?

Sample brand promises

Recently we developed a handful of promises for a small liberal arts college with a strong professional orientation. The promises include:

- Beta embraces change and innovation, providing students with a cutting-edge business education that will help them prosper in the global economy
- Beta educates the whole person, transforming capable students into successful business leaders

- Beta provides individual students the intellectual tools and practical experiences they need to achieve success throughout their lives
- Beta has always been a leader and in touch with the best business thinking and technology, providing students a resource-rich community in which they can master the business tools of the 21st century
- Beta helps students develop the skills, confidence, and personal qualities necessary to succeed in their careers and lives and to make a difference in the world

As you think about these promises, notice how each promise within the set is slightly different from the others. This differentiation is important. Without it, it will be very difficult to test the efficacy of the individual promises.

Importance vs. uniqueness

Before we move on, let's examine two different presentations of brand promise data. Each presentation will focus on just two elements: importance and uniqueness. The example below uses a scattergram to present these data on six different promises. As you can see, there is quite a bit of difference between two clusters of promises. In addition, the second cluster containing promise statements 1 and 2 shows dispersion as well. If I had to choose one promise to use, I would choose promise statement 2 because it is perceived as the second most important of the six promises and the third most unique. Keep in mind, as you look at these data, that you will likely never find one promise that is most important, believable, interesting, and unique. You use research to help increase the odds that the promise you do choose will have as many of these characteristics as possible, but there are no guarantees. As we will see in the next three chapters, it is the execution of promise that is at least as important as the promise itself.

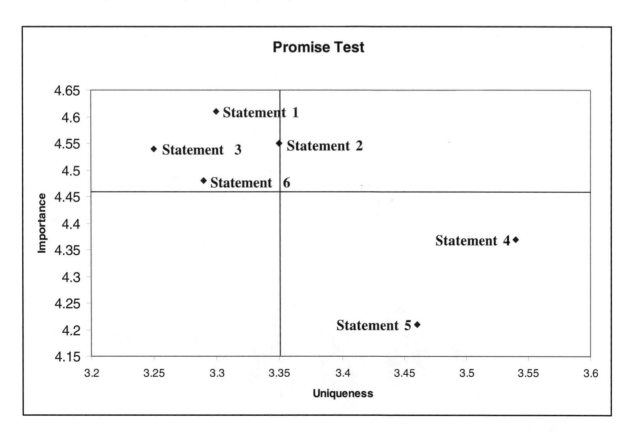

The two graphs below hint at how difficult it is to develop a brand promise that is truly unique. In the first graph, six promises were tested and all scored well on the importance measure. In the second graph, the same six promises were tested on the uniqueness measure. As you can see, the four audiences felt that the promises where much more important than unique.

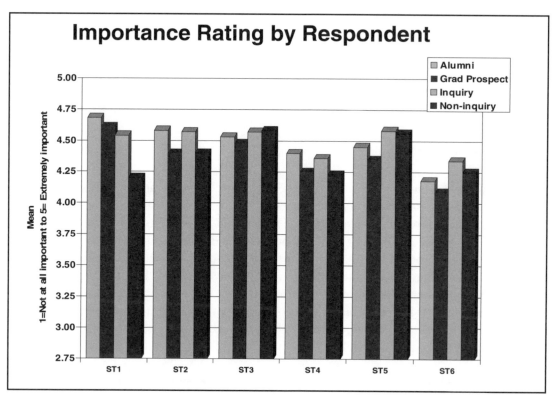

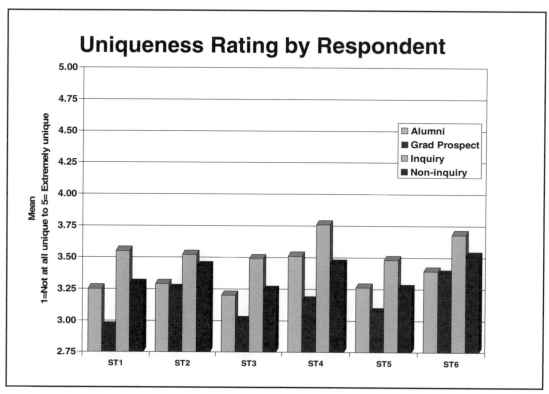

Clarify your brand promise options

Because your research and synthesis will reveal a number of potential brand promises, I would like to offer a handful of suggestions that might help you decide which brand promise has the most potential for you.

First, focus on your mission and vision. For your branding efforts to be truly strategic, they must flow from these two core statements. If prospective students or donors believe you should be doing something that is clearly outside your mission, take a pass. One of the biggest mistakes that colleges and universities make is to continually expand their mission. Smart institutions, however, strive to focus their mission and thereby develop even higher levels of relevance.

Second, consider your organizational culture, values, and people. Ultimately, brands reside in the hearts and minds of your stakeholders so it should be no surprise that it is your people who are the final purveyors of your brand. If your people will not or cannot live your promise, then no matter how enticing it might be to the marketplace, it won't work.

Third, acknowledge your competitor set. If a competing institution is already known for doing something that you aspire to do, you might want to reconsider. Brands and positions are amazingly tough, and if someone else has a lock on a key quality or characteristic, it will take a great deal of time and money to dislodge them. You might be better off heading for unclaimed territory.

Fourth, you want a single brand promise that serves all your key audiences. And while the promise may require slightly different interpretations, it is important for the promise to be meaningful to prospective students of all ages and donors of all ages as well.

Fifth, don't wait for consensus. Chances are you will not find a brand promise that everyone can agree upon. However, you cannot let the disenfranchised few paralyze the willing many who want to proceed.

Next, don't forget collaborations. Your gap analysis research might have identified an issue that you do not have the resources to address. One alternative, then, is to seek a strategic liaison. There is a great number of small private colleges in Boston, and by banding together into a consortium, they are able to offer their students a greater array of resources and opportunities.

──────────Sidebar──────────
Owning a word in the mind and heart of your target audience

In his book, *Focus*, Al Ries says that a brand promise should get boiled down to one word that distinguishes one brand from another in the mind of the consumer. Volvo equals safe. BMW equals sporty. Mercedes equals prestige. Ragu equals thick (spaghetti sauce). Heinz equals thick (ketchup). FedEx equals overnight. These words are "owned" by the brands that represent them, and it's difficult to dislodge that ownership. A brand is vulnerable when it lacks this intense focus. When brands flirt with other promises, when they lead themselves into the temptation of a broader, more all-inclusive appeal, they simply create a dissonance in the minds of the consumer because what they say conflicts with established feelings. It doesn't matter that a Volvo probably isn't any safer than a BMW. Volvo means safe and that's all there is to it!

The idea of owning a word or two is not lost on higher education. A number of years ago, a Pac 10 university developed a list of words that it wanted to own. The words included: boundless, challenging, incomparable, Western/pioneering, stunning, and vibrant. As part of its communication strategy, the university sought to use these words to help position itself in the minds of its target audiences.

Kirk Gohlke, Admissions Marketing Officer at West Point, says the Point wants to own the word "leadership" in the minds of the 11-to-17 year old college bound-market. He says that "one method we use is to insert the word or idea of leadership into every communication from West Point to that market and their influencers. Our tag is 'It's About Leadership' and we believe our target market values this brand," says Gohlke.

Choose a brand promise

The promise testing we completed for Wellspring University indicated that students, donors, and others were most engaged by the fifth brand promise:

Wellspring University will be a partner in the lives of our students, our alumni, and our community

After the promise testing you may want to refine your brand promise even more. This may or may not require revisiting the synthesis stage. Ultimately, however, you want to settle on a single, simple, brand promise that captures the essence of the brand benefits that your most important customers … and stakeholders … value.

Back to Wellspring

Ideally, as noted above, you want to own one word in the minds of your target audiences. Wellspring's brand promise was reduced to a simple two word tag: *Your Partner*. Finally, it was reduced to one word, *Partners*. They decided that this one word reminded external audiences that not only did the institution have a responsibility to be their partner, but that they–especially alumni–had a responsibility to be partners with the institution.

At first blush, *partners* is no more unique to them than *safety* and *refreshment* are unique to Volvo and Coca-Cola. What will make this word unique, however, is how well, consistently, and artfully they are communicated to Wellspring University's target audiences and lived out by the institution and its people.

One institution, one promise

I am often asked whether institutions that serve more than one audience should have more than one brand promise. For example, some deans argue that the law school or the school of continuing education or the graduate school deserve a separate identity. In almost all cases, the driver for this desire is ego rather than strategy. Generally, a brand promise is institution wide. Large, complex institutions might have a super brand. Its expression, however, might vary slightly from school to school. The best analogy for this concept is a team uniform. Everyone on the team wears identical jerseys with the team name across the front. However, each player often has his or her name on the back of the jersey. Within the one brand there is still some room for individuality.

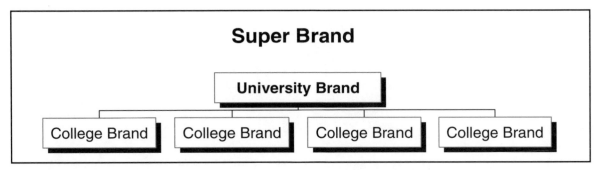

Brand portfolio

After the conclusion of this step, you will have developed at least four of the elements of a brand portfolio. First, you will have your singular brand promise. Second, you will have developed a rationale, or explanation, for the brand promise you chose. This is a critically important part of your portfolio because it helps explain how and why the brand promise was developed.

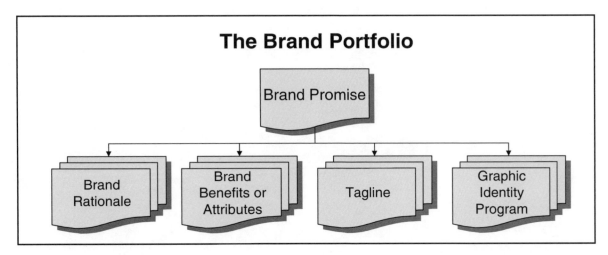

Next, you will have a list of brand benefits that, based on research, are of keen interest to your most important audiences. Ideally, these are words and phrases that you want to own. Fourth, you may have a tagline. A tag is a short-hand version of your brand promise. Finally, in some cases, you will have developed a new graphic identity program to help guide the visual elements of your brand. Historically, the graphic identity program was finalized and distributed in a printed manual. Now it is just as likely to be housed on your Web. Information on the steps for creating a graphic identity program can be found in Chapter 16.

If it was easy, everyone would be doing it.

■■■■■

Chapter 9
Communicating Your Brand Promise[17]

As you can see from the diagram below, the next step in the branding process is the communication of your brand promise to a handful of your most important external audiences and your internal audiences as well. Whereas the first step, creating a brand promise, focuses on relevance, this next step has as its goal the creation and establishment of awareness. While we recognize that how an organization acts and what it does are also powerful communicators, this chapter will focus on issues directly related to messaging and media.

Essential Brand Promise Step #2

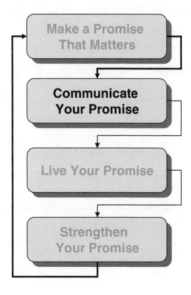

Almost intuitively, we know that successful brand communication strategies, and the messages that bring them to life, have three primary characteristics:

- They are noticed
- They are salient
- They are memorable

First, against the backdrop of the thousands of messages that a person receives each day, the successful brand message is noticed. It arrives with flair. It has texture where others do not. It is contemplative when others are brash. It is received with an "ah ha," a recognition that it is special.

Second, successful messages are salient, or as we have discussed at length, relevant. They strike a cord with the recipient. They meet a need, provide an answer, act on a dream, or resolve an issue. Because they were designed with the recipient–and not the sender–in mind, they resonate.

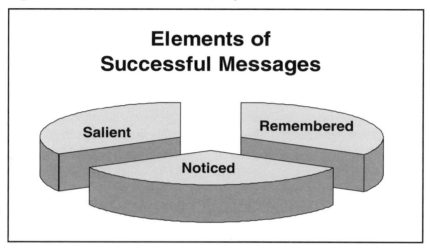

And finally, successful messages are remembered. Initially and cumulatively, they lodge in the memory of the target audience. They nag. They cajole. They are an itch that can't be scratched until they are acted upon.

If a message has these three elements, it is persuasive, but is not the traditional "in-your-face" kind of persuasive. Rather, it is a "we've made a connection" kind of persuasion.

At the same time, if your message is missing one of these critical elements, then there is little likelihood that it will be effective.

Dick Damrow, a colleague at Stamats, suggests that successful messages must be relevant, remembered, and repeated. Slightly different words, but the same basic idea.

Now that we have a sense of what successful messages must do to be effective, let's take a quick look at the creation of a brand communication plan.

Branding Bullet
If your customer isn't aware of your promise,
you will never have a chance to be relevant.

The brand communication plan

The mechanics of a communication plan are very straightforward. They include:

- Prioritize and define your target audience
- Clarify your target geography
- Personalize your brand promise
- Choose your media mix

Remember, it's brand marketing

In chapter 1, I differentiated between brand marketing and direct marketing. Brand marketing, if you remember, is concerned with changing attitudes and perceptions. Direct marketing is concerned with triggering an action or behavior. Brand marketing is all about positioning. Direct marketing is concerned with prospecting. Brand marketing wants to create awareness. Direct marketing wants to generate a response. Brand marketing is about the future. Direct marketing is about now.

Begin with research

Before you can develop your brand marketing plan, you must know how your target audiences perceive you and your brand and compare you and your brand with your competitors. You should also know the brand expectations of your audiences, their media habits, and who influences them. In other words, before you can develop your plan, you must have completed the necessary research. Equally important, if you have not used research to guide the creation of a plan, then you will have no baseline for determining, at a later date, whether or not your plan was effective. Chapters 17 and 18 will help guide you through the necessary research.

Prioritize and define your target audiences

The first step in the brand communication process is to prioritize and then define your target audiences. If you will remember, we discussed defining and prioritizing your target audiences earlier when we talked about creating a brand promise. Even so, we need to spend just a few minutes on this "hen and egg" topic again.

Options for prioritizing

Of course, our marketplaces are filled with a seemingly limitless number of people and groups clamoring for attention. But the fact is, most brand plans would falter if they attempted to establish awareness with more than a handful of the most important audiences. To help you pare the potential list of audiences down to the bare minimum, I suggest asking yourself the following question:

Who matters most?

This is a tough political, and often contentious, question. It is, however, an extremely strategic one because it immediately helps you make some tough but necessary decisions about which audiences are of true importance.

Obviously, the "who matters most?" question has a number of permutations that can help you prioritize potential target audiences. Consider, for example, the following:

- What kinds of students are most interested in your brand promise?
- What donors are most likely to support it?
- Who influences these students and donors?

Defining your target audiences

Prioritizing your plan's target audiences is the first order of battle. Now you must really drill down and define them as accurately as possible. For example, suppose one of your target audiences is donors? Are you referring only to major donors? What about alumni donors? Or lapsed donors? Or potential donors?

Or maybe one of your audiences is alumni. Do you mean all alumni? Or just alumni who actually graduated? What about alumni who completed a specific number of courses? Or alumni who have donated versus alumni who have not?

Not only must you prioritize your target audiences, but you must define them as succinctly as possible so you can avoid any confusion or misinterpretation. Fortunately, there are a number of demographic, psychographic, and behavioral variables you can use to help clarify your target audiences. Some basic demographic characteristics include:

- Age
- Distance from the institution
- Household income
- Relationship to the institution (alumni, parent, faculty, donor)
- Giving history
- Year of graduation

Philip Kotler and others believe that audiences should also be defined psychographically, attitudinally, and, when possible, behaviorally. Kotler, for example, stresses a series of audience characteristics based on benefits sought, user status, loyalty status, readiness stage, and attitude toward the institution. As the table on the next page indicates, these segments have great potential for student recruiting and audiences.

Don't forget the influencers

One audience that is often overlooked is influencers. In other words, while donors and prospective students might be a primary audience, it is also important to keep track of who influences them. For example, we know that parents can have a profound impact on the choice set of traditional-age prospective students, and that peers can apply tremendous influence on donors.

Psychological, Attitudinal, and Motivational Segments	
Benefits sought	Academic quality Job skills Social life
User status	Nonuser Ex-user Potential user First-time user Regular user Former user
Loyalty status	None Medium Strong Absolute Switcher
Readiness stage	Unaware Aware Informed Iterested Desirious Intend to apply/donate
Attitude toward institution	Enthusiastic Positive Indifferent Negative Hostile

Clarify your target geography

After you have prioritized and defined your primary target audiences, it is time to clarify your target geography. Hopefully, the decisions you made at the brand promise development stage will continue to guide your actions. However, recognizing that most colleges and universities think too big when it comes to defining their target geography, I want to reiterate that many brand communication plans fail, or are not budgetarily sustainable, because they tried to address geographies that are too large, too distant, or too disparate. All things considered, it is more efficient and more effective to build your brand in a smaller geographic area than a larger one. We realize that working across town or across the state may not be as glamorous as working across the country, but it is a better stewardship of dollars and time, and will be more beneficial in the long run.

A map on the next page depicts a college that describes itself as "national" because it recruits students coast-to-coast. However, as you can see, these data suggest that it is really much more regional in focus than might first appear. This institution should concentrate the bulk of its branding, marketing, and recruiting efforts in Texas, Oklahoma, Louisiana, and Arkansas and not worry too much about Minneapolis and Madison.

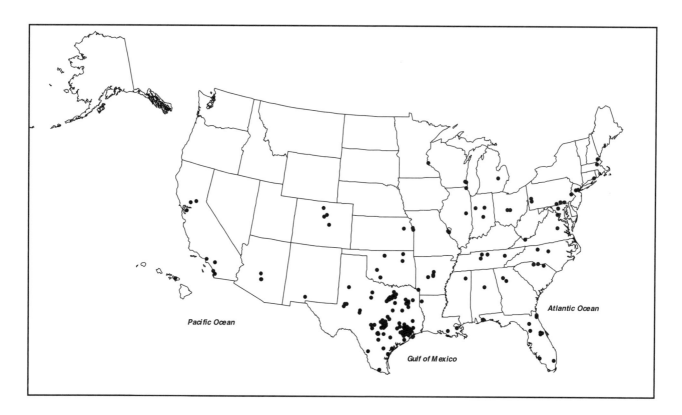

An ill-fated RFP

While I was editing this section of the manuscript, I received an RFP from a small college in the Midwest that wanted to be "nationally known." The request for proposal was ripe with phrases about branding and mind-share. It even included a potential list of audiences (there were 11) and had the broad outlines of a media plan that included:

- Direct mail
- Media consulting and placement
- Special events including a lecture series of "nationally known figures"
- Image advertising on NPR (never mind that NPR doesn't accept "advertising")
- Revitalizing the alumni magazine to turn it into a "think piece"

The RFP did mention that they were not interested in traditional forms of advertising including newspaper, broadcast, cable, and outdoor. They were open, however, to regular "image ads" appearing in such upscale magazines as the *New Yorker, Atlantic Monthly*, in-flight magazines, and golf magazines.

The RFP sought the creation of a brand plan, initial creative, and placement. It also specifically mentioned that it did not envision research "at this time" because it wanted to save those dollars for executing the campaign.

Finally, the college indicated that they were prepared to spend "in excess of $90,000 per year for two years to help achieve this national recognition."

Stamats, and I suspect other consulting companies as well, get RFPs like this all the time. Too little money trying to do too much over too large of an area.

Confessions of an advertising man

A generation ago, David Ogilvy in *Confessions of an Advertising Man*, wrote,

> We were invited to compete for the Rayon Manufacturers' Association account. I duly presented myself at their headquarters and was ushered into a pompous committee room.
>
> 'Mr. Ogilvy,' said the chairman, 'We are interviewing several agencies. You have exactly 15 minutes to plead your case. Then I will *ring this bell*, and the representative of the next agency, who is already waiting outside, will follow you.'
>
> Before launching into my pitch, I (Ogilvy) asked three questions:
>
> 'How many of the end-uses for rayon must be covered in your campaign?' Answer: automobile tires, furnishing fabrics, industrial products, women's clothing, men's clothing.
>
> 'How much money is available?' Answer: $600,000.
>
> 'How many people must "ok" the advertisements?' Answer: the 12 members of the committee, representing 12 manufacturers.
>
> 'Ring the bell!' I said, and walked out.

I wonder how Ogilvy would have reacted to the RFP from the school that wanted a national image?

Personalize your brand promise

The next step in communicating your brand is to make the promise as vivid as possible for each key audience. Let's say for example, that your brand promise is to provide an outstanding education in civil engineering. The next step is to walk that definition of "outstanding" back to your key target audiences by asking such questions as:

- What are the qualities and characteristics that describe an outstanding civil engineering program?
- What other colleges do you think offer outstanding civil engineering programs?
- How can we demonstrate that we have an outstanding civil engineering program?

As you seek to personalize your brand, you also want to capture the verbal and visual vocabulary that will help increase awareness by asking key audiences such questions as:

- What visuals come to mind when you think of an outstanding civil engineering program?
- What words are "quality-laden?"
- How can we better communicate that we offer an outstanding civil engineering program?
- What messages have you received from other institutions offering a similar program that you found particularly compelling?

Choose your media mix

With your list of target audiences and your target geography in hand, it is time to create a media mix. For the most part, developing a media mix involves answering a series of questions. Two of these questions, "who are your target audiences?", and "where do they live?", have already been answered. The other questions are:

- What is their awareness of or attitude toward your institution?
- What are your communication goals beyond creating awareness? Persuade? Motivate?
- What is the character and complexity of your message?
- What are their media habits?
- What media are prevalent within your target geography?
- What media can you afford to use over time?

Traditional media: (advertising) 1. Magazine and newspaper 2. TV/cable 3. Radio 4. Outdoor/out of home	**Constituent relations:** 1. Public 2. High School 3. Alumni 4. Donor 5. Community 6. Business
Interactive media: 1. Web/Interactive 2. CD-ROM 3. DVD	**Media work:** 1. Hometowners 2. Features 3. Wild art
Direct media: 1. Postal mail 2. E-mail 3. Telephone	**Sponsorships, promotions, publicity, and collaborations**
Publications	**Word of mouth**
Internal relations/communication	**Facilities and environmentals:** 1. Buildings and grounds 2. Signage and perimeter marking

Media mix options

As you can see from the above table, there is no shortage of potential media options for you to consider and use. As you review the list of media options presented above, you will quickly discover that I use a very rich definition of "media." This enriched definition is intentional for three reasons.

First, many plans falter because they focus on a media array that is too narrow. Second, it is my belief that the media plan should embrace all communication and outreach, not merely print or broadcast advertising. And third, it reinforces the idea that communication between an institution and its internal and external constituencies should be strategic, comprehensive, and coordinated.

Of course, to pull off a communication effort that includes multiple media will require a true team effort that is supported by the very top administrators and faculty leaders. Only with this kind of demonstrated commitment and support will issues of turf be addressed and even set aside.

As you consider the media options and opportunities presented on the previous page, remember that your mix must be sustainable over the life of the plan and beyond. There are no data to suggest that one-shot media blasts are effective in the long run, and there is little evidence to suggest that they are effective in the short run either. A smaller number of dollars spent over a longer period of time will almost always be more effective than a one-time media blitz.

Creating a communication grid

A useful tool to help you develop an effective media mix is to prepare a simple grid with three columns. In the left column, list your primary target audiences, especially your external ones. In the center column, based on the audience research you have completed, list how each particular target audience defines and interprets your brand promise. In particular, what benefits they believe the brand promise offers them. In the right column, list the media habits, once again based on audience research, of the individual target audiences. This simple grid will help you keep track of the essential elements of the integrated marketing communications plan.

Communication Grid		
Target Segment	Brand Benefits Realized	Communication Media
1. 2. 3.	1. 2. 3.	1. 2. 3.
1. 2. 3.	1. 2. 3.	1. 2. 3.
1. 2. 3.	1. 2. 3.	1. 2. 3.
1. 2. 3.	1. 2. 3.	1. 2. 3.

Some rules of thumb

Without knowing specific context and need, some basic guidelines about media mixes might be useful. First, as noted earlier, make sure the media mix you adopt is sustainable over time. Big splashes are just that–splashes– and seldom have any long-term impact.

Second, avoid the temptation to automatically turn to mass advertising. It is seldom a good first choice unless you have substantial dollars at your disposal and you have carefully matched different media buys to the media habits of your target audiences. Keep in mind, too, that even mass advertising should be supported by other media such as direct mail, special events, etc.

Third, don't overlook "low-end," but incredibly powerful channels such as word-of-mouth or special events. Not particularly sexy, but often highly effective.

Fourth, take the time to test your messages and media on smaller subsets of your target audience before the big rollout. You will almost always be glad that you pre-tested, because this will give you one last chance to catch any mistakes and to refine your concepts one more time.

And finally, and perhaps most importantly, make sure the media you choose, and the messages you craft, target the needs and expectations of your target audiences, not simply those of your president, faculty, or major donors.

Making your media buy

The media mix presented earlier includes a fair number of traditional media. These "purchased" media are typically the most complex and expensive part of a media plan. As you develop this aspect of your plan I strongly suggest that you work with a qualified, ethical, and well-seasoned media planner and buyer. A good planner will help your media dollars go as far as possible. At the same time, a good planner will also tell you when you simply do not have enough money to do the job. For example, we recently completed an advertising campaign for a small college. Originally the president wanted the media buy to cover a five-state region for a period of 12 months. Our media planner, however, showed that the buy, to have any impact at all, would require much more money than the college had available. We were able to refine the plan so the media buy focused on one state for a shorter period of time. This allowed the media to have more impact and achieved much higher penetration.

Predictable, surprising, and courageous[18]

Want to do something really, really, scary? Take your new viewbook and lay it on a table with the books from eight or 10 competitors.

Now step back and ask yourself:

> Is the viewbook noticeable amongst all those other images of smiling kids, green lawns, and academic brownstones?

> Does the cover stand out?

> Do the inside spreads really capture my attention?

If they don't, the odds are high that your publication or Web page or ad or whatever is suffering from ineffective creative.

Before I go on, let me explain that there are actually three levels of creative.

The first is <u>predictable</u>. Predictable creative largely satisfies the problem: we need to get something done.

Predictable creative is task-oriented. It seldom antagonizes or offends. At the same time, predictable creative is more concerned with what the institution wants to say rather than a real understanding of what the audience wants or needs to hear. Sadly, predictable creative is the most expensive kind of creative of all because no one notices it. It is lost on the table with all the other view books.

The second level of creative <u>surprising</u>. Surprising creative is a bit more market-oriented and is more interested in creating a dialogue than in merely promoting. In this respect, it has more of an audience orientation than institutional orientation. Surprising creative probably causes some consternation among senior faculty and administrators, but in the main, students receive it and say, "oh." Surprising creative gets noticed.

The final level of creative, <u>courageous</u>, gets noticed on the one hand and talked about on the other. It is edgy. It gets buzz. It also causes the most consternation among senior administrators and faculty. Fortunately, these people are usually not your target audience.

Whether you are designing publications, direct mail campaigns, or Web pages, consider the three levels of creativity. At the very least, your work needs to be surprising. And when you do enough surprising work, courageous starts looking attainable.

Let's see how this might work for taglines.

Not too long ago, I spent a day at a small church-related university in the Northeast. During part of my visit they wanted to work on a possible tagline. Because I had been on campus several times before, they were well-versed in the idea of predictable, surprising, and courageous.

Before we began talking taglines, however, I wanted to spend some time talking about the intended audience so I asked several key questions.

Question #1: Who is the singular audience? Who are you trying to influence or inform?

> <u>Comment</u>: This helps focus the creative on the most important audience and away from the institution.

Question #2: What is the one thing this singular audience is most likely to say about you right now?

> <u>Comment</u>: Where is the audience now? What do you know about what they are thinking?

Question #3: What do you want the singular audience to say about you?

> <u>Comment</u>: Recognizing that a tag is part of a larger campaign, where do you want the audience to be after the campaign is executed?

The purpose of these three questions is to help you focus as completely as possible on the audience and the intended result. These questions also help keep the creative on track.

With the answers to these three questions firmly in place we came up with three tags, one for each level of creative:

- Predictable   Our Goal. Your Future.
- Surprising   Think. Ahead.
- Courageous   By God. We're Good. (remember this one from earlier in the book?)

It was very interesting that the group thought the surprising tag was courageous until they came up with the final tag. While they will likely not use the final tag (perhaps too courageous, or even outrageous), it does make the surprising tag more OK.

Of course, now you would want to test these tags with the prospective target audience.

The idea of sticky messages

In a wonderful little book, *The Tipping Point: How Little Things Can Make a Big Difference*, Malcolm Gladwell introduced us to the idea of sticky messages. Sticky messages are those messages that, once heard, almost immediately become part of our culture, pop or otherwise.

"Where's the beef?" is a sticky message.

So is "Just Do It."

Sticky messages seem to have a life of their own. They stand out from the cacophony of other messages. And long after the campaign is over, they are remembered.

Higher education has had some wonderfully sticky messages. On the next few pages let me offer some examples–both current and historic–some with a brand marketing orientation and others with a direct marketing orientation.

More than a decade ago, Harvey Mudd University introduced us to the Harvey Mudd Junk Mail Kit, a search piece that raised search to the next level.

In the mid to late '90s, Rider University sent inquiring students its duck tube. The tube was designed as a campus visit piece and was filled with an invitation to visit . . . and croutons. Students were invited to visit and feed the ducks that wander around the Lawrenceville campus. During that period, the Rider duck tube was one of the most successful campus visit pieces ever created. In fact, even students who didn't visit Rider remembered receiving the tube in the mail.

In 2000, Albertson College of Idaho offered prospective students "info chips" as part of its recruiting strategy.

In the late 1990s, Meredith College, a college for women in North Carolina, used courageous advertising to help build its M.B.A. program.

The Minnesota State Colleges and Universities reminded better and brighter students what happens when they "do math."

The Franklin W. Olin College of Engineering extended an invitation to students to come and help build a campus and an educational experience.

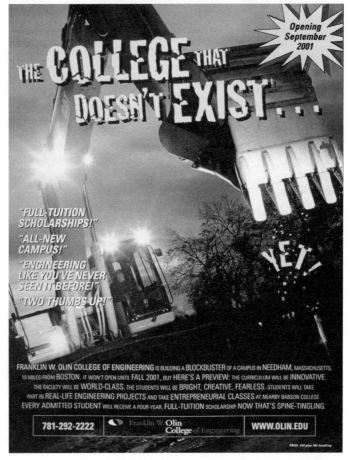

In the example at the top of the page, Houston Baptist University is positioning itself as Houston's blessed university, an acknowledgement that it is a Christian university. This particular ad was designed for placement at a baseball field. In the ad immediately below it, a community college in Reno reminds prospective students that there was more to life than flipping burgers. This billboard was strategically placed. One arrow pointed across the street to a fast-food restaurant. Another pointed to the college campus.

The concept is king ... and queen

Unfortunately, Gladwell does not provide us with seven keys to sticky messages or even a list of six steps to surefire stickiness.

However, when you look at them, you will notice that they were all built around an elegant yet simple out-of-the-box concept. All of these concepts were surprising. Maybe even courageous.

Note: These black and white renditions do not do these samples justice. To help give you a better idea of how good this creative is, I have posted samples on the Strategy Publishing site at www.strategypublishing.com/branding/samples.

Dancing the tagline tango

I have long wanted to write a short article on the use and misuse of taglines in higher education marketing. Last fall, Dick Damrow, an associate at Stamats, and I had an opportunity to work together on a short piece we called "Dancing the Tagline Tango." Here it is.

The universal marketing balm

At times it seems as if taglines are perceived as a sort of universal marketing balm. When things aren't working, when you feel like a change, or when you just want to do something, a new tagline is often perceived as the answer. Have a problem getting the class? Maybe you need a new tag. A capital campaign coming up? Spice it up with a tag. New president? New tag.

Of course, we are overstating the problem... but probably not by much. Higher education is infatuated with taglines. And when colleges and universities don't know what to do—or when the people in charge ride roughshod over the people that do know what to do—taglines seem to be the result.

Unfortunately, the taglines that emerge from this misguided approach to marketing almost never live up to expectations. They fail at the outset because they are not relevant, not easy to remember, and not likely to be repeated. They are perceived as the marketing end when, in fact, they are one element, and a minor one at that, of the overall marketing means.

By way of illustration, consider an experiment run by Curt Cichowski. In his role as Associate Dean for the Valparaiso University School of Law, he asked a law student to go through a collection of law school tags and see if he could identify which tag came from which school. The taglines the student looked at included:

- Combining great tradition with great promise
- New frontiers in the law
- Leadership for the new era
- On the move
- Education for a lifetime
- A tradition of pioneering
- Lawyers for the future
- Embracing the real world
- An education that works
- Faithful stewards of the law
- Building for your future
- Connecting the mind to what matters
- The dawn of a new era
- Lawyer's law school
- Expect a difference
- Real world, real law
- The best kept secret in legal education
- Why XYZ law? Why not XYZ law?
- Learning. Leading.
- Law lives here

At the conclusion of the exercise the student could not match a single tagline with the school that spawned it. On their face, these tags seem to have all the right stuff. They are short. Punchy. Even a bit daring. But they did not find a place in the minds of their target audiences.

A bit of marketing misdirection

Taglines are a bit of a marketing misdirection. They can distract us from the real marketing and branding issues that many campuses are facing. We make this statement for a number of reasons.

First, it is often easier to focus on the creation of a tag when the real focus ought to be on the resuscitation of your academic programs, an evaluation of your competitive positioning strategy, or a review of your pricing policies.

Second, creating a tagline can generate a profound sense of accomplishment, the feeling that you are doing something when you sense that something needs to be done.

Third, when most people think of brand marketing, they think of promotion and they see words and logos and marks. Taglines fit neatly into this loose verbal/visual definition of marketing. "After all," they seem to be saying, "isn't it really just a message issue?"

And finally, like a canine marking his or her territory, taglines quickly follow new people in new positions. Tags let the new dog announce to the other dogs in the pack, "Hey, I'm here and I'm doing stuff."

How tags fit into the grand scheme of things

Before we can discuss how to create and execute a tagline, we want to take a minute to give you a sense of how a tag fits into the grand scheme of things.

First, it is important to recognize that a successful tagline is a derivative of a successful brand promise. By way of review, remember that your brand promise occurs at the juncture of what you do well as an institution (your mission, vision, and strengths) and what your target audiences value. It is at the merging of these two that relevance is found.

Second, remember that your brand promise, like a supernova, "throws off" four key elements including your:

- Brand rationale
- Brand benefits
- Tagline
- Graphic identity program

Of course, we remember this as your brand portfolio.

Qualities and characteristics of a great tagline

Now that we have come this far, let's spend a few minutes describing the qualities and characteristics of what makes a great tag. We know that great tags:

- **Know their place.** They are not the heavy lifters. They are tactical extensions of strategy, not strategy themselves. A successful tag showcases a meaningful brand promise, it does not stand in place of one.

- **Are known by the company they keep.** They are publicly, regularly, and thoroughly used. They are part of the larger merchandising of the brand promise, especially the visual and verbal vocabulary that communicates the promise.

- **Unify, not divide; clarify rather than confound.** One tag is sufficient for the entire organization. You should not have competing tags any more than you would have competing brand promises.

- **Are alive and life giving.** They galvanize an organization and its people, they captivate a marketplace, and done well, they make competitors nervous.

- **Endure.** They are not temporary, but long-lasting. If a brand promise is part of a never-ending story, the tags that announce them must be just as enduring.

- **Are relevant, remembered, and repeated.** They are invited in. They capture imaginations. They get buzz.

Some solid taglines

Recognizing that it is the context and relevance of a tagline, and how well it is executed that matters most, we would like to offer a handful of exceptional tags:

- Life-long, world-wide–The USC Alumni Association
- Why not change the world?–Rensselaer
- Invent yourself–Beloit College
- Forge the future–Valley Forge Military Academy
- Engage–Furman University
- A college in formation–Southern Catholic
- Women first–Wesleyan College

Note how all are big yet small. They support a big promise but do so succinctly. They stress audience benefits, not institutional ones. The word choice is inviting, even enticing. And all are enduring and fully able to grow as the institution does.

Creating great taglines–some final thoughts and guidelines

Before we close, we want to present some final thoughts about creating great taglines that should help your efforts go more smoothly.

1. First and foremost, manage those expectations. Everyone involved needs to understand how a tagline fits into the larger marketing and branding strategy. Again, it is not an end. It is a means. Ask early and often: What problems are we trying to solve with a new tagline?

2. Make sure your tagline follows your overall marketing and branding strategy. It should neither lead strategy nor be created without a larger strategy in mind.

3. Remember that good tags are not created with your most important audience in mind. Rather, they are created with the input of that audience. Gather their insights. Seek their input. Suffer their criticisms. Listen well and long, and when you do, magic will happen.

4. Your goal is not to develop a tagline that everyone will like. Your goal is to develop a tagline that captures the hearts and minds of your most important audiences, especially those audiences that are external and pay the bills. Your most important audiences must find it important, believable, interesting, and if possible, unique.

5. Before you settle on a tag, test it by asking your most important target audiences: a) Is it relevant? b) Is it easy to remember? c) Is it likely to be repeated? If you can't answer each question with a resounding "yes!"go back and begin again.

6. Make sure your tag is vital enough to serve the entire institution. It needs to be big enough for recruiting, fundraising, continuing education, and even those folks in the law school. Remember the simple math: One institution equals one tagline.

7. Check to make sure none of your competitors are using a similar tag.

8. Take the time to operationally define your tagline so your faculty and staff know what it means, how it was created, and how they are supposed to live it out. Create a brand portfolio as part of a successful internal launch.

9. While tags are verbal, they are often played out visually. Keep the design in mind when you develop your tag.

10. Register your tag and then merchandise it regularly, publicly, and thoroughly.

11. When your research and external audience feedback confirms that your tagline is still relevant, remembered, and being repeated, resist internal pressures to change it. Your internal audiences will tire of your tagline long before your external audiences do, so stand firm.

12. Remember, taglines are not heavy lifters. They will never save an institution that does not seek to become more relevant to its most important target audiences each day. For brands and tags alike, relevance with your target audience is king … and queen.

A final thought on taglines

It is truly the wisdom of 16-year-olds that keeps us all on our toes. While helping a client develop a tagline, a prospective student summarized the whole discussion when she said she was tired of taglines that hyped some institutional feature. She said with more than a hint of frustration in her voice, "Don't talk to me about you, talk to me about me. That's what I am most interested in."

She nailed it.

You can't semantic your way out of a strategic fuddle.

■■■■■

Branding Case Study
Rensselaer Polytechnic Institute
A Comprehensive Brand Rollout

A few years ago, Rensselaer Polytechnic Institute (RPI) realized that they had a problem. Like many colleges and universities in the United States, RPI believed that it was a much better school than most people realized. But unlike other institutions facing a similar problem, RPI decided to do something about it. The result is one of the most comprehensive university brand communication strategies created in the last decade.

To find out more about Rensselaer's brand campaign I interviewed Tom Torello, RPI's Director of Marketing.

By almost any measure, the RPI brand development story is a textbook case on how to do things right. It begins with initial brand research, moves on to campaign execution, and then returns to evaluate the effectiveness of their campaign.

Sensing something was amiss with their brand, RPI created a Strategic Marketing Committee made up of top administrators that had "ownership" of their key audiences. The committee included their provost, vice president for institute relations, the vice president for student life, and the dean of students. The fact that the Institute's heaviest hitters were on the committee sent an important signal about how much importance RPI placed on its branding efforts. In addition, the committee was critical in helping ensure campus buy-in and cooperation. It also laid the groundwork for the initial research completed in Spring 1998. This research was directed at five key audiences, including:

- Alumni
- Faculty
- Potential students
- Current students
- Corporate recruiters

Using focus groups and individual interviews, the research sought to answer the important question: "Who do we think we are?" The research revealed that there was a gap between who RPI believed it was and how it was perceived by key audiences. Importantly, this initial research not only helped RPI refine its brand, but it created an important baseline against which the effectiveness of its brand campaign could be later determined. The research also helped RPI clarify some of its core values. Rensselaer felt very strongly that its history of combining creativity with practicality, and an institutional "roll up your sleeves and get it done" attitude, defined exactly what made the school unique. Research showed that stakeholders concurred.

Positioning statement and the brand tag

The next step in the brand development process was to develop a positioning statement. According to Media Logic, RPI's branding partner, a positioning statement is a phrase that forms the foundation of your brand. It must "ring true" to your primary stakeholders. It establishes the primary point of difference between your school and competing schools. Most importantly, it warrants repeating in all communications.

Rensselaer found the inspiration for their positioning statement in the words of one of their founders who said that RPI's mission was "to apply science to the common purposes of life." The modern day equivalent became their simple positioning statement: Technological creativity.

Technological creativity was one of RPI's core values. Says Torello, "We really felt that our students wanted to be challenged rather than told what to do. That's why we went with 'why not change the world?' rather than the more pedestrian 'change the world.'"

It is this simple tagline that brought RPI's brand campaign into focus.

Graphic treatment

After the tagline was finalized, RPI and Media Logic turned to the graphic treatment. They settled on a treatment that melded high concept with extraordinarily high production values. The concept focused on RPI's biggest stars–world-class faculty doing world-class work. By showcasing faculty of the highest quality, RPI helped blunt the criticism that they were more interested in quick promotion wins rather than a long-term branding campaign.

Eventually, the campaign would embrace the following:

- Rensselaer logo and tagline
- A direct mail piece for alumni that explained the message, "why not change the world?"
- Television spots on CNBC, MSNBC, and CNN
- Print ads in *The Wall Street Journal, The Washington Post, Time, Newsweek,* and *Sports Illustrated.* The print ads demonstrated the "why not change the world?" position by focusing on actual stories of innovation and achievements at Rensselaer
- Admissions brochures
- Admissions direct mail
- Web site
- Brochures for the School of Engineering, the School of Science, the School of Architecture, the School of Humanities & Social Sciences, and the Lally School of Management & Technology

Rollout

The campaign rollout began with a three-day public relations event that featured the unveiling of the University's new branding campaign. The on-campus rollout included workshops on the new graphic standards as well as the distribution of a graphic standards tool kit. This allowed RPI to maintain a fully integrated look for work created by multiple in-house and out-of-house resources.

Even as RPI was settling on a graphic treatment, they identified 20 stakeholder groups, including prospective students, current students, alumni, parents, faculty and staff, and others at whom the campaign would be directed.

One very important audience was alumni. Torello says that garnering alumni support was a critical campaign goal. With this in mind, a special alumni publication was developed that included campaign specifics as well as where the ads would be running (see below).

The first ads ran in *Time, Newsweek, U.S. News & World Report,* and *Sports Illustrated.* As mentioned earlier, the print ads demonstrated the "why not change the world?" position by focusing on actual stories of innovation and achievements at Rensselaer. RPI also ran TV spots on cable systems in its top alumni markets on CNBC, CNN, and MSNBC.

As you can see from the examples on the next page, the print ads are highly visual and use attention-grabbing, sometimes quirky headlines. Great art and copy were also used.

Headlines from the print ads included:

- Can you work on a computer that won't be built for 10 years?
- First chess, now literature
- One little student project turned into a $60,000,000 company
- E-merging traffic ahead
- Employers, commence wooing
- Research mussel(s)
- The only real thing is the human
- Wired science
- IEAR U
- Future tech
- Heidi in the sky (with data)

Sidebar
The essential need for focus

Torello says that the brand campaign benefited with the election of Dr. Shirley Ann Jackson in July 1999 as RPI's 19th president. Almost from the beginning, Dr. Jackson believed that RPI must be more consistently known as a world-class research institution. She also wanted RPI to catch up with its peers on dollars earned from research grants. Her aspirations were spelled out in the visionary Rensselaer Plan. To that end, she wanted RPI to focus in two research areas:

- Biotechnology
- Information technology

The Rensselaer Plan was strategically important and played a pivotal role in clarifying the main themes of RPI's emerging brand campaign. According to Torello, the key themes established by the committee and refined by the president meant that instead of trying to tell the whole RPI story, they could focus their efforts and tell a smaller story, but tell that story more completely.

Torello notes that Dr. Jackson joined RPI after the initial branding efforts were underway. However, he believes that her leadership helped focus RPI even more.

Evaluative research

In addition to the research undertaken as part of the initial brand development, RPI also undertook evaluative research in the spring of 1999, 2000, and 2001. These studies sought to measure awareness and perception of RPI after the initial flights of advertising. Later studies helped clarify two important drivers of university prestige: the quality of the faculty and the quality of research. These studies showed that audiences were especially responsive to the print ads that appeared in the science and technology sections of *The Wall Street Journal* and other major print media.

Branding timeline

- 8/97   Internal "perception study" interviews
- 12/97   Board approves development of Institute-wide marketing initiatives
- 1/98   News and Communications reorganizes to include strategic marketing functions and changes name to Marketing and Media Relations
- 4/98   External "perception study" (focus groups)
- 4/98   Strategic marketing committee formed
- 4/98   President Bryon Pipes leaves
- 7/98   Creative partner is hired after an extensive search process
- 8/98   Tagline, graphic standards, advertising creative, and media plans are developed and presented to faculty
- 1/99   Focus groups to test creative with alumni
- 3/99   Open house for campus to preview new campaign
- 3/99   Alumni brochure sent out in alumni magazine to all alumni
- 3/99   Perception survey mailed (to establish benchmarks for campaign evaluation)
- 3/99   First flight of advertising aimed at alumni begins
- 3/99   New graphic standards tool kit introduced to campus
- 7/99   Dr. Shirley Ann Jackson takes over as 19th president
- 10/99   First draft of "Rensselaer Plan" outlines Institute's future focus on information technology and biotechnology
- 11/99   Campaign revised to focus on "opinion leaders"
- 3/00   Second phase of campaign runs in the *The Wall Street Journal* and *The Washington Post*
- 4/00   Second perception study mailed
- 4/01   Third perception study mailed
- 7/01   Media refined to include special placement in *U.S. News & World Report* and additional media in Washington, D.C.

A shift in the go-to-market strategy

The brand communication plan launched by RPI was part of a larger shift in marketing at the Institute. Historically, RPI operated the traditional News and Communications Office. Now, as part of the institution-wide commitment to marketing and branding, this office has been reconfigured. It's new title, Marketing and Media Relations, reflects its larger mandate. As part of this shift, RPI brought in staffers, titled "account executives," who were assigned to different campus clients, much like an advertising agency. Clients include individual schools at the Institute as well as major divisions. The chief client contact is typically a dean or department head. Says Torello, "This approach has gone over so well on campus that the demand is greater than our ability to keep up."

Evaluating the campaign's success

After three years it was time for RPI to ask the important question: Has the brand communication campaign been successful? The following facts and insights provide much of the answer:

- Based on ongoing research, perception gaps are closing
- Inquiries and applications to RPI are at an all-time high
- The tuition discount rate is edging down
- The average SAT scores are at a 16-year high
- Fundraising is at record levels, including an increase in annual contributions from $40 million to $60 million
- RPI recently received the largest individual gift ever to a university, $360 million from an anonymous donor (completely unrestricted). This ranks second only to the recent gift by the Hewlett Foundation to Stanford of $400 million
- Research funding is at a new high
- RPI's students are in demand more than ever. They receive an average of seven job offers before they graduate with an average starting salary for a B.S. degree of $53,000
- The campaign has reinvigorated the morale of the staff and faculty

While it is still early, it looks as if RPI is receiving positive overtures from key research grant funding bodies. Says Torello, "RPI just won a major NSF research center in nanotechnology. We're one of only six schools to get one of these centers as part of the NSF's National Nanotechnology Initiative. The other schools (some pretty good company) are Harvard, Columbia, Cornell, Rice, and Northwestern."

Why the campaign was successful

Torello cites three key reasons why the campaign has been so successful. First, focus. The decision by the president to stress information technology and biotechnology allowed RPI to do a more thorough job, telling fewer stories.

Second, the decision to conduct faculty research early in the process, and to then rollout the campaign to faculty beforehand, was critically important for generating ownership. Says Torello, "I would never attempt to rollout any campaign without obtaining that initial buy-in before the creative."

And third, RPI committed to enough resources to do the job. Unlike many colleges and universities that dream big and fund small, RPI chose to dream modest and fund big.

Resources

In addition to a series of conversations and e-mails with Tom Torello, RPI's Director of Marketing, I had access to the nicely done publication, *Not Just Another Viewbook: A Study in Branding for Higher Education,* prepared by RPI's creative partner, Media Logic.

■■■■■

Chapter 10
Living Your Brand Promise

Successful brands know that they must deliver on the promises they make. As a consequence, they make their promises very carefully and commit themselves philosophically, organizationally, and economically to delivering on the few promises they do make.

The delivery on your promise is the most important litmus test of a successful brand leadership strategy. When students, donors, and others find a college brand that they believe in, and their experiences at that institution support their beliefs, then their loyalty, word-of-mouth, and economic support will prove invaluable. At the same time, if you do not live up to your promises, then students and others will withdraw from the promise relationship and your institution will suffer.

Essential Brand Promise Step #3

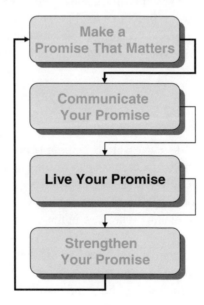

The organizational implications of brand

Mary Lou Zievis, writing in, "Beauty Is Only Skin Deep. It's What's Inside That Makes a Brand," reminds us that if the brand is to deliver its desired value and impact, then the organization standing behind it had better ensure that it lives up to what the brand stands for.

She goes on, "You can create award-winning advertising campaigns until the cows come home or design a logo for the ages. Yet if daily activities don't support and reinforce such messages, they won't mean a thing. Far more powerful are your customers' experiences and in perceptions they prompt."

In other words, you must walk the talk.

Living the brand can be difficult, especially if some people on your campus believe that a brand is just a look, logo, and tagline. To be successful, however, the brand promise must have the power to change the institution, its policies, and its people. For example, if your promise is to provide an outstanding engineering education, then this promise must guide how you are organized, the program you offer, the allocation of financial aid, your facilities plan, even who you hire, how they are evaluated for promotion, and when some are even let go. It is this aspect of a brand, its ability to change the behavior of stakeholders, that is one of the truest tests of a successful brand promise.

Brand stewardship

At Stamats, we use the phrase "brand stewardship" to describe how the stakeholders–faculty, staff, administrators–of a college or university work together to live the brand promise. A colleague once describe brand stewardship as "inside-out branding" when he mentioned that brand stewardship focuses on internal audiences with the idea that changing how internal audiences think and act will impact external audiences as well.

Instead of attitudinal, the problem with brand compliance is usually informational. Sometimes faculty, staff, and administrators simply do not know how the brand promise should impact how they teach, work, and administrate. Because of this, most brand stewardship programs tend to have two primary goals. First, to explain the brand promise to people on campus. And second, to help people understand how the brand promise should impact their jobs and how they interact with your most important audiences.

Explaining the brand promise

One of the most important aspects of brand stewardship is helping people on campus understand and apply the brand promise to their everyday responsibilities. Often, as part of the brand rollout, we will work with different groups and teams on campus and talk through how the brand promise might apply to them. For example, if we were working with security we might explore their motivations for giving tickets, how they respond to students who are unruly, or even how they react to visitors who park in the wrong spaces while on campus.

It is very important as part of the brand stewardship program to make the brand promise meaningful for each different cohort on campus and then to create customized discussions. One of the best ways to obtain insights into how different groups might do a better job living the brand is to talk to that group's customers. For example, before you talk with faculty, talk to students. Before you talk to food service, talk to people who eat in the cafeteria. And before you talk to senior administrators, talk to middle managers.

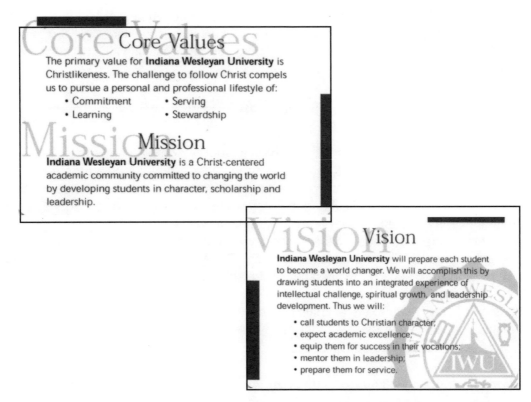

The little plastic card presented above illustrates how Indiana Wesleyan University helps deliver on its brand promise. This wallet-sized card is distributed to all employees, is discussed during the hiring process, and is also given to vendors. The purpose of the card is to help Indiana Wesleyan do a better job living its brand promise by reinforcing its most important brand messages.

Dr. Thomas Corts, President of Samford University, says that "Once established, a brand is a symbol for all that the organization represents: integrity, high standards, good value, fairness, courtesy." He goes on to say that a former staff member, in frustration, once used some inappropriate language to a vendor. The vendor reported it, saying, "He doesn't act like he's a Samford person." The message conflicts with the brand which had been well-established in the vendor's mind. Anything contrary to that symbol causes dissonance.

Corts believes that "branding is too important to be targeted at only for those outside the enterprise. If the faculty, staff, administration cannot buy into the key elements of an institution's identity, if they cannot own the mission, it is unlikely you can be convincing with external publics."

Translating the brand promise into improved performance

Another interesting approach to brand stewardship is to actually develop metrics through which you can measure whether or not the brand promise is impacting performance. For example, you might measure two important metrics that help define faculty and student interactions:

- Faculty evaluations
- Freshmen to sophomore retention data organized by department and individual faculty advisors

Of course, it is important for the people and groups who are being evaluated to have buy-in on the metrics and the evaluation process. It is also important for these groups to have buy-in on the rewards that improved performance will generate. At the same time, there must be some understanding about what happens when performance does not improve.

Sidebar
Fix what needs fixing

There's a famous story about the British Rail Service's search for a new advertising agency. When they went to the offices of Allen Brady & Marsh in London, they were met by a rude receptionist and were told to wait. Finally, an ill-kept person arrived to show them into the conference room. The room was dirty and cluttered with plates of stale food. They waited some more. A few agency people arrived one at a time in a lackadaisical manner, showing very little interest in what the BRS execs had to say. Just as the railway people were about to walk out in disgust, one of the agency people piped up and said, "Gentlemen, your treatment at Allen Brady & Marsh isn't typical. We behaved this way to point out what it is like to be a customer of British Rail."

He went on to say, "The real problem at British Rail isn't your advertising. It's your people. We suggest we help you fix the attitudes of your employees before we attempt to fix your advertising."

Determining whether or not you are delivering on your promise

There are a handful of metrics that help colleges and universities know whether or not they are delivering on their brand promise. Monitoring these metrics, like monitoring any barometer, can tell you what's working and what's not:

- Do prospective students refer themselves to you?
- Do students who apply go on to enroll?
- Do students persist?
- Do current students tell prospective students good things about you?
- When students leave, is it because they felt misled or uninformed?
- Do your graduates participate in alumni activities?
- Do your graduates support the institution?
- Do current donors commit to giving again?
- Do foundations who might be interested in your mission seek you out? Are they even aware of you?

Strategies for gathering feedback

There are a number of strategies for gathering feedback, including:

- Get out and have some conversations with your faculty, students, administrators, staff, alumni, donors, community residents, and others
- Organize focus groups or surveys
- Use suggestion boxes
- Read campus bulletin boards and newsletters
- Initiate a customer newsletter or computer bulletin board

The classroom experience

Most colleges and universities do an excellent job delivering their core promise: a quality education. In fact, study after study I have done for clients indicates that students are generally very satisfied with what goes on inside the classroom. More often than not, it is a poor secondary experience, or multiple poor secondary experiences, that are the source of frustration. Often, these failures to live the brand involve such areas as:

- Advising
- Financial aid (both amount of aid and timing and accuracy of aid information)
- Residence life
- Bursars office
- Registrar

Moments of truth

In the early 1970s, Jan Carlzon introduced the world to the idea of *moments of truth*. Carlzon was head of SAS Airlines and he recognized that 30 seconds with an agent at the counter is all it takes for customers to conclude that they're dealing with a great or a lousy airline. Even as we recognize that keeping your promise is more than customer service, we realize that a commitment to customer service can go a long way to helping you live your brand promise. We know, for example, that institutions with a strong commitment to its customers:

- Are attuned to the needs of their students, donors, and other stakeholders
- Are obsessed with making a positive impact at every moment of truth
- Have staff who keep policies and procedures in perspective
- Support frontline employees in every conceivable way
- Hire people who can and will exercise judgment
- Encourage employees to bend rules in order to resolve problems
- Are more interested in fixing the problem than in affixing the blame
- Keep their promises
- Have initial and ongoing orientation programs
- Reward and fire for quality
- Realize that we are all someone's customers

Several times each year I deliver a PowerPoint presentation on customer service called "Move Over Nordstrom: How to Build the Best Customer Service Program on the Planet." During the presentation, I outline a 10-step, sure-fire customer service program. The steps are:

- Obtain commitment from the top. The administration must send a clear message that customer service is critical to institutional success
- Designate a customer service champion
- Listen to your customers. Conduct research to determine:
  - Which programs, processes, and services are most important to your customers
  - How your clients perceive these services now
  - How your customers believe these services should be improved
  - Examine policies and procedures that inhibit service
- Within reason, and based on your research, define quality from the perspective of the customers
- Set service standards and be prepared to enforce them
- Select and train employees to work for the customers
- Create an ombudsman
- Empower employees to act
- Develop a reward and recognition system for frontline staff that is attractive and meaningful
- Remove people who do not perform

The ombudsman

An important step that a college or university can take to more effectively live their brand promises is to designate someone as the campus ombudsman. An ombudsman serves as a central clearinghouse for conflicts and problems that arise between the institution and its constituents, including students, faculty, staff, donors, and others. When someone on campus feels that they have been taken advantage of, abused, or ignored, they can visit or place a call to the ombudsman who is tasked with resolving the problem quickly and fairly. In some respects, an ombudsman is a "court of last resort." The brochure on the next page, from Bethel College and Seminary in St. Paul, outlines one such program.

Bless thy complaining customer

Oren Harari, writing in *Leapfrogging the Competition: Five Steps to Becoming a Market Leader*, emphasizes the need to look at complaining customers as an asset. Says Harari, "Every complaint is a golden nugget of information" for any organization. This is why leaders should gratefully pounce on them."

He goes on to say that there is a critical difference between a customer from hell and a customer put through hell. These customers often look alike, he says, "But each time we respond inappropriately to customers who have gone through hell, we push them closer to the door marked 'customer from hell."

Harari believes that complaining customers tell us three important things. First, that they are still wooable. In other words, they still desire a relationship. Second, that they represent other, often quieter, customers who just move on without voicing a complaint. And third, complaining customers tell us about glitches in our system. In this manner, they should be considered a fire alarm that's letting you know that whatever you are doing is not working and that you had better change, and fast.

The author then presents a series of strategies for turning complaining customers into allies. These strategies include:

- Make it very easy for customers to complain. In some cases, proactively solicit complaints
- Work like mad to respond to each and every complaint and make sure complaints are handled fast and in a friendly manner
- Make sure you change the structure so the policy or procedure that created the complaint is fixed
- Make complaints visible. Post quantitative data, unedited letters, and telephone transcripts. Read and discuss these complaints at meetings and then publicize how the complaint was resolved.
- Adjust performance review and compensation accordingly
- Reward complainers

Some final thoughts on keeping your promise

Not too long ago I was working with a client in Montana. Their brand promise centered around students. During one afternoon meeting we were talking about living the promise. I read some passages from the student handbook and posed this question: how many of these rules and regulations are designed to serve students and how many are designed to protect the institution from students? When I left they were making plans to not only review the student handbook but the faculty handbook, the manual from campus safety and security, the guidelines for operating the bookstore, the student center, the wellness center, and the library. More than simple words on paper, this school wanted to live its brand.

■ ■ ■ ■

Branding Case Study
University of Southern California
Doing Good Things

There are good neighbors. There are great neighbors. And there is USC.

The University of Southern California has built its brand around the notion of a being a good neighbor in the community immediately surrounding its two campuses in Los Angeles.

Most of us know that universities, particularly members of the Association of American Universities (AAU), are like a stool with three legs. One leg is education. The second is research. The third leg, often ignored or undervalued at many universities, is service.

Martha Harris, Vice President for University Public Relations at USC, says that when Steven Sample became president in 1991, he wanted to build on the legacy of James H. Zumberge, the previous president of USC. While Sample was keenly interested in the first two legs of the stool–research and education–he sought to elevate and focus USC's commitment to service. Says Harris, "An important breakthrough came when Sample said, essentially, 'Let's not try to save the world, but let's work in our neighborhood. Let's expand the service dimension even as we continue to do great research and offer an exceptional educational experience.'"

According to Harris, "Sample not only believed that the decision for USC to serve the community was best for the University, but felt that we would find that a lot of our work would be exportable and that many other universities–and their communities–might benefit."

The decision to focus on USC's immediate neighborhood would prove to be a pivotal decision for the University.

The neighborhood

Martha Harris loves maps and if given half a chance, she is quick to sketch the boundaries of USC's neighborhood. It is a 3.4 square-mile area bordered by the 10 Freeway on the north, the 110 Freeway on the east, Martin Luther King Boulevard on the south, and Western Avenue on the west.

The geographic boundaries of USC's neighborhood only tell part of the story. Those who are familiar with Los Angeles will recognize this area as one of the city's toughest. When Sample became president, unemployment was rampant. The available jobs were largely blue-collar or low-end service. Crime was high. By any stretch, this part of Los Angeles was a troubled, sometimes dangerous place.

But it was also the home of USC's main campuses. Rather than cut and run as other colleges had done, abandoning its neighborhood, USC decided to become a partner.

Harris says that many USC faculty were initially skeptical about Sample's idea to focus on the immediate neighborhood. Faculty had been used to doing work around the city, the nation, and even around the world. Importantly, Sample didn't try to stop faculty from doing their own thing. Instead, he began to focus institutional resources. He committed institutional dollars, and staff, and he committed the cloak of his presidency. The result was a critical mass of resources and institutional momentum directed at the neighborhood that made it possible for others to join in.

While progress was sometimes slow, eventually Sample discovered that faculty were directing their own resources, and research, to the neighborhood to which he had committed the University. Kenneth Weiss, in an article about Sample in the *Los Angeles Times Magazine*, says that being a college president is like herding cats. Says Weiss, "Sample's strength is his ability to sell his vision of where USC needs to go. He laid out a clear agenda soon after arriving and stuck to it, refusing to get sidetracked by day-to-day crises. He coaxed and cooed, snarled and snapped until most of the cats headed his way."

The inauguration of Steven Sample

Steven B. Sample was inaugurated as USC's 10th president on September 20, 1991. During his inauguration speech, Sample outlined six priorities. One of those priorities was to "continue and expand the USC tradition of public service in Southern California, with special emphasis on the neighborhoods in the immediate vicinity of our two campuses."

This was one of the first public pronouncements of Sample's intent, and it was this simple declaration that would become the heart and soul of USC's brand as a good neighbor.

Defining his neighborhood policy

Sample's neighborhood priority was refined during a year's worth of conversations with staff, faculty, students, neighbors, clergy, and area leaders. During that year, he listened carefully and discovered that USC's neighbors didn't want (and didn't trust) handouts. They were tired of programs that were created without their input and managed without their involvement. Sample's neighbors told him that they wanted USC to be a true partner, and that they wanted this partnership based on mutual respect and trust.

Eventually, USC's good neighbor policy crystallized around five important initiatives:

- Hire neighbors
- Provide incentives for USC employees, especially low-level employees, to buy housing in the neighborhood
- Use USC's expertise and energy to partner with the community to create great public schools
- Stimulate business development, especially for small businesses
- Help assure safe streets

And while these initiatives were important, no one could imagine how this commitment would be tested during the next few months.

The week that LA rioted

Six months after Sample's inauguration, and six months after he emphasized anew USC's commitment to its neighborhood, tragedy struck Los Angeles. During the last week of April 1992, following the Rodney King incident, LA rioted.

One short week after the riot, on May 8th, , USC held its 109th commencement. In part because of the riot, and wanting to distance himself from the troubled city, the commencement speaker cancelled. Instead of searching for another speaker, Sample chose this opportunity to draw an important line in the sand.

Standing before a restless crowd of 8,000, Sample began his speech, portions of which I have excerpted below:

"Rather than deliver a conventional commencement address, I want to talk about the events of recent days, about the city of Los Angeles, and about the role of the University of Southern California in this city. Commencement is a deeply symbolic event in the life of a university. It is a time when the academic community comes together to celebrate shared values and to send our most recent graduates out into the world. It is a time of rejoicing for families and extended families, and a time to celebrate new beginnings.

"Today, however, we are experiencing this ancient rite of passage in a sobering context. Our city, the City of Angels, has undergone a massive trauma. I would venture to say there is not a person here today who does not feel the events of the recent week in a deeply personal way. Speaking for myself, I can say that I feel a great sense of sorrow, not only for those who directly experienced violence and loss, but for our whole community. We have been reminded in a vivid and dramatic way that there are major problems yet to be solved in our society. Today we are sending nearly 8,000 of you, as newly minted graduates, out into the world to see what you can do about these problems.

"You are probably better equipped to take on these challenges than any other graduating class in the nation. You have received a first-rate education in one of America's finest universities. And you have had an opportunity to be engaged directly in the issues of a multicultural society–issues that everyone in our country will have to confront in the very near future.

"My message today is simple and hopeful. We have an opportunity to build our city anew–not as it was, but as it should be. We have a chance to create a new kind of city, with justice for all, with broad access to quality education, and with real economic opportunities for everyone; a place in which every child has a chance for a decent and productive life. Thus we must begin to look through the crisis of the moment toward a larger goal.

"Our city went berserk last week. It has happened before in our country. It happens routinely all over the world, but when it happens here at home we feel let down, betrayed, frightened, and lost. We feel that our deepest values as a nation have somehow failed us. There is a paradox here. No nation in the world has been as successful as ours in bringing together so many different people from so many different places with so many different mother tongues. And yet our history is replete with examples in which these ongoing efforts at incorporation have been temporarily derailed by violence.

"I am fond of reminding people that we are an <u>anchor</u> institution in Los Angeles. Being an anchor institution means we are here for the long pull. Unlike so many of the other private-sector institutions on which cities have traditionally depended, USC will not be sold or merged or moved to Phoenix.

"Being an anchor institution also means being one of the largest employers in the city of Los Angeles, and perhaps now the city's single largest employer in the private sector. We have some 13,000 employees on our two campuses in downtown L.A. More than 40 percent of our full-time staff are people of color, which may well make us the largest private employer of minorities in Los Angeles.

"And finally, being an anchor institution means we are a magnet for new dollars coming into this community. We attract tens of thousands of students and patients and hundreds of millions of dollars in gifts and contracts from outside Los Angeles. It is estimated that USC contributes nearly $3 billion a year to the gross regional product, which in turn generates some 40,000 total jobs.

"Ladies and gentlemen, we face a special moment in history. If your house went up in flames, would you restore it exactly as it was before? No. You would probably build a somewhat different house, one that was better suited to your current needs and circumstances, and that was more adaptable to future possibilities. We now have just such an opportunity to work together to build a new and better city. We have an opportunity to take all that is good about Los Angeles–the creative spirit, the optimism, the essential decency–and create a community in which our children and grandchildren will be able to live together in peace and mutual prosperity.

"As a university we can be a catalyst for action, an important and central player in the creation of a new kind of urban environment here in Los Angeles. Our faculty and students are brim full of ideas and enthusiasm for this project.

"But before we get too far down the road we all have a lot of listening and learning to do. We need to approach our task in the spirit of partnership, and work in concert with Angelenos from every walk of life. Let me tell you what I have been hearing during my first year here in Los Angeles. It's been my good fortune to meet and talk with hundreds of people in our city–workers, professional people, politicians, religious and ethnic leaders, and business people. I've been struck by the similarities among their basic desires and aspirations.

"When I ask people what they want for Los Angeles, I hear these five points over and over:

1. **Safe schools.** Schools that are not just physically safe, but emotionally safe as well. Schools that are free of violence and gangs and drugs and sexual coercion. Schools that are safe for teaching and learning. Schools in which children can safely be children, sheltered from premature pressures to be parents and warriors.

2. **Safe streets.** The people I've talked with are sick and tired of their children and spouses being mugged, shot, raped, and run over on the streets. They're sick and tired of their streets being controlled by gangs and hoodlums, instead of by homemakers and neighbors.

3. **Jobs.** I have talked to hundreds of people out in our community, and what I hear people say they want are jobs. I have not heard a single person say that what we need is more handouts. Instead, the vast majority want the chance to work for a living.

4. **Ownership.** I sense a hunger in Los Angeles for ownership, for achieving a real economic stake in our society. People want to own their own businesses and homes–and most especially their own homes. The American dream of home ownership isn't dead, but for many Angelenos it's simply out of reach.

5. **Respect.** The desire for respect is a basic human need. Not surprisingly, Angelenos of every color and creed and from every economic stratum want to be treated with respect as individuals, and not judged or dismissed as a group. They want this basic respect from the police, from store clerks, from bureaucrats, and from each other.

"Remember, the foregoing five points are not my list of priorities for Los Angeles; rather, they are what I've been hearing from other people. But the good news is this: If what Angelenos really want is safe schools, safe streets, jobs, home ownership, and basic respect, then those goals are truly within the realm of possibility. Other people in this country–tens of millions of other people–already have these five things. And there's no reason why we here in Los Angeles shouldn't have them too, and have them in abundance for all our citizens."

Concludes Sample, "My friends, this is not an easy time to be earning your degrees and entering the real world of work and worry. But I don't really pity you. Because while the challenges you face may be daunting, the opportunities are almost limitless. With your energy, enthusiasm, and expertise, we will surely be successful in transforming this wounded city of ours into something of which all of us here today, as well as those who will follow us in generations yet unborn, can be justifiably proud."

Kicking it up a notch

In 1993, USC hired Dr. Jane Pisano as Senior Vice President for External Relations. Her job was to coordinate and focus the many neighborhood programs that USC already had on line and to develop a handful of programs that would be truly stellar.

Prior to that assignment, Pisano was the Dean of Public Administration at USC. Her interest was community development and she was the ideal person to lead USC's good neighbor program. Described as an "implementer," "guru," and "lightning rod," Pisano helped institutionalize USC's commitment to its neighborhood.

While there are now more than 300 neighborhood programs, 10 programs were recently highlighted in a thoughtful publication, *Neighbors and Friends: Living and Working in University Park*, produced by USC. Those 10 programs are:

- Family of Five Schools
- Kid Watch
- Neighborhood Academic Initiative
- Joint Educational Project
- Good Neighbors Campaign
- Troy Camp
- Business Expansion Network
- USC Local Vendor Program
- Building and Development in University Park
- Neighborhood Watch

To help you more completely understand USC's commitment to its promise to be a good neighbor, I would like to briefly touch on a handful of these programs to give you a sense of what they are, how they work, and what they have accomplished.

Family of Five Schools

There are five elementary schools in USC's neighborhood. Almost immediately, USC began to focus its attention on those schools through its Family of Five Schools Program. The reason for this commitment is simple: USC understood that working closely with students long before they were able to attend college was one of the best ways to encourage and position them to attend college. The outcomes of that program have been both neighborhood–and life–changing. Consider:

- Each year, more than 1,500 low-income children and their families who live near a USC campus receive dental screenings, dental care, and dental education at no cost
- Two schools in the Family of Five School program were designated a *California Distinguished School*, an honor reserved for the top 10 percent of all California public schools
- The principal of one of the Family of Five Schools was selected as the 1998 California secondary school Principal of the Year
- More than 30 teachers from the Family of Five Schools have participated in USC's Web Master/Info Master program, an Internet training program
- All Family of Five Schools have been wired for the Internet with the help of USC's Information Services Division
- Some 98 percent of the 1998 graduates of the 32nd Street/USC Magnet Center and Foshay Learner Center were accepted into college

Kid Watch

A second program is Kid Watch. Kid Watch mobilizes volunteers to provide safe corridors for more than 8,000 neighborhood children as they walk to and from school, local parks, museums, libraries, and other neighborhood cultural and recreational facilities.

Almost 750 volunteers water their lawns, sweep sidewalks and perform other outside chores, keeping alert and informing law enforcement officials of anything that might harm a child. Children who were interviewed on their way to and from school report that they feel safer, and residents report that they have an increased sense of community togetherness and pride. The city's overall decline in crime has been more dramatic in University Park than in any other part of the city. Local law enforcement officials say Kid Watch and programs like it made the difference.

Harris says that as part of Kid Watch, homes were declared "safe havens" for children who felt threatened as they went to and from school. In addition, program leaders discovered a pedestrian tunnel under a road that children avoided because it was dangerous. As a consequence, students were forced to cross an extremely busy street. "As part of Kid Watch, the principal of a nearby school organized a 'Tunnel Brigade' so that kids would feel safe using the tunnel. Since the brigade has been on guard, there has not been one incident." Concludes Harris, "We now have 750 neighbors watching out for kids, and the program is growing."

One neighbor volunteer is Virgie Simon. Says Simon, "When children see the Kid Watch emblem in the windows, they know that there is someone watching them, that there is someone very interested in their safety. I can't wait to get up in the morning and put on my Kid Watch shirt."

The Neighborhood Academic Initiative

The goal of the Neighborhood Academic Initiative (NAI) is to prepare neighborhood children to succeed in college and in life. To accomplish this goal, NAI offers a full complement of educational and social service programs to low-income, at-risk, minority scholars and their families living in the University Park area. Counselors, teachers, and tutors work with the youngsters and their parents before and after school, weekdays, and on Saturday mornings.

NAI students are now scoring at the top of their high school classes and are going on to pursue their dreams in higher education. Those who meet USC's admission criteria are guaranteed a four-and-one-half-year tuition scholarship. From 1996 to 1998, USC awarded $2 million in NAI scholarships to students from the neighborhood.

Neighborhood Outreach

Since 1994, USC faculty and staff have donated more than $2 million of their own money to USC's Neighborhood Outreach program in part because they know that every cent they donate goes directly to a neighborhood-based organization or agency.

To help guide funding, a 12-member committee of faculty and staff allocates neighborhood outreach funds in response to grant requests developed by organizations in the neighborhood. These organizations work in partnership with USC to improve the quality of life and education for area children and their families, to improve public safety, and to boost neighborhood economic development. USC faculty and staff often work with neighborhood groups to write grant proposals.

Harris says that financial contributions from USC faculty, staff, and administrators increased tenfold in eight years in large part, she says, because "we can see how those dollars are directly impacting and improving our immediate community."

Local Vendor Program

One way that USC demonstrates its commitment to its neighborhood is its decision to purchase as many supplies and services as possible from local vendors. In 1998, USC purchased $47.2 million in goods and services from local vendors; $7.2 million from more than 250 small local businesses; $15 million from large community businesses; and $25 million from minority and disabled veteran business enterprises.

The intent of the Local Vendor program is to help local vendors create employment opportunities that are filled by residents living and working in neighborhoods close to the University Park and Health Sciences campuses. Vendors who participate in the program have an opportunity to competitively bid for USC projects. The program is part of an initiative that concentrates on a designated catchment area near both USC campuses. By 1999, more than 8,000 small businesses located within one of 15 zip codes in USC's two neighborhoods had received information about the program.

Program highlights

Recently, USC published a 170-page annual report on its good neighborhood programs. The report concludes with a series of "did you knows?":

- There are over 315 community outreach programs administered by USC and affiliated institutions
- USC serves over 696,329 people a year through those 315 programs, which range from education to health service
- Over 13,642 USC students, staff, faculty, and alumni volunteer through these USC programs in one year
- USC employees have contributed $2 million through USC's Good Neighbors campaign since 1994. Some $1.7 million has been invested in 82 USC-community partnerships near the two USC campuses
- USC did about $7 million in business with over 311 local small business vendors in the last year
- 10,127 USC undergraduate student volunteers worked in our neighborhood in 1998-1999 with more than 300 human service agencies

Do good work and get noticed

Harris says that while USC is wholly committed to its neighborhood, it is also committed to getting noticed for its good works. As a result, Harris says that USC had a number of important communication goals as part of the good neighbor program. "We want people to understand that our University Park neighborhood is a vibrant, safe urban community that is architecturally and historically interesting. In addition, we wanted to communicate that the people in our neighborhood–and USC itself–understand what it means to be a good neighbor, working respectfully together to transform our community. Finally, we wanted to get the word out that USC faculty, staff, and students are part of a culture of caring."

To help get the word out, USC developed a unique, three-tiered communication pyramid. The top tier–USC Ambassadors–is comprised of 6,000 opinion leaders and stakeholders; people whom USC wishes to inform and influence. The second tier, some 40,000 parents, faculty, volunteers, and donors, receive the Presidential Communiqué. The bottom tier, some 200,000 people in size, receive USC's quarterly *Trojan Family Magazine*.

While all three tiers are important, it is the top tier–the Ambassadors– that is the most influential. The purpose of the Ambassador program is twofold. First, Ambassadors serve as a sounding board to help test USC messages. Second, they serve as "ambassadors" to various external stakeholder groups. This helps USC influence the influencers who will in turn influence others. The result is a viral approach to marketing and communication that helps spread the word about USC.

Harris believes that USC must do good works ... and get noticed for doing so. In the last couple of years, USC has received some pretty impressive "buzz" about its good works and overall increase in student quality. First, there was the naming of USC as the *Time Magazine-Princeton Review* College of the Year in 2000. And then there was the exposure in *The Los Angeles Times Magazine*.

Let's begin with the *Los Angeles Times Magazine*, (see cover, left).

The Los Angeles Times Magazine

In September 2000, the *Los Angeles Times Magazine* presented a cover story on USC's president Steven Sample under the headline, "Engineer-Drummer-Pitchman, Steven Sample is Staging a Surprising Production: The Make-Over of USC." The lengthy article heralded USC's commitment to its neighborhood, but it also acknowledged USC's climb into the top tier of academic institutions in the United States.

If USC had written the article itself it couldn't have done a better job than did *Los Angeles Times* correspondent Kenneth Weiss. At one point in the article Weiss wrote, "In what until recently was one of the best-kept secrets in academic circles, USC has become a hot school. No longer does it go begging for qualified students, as it did a decade ago before Sample arrived. This year, it turned away two-thirds of its freshmen applicants. The once largely white student body has evolved into one of the most racially diverse in the nation. Average SAT scores of incoming students, once so low that in 1987 the irreverent Stanford marching band spelled them out with just three digits, soared this fall to 1,309, eclipsing those of UCLA freshmen for the first time. There are other signs:

- USC faculty bring in nearly twice as much each year in research grants as a decade ago; they have almost doubled the number of memberships in prestigious national academies; and they landed the school's first Nobel Prize, in 1994 for chemistry.

131

- The school's financial fortunes have soared. The haul from a seven-year fundraising campaign stands at $1.7 billion in cash and pledges, and is growing.
- The university's endowment has quadrupled.
- Even the surrounding neighborhood, for years a danger zone that gave the school an abrupt and jagged edge, is on the upswing as thousands of USC staff and volunteers have reached out to help reduce crime, improve area schools, or otherwise aid their poor neighbors."

Part of what landed the *Los Angeles Times Magazine* article was an earlier, and much more important accolade; USC being named College of the Year by *Time.*.

It's about Time

On August 22, 1999, USC was named the *Time-Princeton Review* College of the Year. As part of the honor, USC was featured in an extensive article in *Time*. That article chronicled the dramatic rise in USC's stature and prestige in the academic community. At the same time, the article also made extensive mention of USC's commitment to its neighborhood. In fact, many suggest that it was the scale of this commitment to its neighbors that distinguished USC from the other schools in the running for the same honor.

Says Harris, "We have shamelessly exploited the honor we received from *Time*, distributing half a million copies of the reprint to our closest friends. We reached millions more–most of them classical music listeners–when we incorporated a mention of the recognition in the on-air ID for our public radio station, KUSC, during a yearlong promotion."

The key message

At the conclusion of our interview, Harris was careful to mention that USC already had a significant culture of outreach that preceded Sample. "What Sample helped us do in 1991 was to focus our outreach efforts into our immediate neighborhood. At the same time, we wanted to do a much better job celebrating this outreach, and this celebration had to be internal–we needed to do a better job telling our own faculty and staff–and external– we wanted to tell the world."

It was important, says Harris, to focus and celebrate on things that were real and working. "We didn't talk too much about what we were going to do but instead stressed what we did do. Our promise was to help our community. Our promise was to be good neighbors. We have lived up to that promise and we will continue to live that promise."

The University for Spoiled Children

Doing good things and getting noticed.

These twin emphases have served USC extremely well during the last 10 years. And as USC continues its march up the ranks of America's best colleges, it can't help but poke fun at itself … and its detractors. On the back cover of the small publication that contains the *Time-Princeton Review* College of the Year excerpt is a full-page ad featuring an attractive young man and woman in a Mercedes convertible.

The copy for the ad begins, "A favorite stunt of rival football fans from UCLA, Stanford, and Notre Dame is to wave their car keys and credit cards in cadence to the Trojan Marching Band as it plays "Tribute to Troy," a march our opponents love to hate. This amusing ritual is meant to symbolize their contention that USC is the "University of Spoiled Children." If you have heard the myth promoted by students at other colleges that USC's student body is rich and spoiled, consider this:

- Among the nation's most selective universities, our student body is also one of the most ethnically and racially diverse and draws students from all 50 states and more than 100 countries
- USC distributes $200 million in financial aid; over 60 percent of our students receive assistance
- More than 60 percent of USC students volunteer in community-service programs in neighborhoods around campus and throughout LA

And consider this:

- The student-to-faculty ratio is 14-to-1
- The average class size is 26 students
- Full-time faculty teach the vast majority of our courses
- Students can get all the classes they need in order to graduate in four years
- USC grads get great jobs, attend the best graduate and professional schools in the country (including our own), and are supported by the Trojan Family, a network of nearly a quarter million alumni

Concludes the ad, "So, maybe we *do* spoil our students–and we intend to keep it that way."

A final word

It is clear that USC has received significant national press about its commitment to its neighborhood. But it is also clear that it is the nod from the people in that 3.4-square-mile area that USC treasures most.

In the *Time* article, author Margot Hornblower quotes the Rev. Cecil "Chip" Murray, senior minister of the First African Methodist Episcopal Church. Says Murray, "USC was once perceived as hoity-toity. And some people from the lower-crust are afraid to enter an upper-crust school." By the time the riots exploded, many families in South Central Los Angeles–as a result of the University's neighborhood programs–had begun to adopt USC as their own. In the years since, relations have only deepened. The Rev. Murray goes on, "Other schools say, 'You are free to come to us if you wish.' USC goes out and puts their hands in yours and brings you to them."

Resources

In addition to interviewing Martha Harris, USC's Vice President for University Public Relations, a number of resources were used in preparing this case study including:

- Kenneth Weiss's "Engineer-Drummer-Pitchman: Steve Sample is Staging a Surprise Production: The Make-Over of USC." *Los Angeles Times Magazine,* September 2000
- Presentation on USC's good neighbor program at CASE VII on December 1, 2000, by Martha Harris
- *Time-Princeton Review College of the Year* issue, 2000
- USC's *Friends and Neighbors* report, 2000
- USC's *Good Neighbor* annual report, 2000

■■■■■

Chapter 11
Strengthening Your Brand Promise

Brands are organic and their story is never ending. As such, you must make an ongoing commitment to continually strengthen your brand promise. At its most basic, strengthening your brand promise involves continually asking and seeking the answer to the following three questions:

- Is our original promise still relevant to our most important internal and external audiences?
- Did we live our promise as well as we could?
- Did we communicate our promise effectively?

In other words, "did we live up to expectations?" and "how can we do this better?"[19]

Essential Brand Promise Step #4

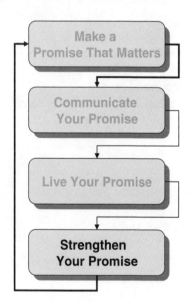

It shouldn't be surprising that answering these questions will require a commitment to systematic, ongoing, formal and informal market research. In addition, these research data must be used to not only assess your current situation, but also to look for new opportunities to make your brand promise even stronger and more vibrant.

The following three sections, oriented around making, communicating, and living your brand promise, contain a series of questions that will help you strengthen your promise.

Possible research questions: making a brand promise

- Based on research with our target audiences, our internal audiences, our competitors, and our marketplace, is our brand promise still meaningful?
- Are prospective students and donors–based on tuition revenue and fundraising data–willing, even eager, to support it?
- Can another college or university make the same promise we are making? Is anyone trying?
- Is there a chance they will be able to do a better job delivering on this promise than we do?
- What data do we have to suggest that our brand promise needs refreshing?

Possible research questions: communicating your promise

- Can such internal audiences as faculty, staff, and administrators recite the basic tenants of our brand promise?
- Can such customers as students and donors recite the main elements of our brand promise?
- Is there internal confusion about the brand promise?
- Do prospective students notice our brand promise amidst all the other messages they receive?
- Do prospective students and donors find the promise–and how it was conveyed–meaningful? Do they tell others about it?
- Do the people who influence our target audiences (parents, high school counselors, employers) recognize our brand promise?
- Are competitors responding to our brand promise?
- How effective are we at using an enriched media array to communicate our brand promise?
- How are we communicating our brand promise via:
  - Special events?
  - Sponsorships?
  - Outreach?
  - Internal messaging to faculty, staff, and administrators?
  - Internal messaging to current students?
  - External messages to prospective students?
  - External messages to donors?
  - External messages to alumni?
  - External messages to community residents?
- How have we segmented our brand communication strategy to reflect the different expectations and media habits of our different target audiences?
- Have we implemented a graphic identity program, and is this program being followed?

Possible research questions: living your brand promise

- Can faculty, staff, and administrators point to how our brand promise has changed their behaviors?
- Are our brand stewardship programs well attended and having an impact?
- Has our brand promise affected our hiring and promotion practices?
- Do our graduates and donors feel that we lived up to our brand promise?
- Do graduates and donors believe that our brand promise is still valuable and unique?
- Are graduates and donors "recommending" our brand to others?
- Is the cost of recruiting a student or raising a dollar going down?
- Are our retention rates increasing?
- Is the average annual fund contribution going up?

Time to revise your mission, vision, and original brand promise

If the research you are conducting on your brand promise indicates that there is a serious disconnect between the brand promise you are making and the promise that is communicated or delivered, then it is time to look at your originating document: Your mission, vision, strategic plan, and brand promise. If the research that supported the creation of the brand is solid, then the disconnect is likely occurring at the communicating or living stages. However, some brand promises, no matter how thoughtfully developed, communicated, and lived, simply fail to capture the attention of the intended target audiences. This failure in the middle will require you to go back to the beginning of your brand creation strategy and identify where change is needed.

Not just data, but action

As you consider the creation of a research agenda, to ask and answer the questions that will help you strengthen your brand, it is very important to remember that your aim is not simply to conduct market research. Rather, your goal is to gather information upon which you can act and improve performance. With this goal, it is recommended that your research be broadly focused across multiple audiences with slightly less validity.

The importance of a research cycle

One of the best ways to keep your finger on the pulse of your marketplace is to conduct ongoing research. To help in this endeavor, a research cycle is presented in Chapter 17.

The brand report card

As part of our branding work with colleges and universities, Stamats often conducts evaluations of a college or university's overall brand strategy. This audit is different than the strategic brand audit that is undertaken at the brand creation stage. This audit is more evaluative in nature, and at its conclusion we present the client with a branding report card that grades them on different aspects of their brand and offers insight and advice on any weaknesses that are uncovered.

While the categories covered in the report card are dependent on the institution and its context, typical categories include:

- The president, board, and senior administrators understand and agree on the definition, role, and function of branding at the institution and they use a common language to discuss marketing and branding
- The institution demonstrates a commitment to building brand equity with a sufficient allocation of time, talent, and dollars
- The most important target audiences and competitors have been clearly identified
- Your most important external target audiences find your brand promise relevant and demonstrate their commitment to your brand promise
- Internal stakeholders understand and value your brand promise
- You consistently deliver on your brand promise
- Your price is competitive and consistent with public perception of what people think you are worth
- Your brand promise properly positions you for the future
- Your brand image is consistent and distinctive and supports messages that are relevant, remembered, and repeated
- You consistently measure whether or not you are increasing brand equity

Sidebar
One short month to brand ruin

The March 2001 issue of *Promo* magazine contains an insightful, even humorous article titled, "One Short Month to Brand Ruin", by Peter Breen. Breen opens the article by saying, "Follow these helpful hints in any order you'd like; there are many paths to failure."

His calendar for brand ruin, abbreviated for higher education, includes:

Day 1: Integration schmintegration. Trying to coordinate advertising, promotion, Internet activity, blah, blah, blah, is simply too difficult a task. As Homer Simpson once said, "Anything that's hard isn't worth doing."

Day 3: Start with the creative. State-of-the-art graphics and killer copy–most importantly, a really cool tagline–can be tailored to meet the needs of just about any future plan.

Day 15: Obtain a digital file of your competitor's ad. Painstakingly replace all references to their brand with yours. Tell your media buyer to run it "everywhere they were."

Day 17: Make every decision based solely on cost. Devise a spreadsheet that will tally all the money you save. Use lots of colors.

Day 19: Change your unique selling proposition to, "We're cheaper." (Hey, it works for Wal-Mart, right?)

Day 21: Plan your itinerary (tour), starting with the cities you've never visited, then the ones containing relatives.

Day 22: Never let your advertising agency meet with your consultant. Better yet, encourage competition between them. That'll inspire creativity.

Day 26: Never repeat a promotion, no matter how successful. How will you get noticed if you keep using the same old concepts? If that tired execution can keep lifting awareness, imagine how a new idea–whatever it is–will move the needle.

Day 28: Don't bother developing measurement tools. They'll just cause trouble. If anyone asks, tell them "awareness went through the roof." Besides, whomever they get to replace you can dig for results.

Conducting postmortems

One of my favorite tools for strengthening brand performance is the completion of a postmortem on any complaints you hear from your target audiences. Postmortems work like this:

- Someone has a problem
- The problem is communicated to the responsible administrator (or the campus ombudsman)
- The administrator, often working directly with the person who made the complaint, as well as the others who are involved, determines what went wrong
- The problem is addressed, the fix is communicated back to the person who complained, and the relationship is restored
- The fix is also communicated back to the organization, so changes in the system can be made to ensure that the mistake is not repeated

For the postmortem to work, the organization and its people must be sensitive to the needs of both internal and external audiences and must look at complaints as opportunities to learn rather than something to ignore or avoid.

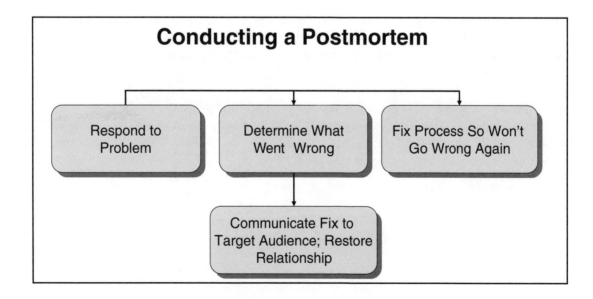

Conducting a Postmortem

Respond to Problem

Determine What Went Wrong

Fix Process So Won't Go Wrong Again

Communicate Fix to Target Audience; Restore Relationship

Interestingly, while most postmortems are directed at handling complaints, they can also be used to more completely understand why something went better than expected. Communicating this kind of information has a tremendous impact on improved performance as well.

Branding Bullet

There is a big difference between a customer from hell
and a customer that has been put through hell.

The parable of the black belt

Sometimes when I think about the ongoing commitment to living your brand promise, I am reminded of the parable of the black belt. I first read this parable in James Collins' *Built to Last: Successful Habits of Visionary Companies.*

Collins writes, "Picture a martial artist kneeling before the master sensei in a ceremony to receive a hard-earned black belt. After years of relentless training, the student has finally reached a pinnacle of achievement in the discipline. 'Before granting the belt, you must pass one more test,' says the sensei. 'I am ready,' responds the student, expecting perhaps one final round of sparring.

"'You must answer the essential question: What is the true meaning of the black belt?'

"'The end of my journey,' says the student. 'A well-deserved reward for all my hard work.'"

The sensei waits for more. Clearly, he is not satisfied. Finally, the sensei speaks. 'You are not yet ready for the black belt. Return in one year.'

"A year later, the student kneels again in front of the sensei, 'What is the true meaning of the black belt?' asks the sensei. 'A symbol of distinction and the highest achievement in our art,' says the student. The sensei says nothing for many minutes, waiting. Clearly, he is not satisfied. Finally, he speaks. 'You are still not ready for the black belt. Return in one year.'

"A year later, the student kneels once again in front of the sensei. And again the sensei asks: 'What is the true meaning of the black belt?' 'The black belt represents the beginning–the start of a never-ending journey of discipline, work, and the pursuit of an ever-higher standard,' says the student. 'Yes, says the sensei, 'you are now ready to receive the black belt and begin your work.'"

■■■■■

Section Three
Brand Mechanics

The following section will contain a handful of marketing strategies that will help you refine your brand strategy.

■ ■ ■ ■ ■

Chapter 12
Differentiate or Die[20]

Why differentiation is important

Sometimes I think that 99.99 percent of the colleges and universities in the country describe themselves as friendly, caring, and supporting. And according to their recruiting literature, all offer outstanding academic quality.

While these qualities are exceedingly important, they are hardly distinctive. Unfortunately, a lack of distinctiveness is at the heart of many brand failures. To help remedy this problem, I would like to offer a handful of strategies that will help you become more distinctive in ways that your target audiences value and will pay for.

These differentiation strategies involve:

- Communication
- Curriculum
- Co-branding

Before we begin discussing these strategies in the next three chapters, I would like to offer one suggestion; follow through on the brand promise.

The glory is in the follow-through

Sadly, we live in an increasingly trust-less society, and branding, like any other promise, will likely be perceived with skepticism unless you actually keep your word and deliver on your brand promise. To do this, of course, your brand and its promise must be embraced–and lived out–by your faculty, staff, and administrators. If it isn't, then the promise of your brand becomes just another bit of hype in a hyped up marketplace.

It is relatively easy to come up with a brand promise.

And it is relatively easy to write a brand communication plan.

But the fact is, more people talk about brands and brand communication than actually follow through. In other words, when all is said and done, more is said than done.

As a whole, colleges and universities are not very good at follow-through. It seems at times as if they spend all their time and expend all their energy concocting plans, but they seem to run out of gas when it comes time for implementation.

As I think about the problem of follow-through, I am reminded of a paper by Amar Bhide. It was titled, "Hustle as Strategy" and ran in the 1986 September-October *Harvard Business Review*. While the context of the article is business in general and the financial services industry in particular, its application to our discussion is obvious.

Writes Bhide, "Strategy, its high-church theologians insist, is about outflanking competitors with big plays. It is questionable whether this proposition is itself sustainable. Strategy involves a lot more and also a lot less. The competitive scriptures almost systematically ignore the importance of hustle and energy. While they preach strategic planning, competitive strategy, and competitive advantage, they overlook the record of a surprisingly large number of very successful companies that vigorously practice a different religion. These companies don't have long-term strategic plans with an obsessive preoccupation on rivalry. They concentrate on operating details and doing things well. Hustle is their style and their strategy. They move fast, and they get it right.

"Are administrators in these organizations living in the managerial dark ages? Wouldn't they do even better if they linked their hustle to big, powerful strategic plans? I believe the answer is 'no.'"

He goes on, "Opportunities to gain lasting advantage through blockbuster strategic moves are rare in any business. What mostly counts are vigor and nimbleness. These traits are always needed and always important, yet strategic planning theologians largely ignore them.

"Countless companies in all industries, young or old, mature or booming, are finally learning the limits of strategy and concentrating on tactics and execution. In a world where there are no secrets, where innovations are quickly imitated or become obsolete, the theory of competitive advantage may have had its day. Realistically, ask yourself: If all your competitors gave their strategic plans to each other, would it really make a difference?"

To his wise counsel I add a simple, "Amen."

■■■■

Chapter 13
Differentiation Through Communication
(or the Big Dog Theory of Differentiation)

The Big Dog Theory of Differentiation means that on one of the 4 Ps (or 4 Cs) you must differentiate yourself from your competition and be known as the Big Dog.

You must have the best academic product on the planet (or at least in your target geography), or ... .

Offer the best price, or ... .

Hold your courses in the best place (or in the most unique way), or ... .

You must have the best marketing communication strategy under the sun.

In theory, you can differentiate along any of the 4 Ps or Cs. But reality is different. While it pains me to say it, most colleges and universities are really not that different.

They offer the same basic programs as their competitors and teach these courses in the same basic way.

If you look closely, you typically find that within their cohort, their costs are not that different.

While some locales might be more attractive than others (my nephew chose UC-Santa Barbara in part because he could surf), location is seldom the Big Dog in the college choice process.

More often than not, for institutions that are largely similar, the Big Dog will likely be how well, consistently, and creatively you market and promote yourself. In other words, how well you communicate your brand; how well you create top of mindshare.

There are countless examples in business about commodity products differentiating themselves on promotion alone. For example, is Sunkist really different than any other orange? Probably not, but how many other brands of oranges can you name?

Is Mount Blanc the only great fountain pen? Likely not, but can you name another?

Aren't most t-shirts alike? Of course, but try telling that to a "gotta have the latest Tommy" 17-year-old.

So what makes these brands, brands? In some measure, it is because they have extremely aggressive and effective brand communication strategies.

Why consider a communication-based differentiation strategy

There are a number of reasons why a communication-based differentiation strategy can be extremely effective.

First, it is typically much less political than differentiating yourself by changing your curriculum, because faculty have a tendency to dig in and resist any efforts to change programs. This is especially true when the impetus to change seems to be coming from those Visigoths in marketing.

Second, while a communication-based differentiation strategy is based on four essential ingredients, these ingredients, while not common, are available if you really look for them. These ingredients are:

- The institutional will to commit yourself and your institution to a communication-based differentiation strategy
- The dollars to fund the strategy over a long period of time
- Finding a person who has the experience and creativity to run your communication strategy
- Follow-through

Of the above four, the easiest is the dollars. Having the institutional will and finding the right person will prove to be the main hurdles. And of course, there is follow-through.

Third, a strategy based on differentiated communication can be ramped up quickly. It takes time to change your programs, adjust pricing, or even enhance your location. But a communication-based differentiation strategy is largely a function of talent and dollars. If you have both, you can move very quickly.

A few words of caution

Before we move on to a discussion of the elements of a communication-based differentiation strategy, a few words of caution are in order. First, it is important to remember that any advantage that a communication-based differentiation strategy might generate for you is also available to your competitors, if they have or can acquire similar resources. In other words, you run the risk of being outspent.

With this in mind, a communication-based differentiation strategy might buy you some time, but eventually you will need to work to differentiate yourself on the melding of your three strategic assets: product, price, and place, or customer, cost, and convenience–assets that are uniquely yours and yours alone.

Second, and perhaps more importantly, your communication strategy must be built on true academic quality. If the marketplace senses smoke and mirrors, you will likely never recover. If you are a flawed institution with a moribund curriculum, and aggressively carry your message to the marketplace, more people will find out you are flawed.

Some elements of a communication-based differentiation strategy

The key to a differentiation strategy based on communication is how well, artfully, and consistently you communicate, or promote, your brand promise. As noted earlier, this is often a function of institutional will, dollars, and the creativity and experience of your chief branding officer.

While I don't want to repeat the elements of a brand communication plan (see Chapter 9), I do want to highlight a couple of things.

First, let's turn our attention once again to the utilization of an enriched media mix. As you look at the mix you should immediately notice that many of these functions report up through different vice presidents. The first challenge will be to work from an institutional perspective, not solely a marketing, recruiting, or fundraising perspective. This means a single, coordinated, cross-functional team.

Second, remember your prioritized target audiences. Reaching a handful of audiences with a saturation-level campaign is more effective than dribbling out a little creative across too many audiences.

Third, I would rollout my campaign in three phases. It is critically important to remember that you will be adding phase two in the second year and phase three in the third year so that in three years you are running a campaign that might look like this:

Phase one

- New graphic identity system including an internal launch of your new brand
- Signage and environmentals, especially perimeter markings, maps, and directions to campus
- High school relations:
    - Database of where your graduates are teaching and administrating
    - E-mail distributed newsletter to high school influencers
    - High school visit program
    - Faculty (yours) to faculty (theirs) program
- Internal communications
- Concentrated regional media buy for the final three months of Phase One:
    - Billboards
    - Regional magazines
    - Regional newspapers including high school and community college newspapers
    - Drive-time radio

Phase two

- Media relations work
- Web strategy
- Donor relations
- Direct mail including broadcast e-mail
- Concentrated regional media buy for the first six months and final three months of Phase Two:
    - Billboards
    - Regional magazines
    - Regional newspapers including high school and community college newspapers
    - Drive-time radio

Phase three

- Special events and symposia
- Collaborations
- Co-branding
- Concentrated regional media buy for the first six months and final three months of Phase Three:
  - Billboards
  - Regional magazines
  - Regional newspapers including high school and community college newspapers
  - Drive-time radio

Note that the three phases go from simple media to more complex media. However, by beginning with the simple, you will generate momentum that will help you move through the more complex issues in a more expedient manner.

Note, too, that I am not addressing matching messages and media to specific target audiences. Earlier we discussed the need to hire a seasoned professional to run your campaign. No doubt this is one of the first things he or she will do.

Finally, remember that these three phases must be customized and refined based on your institution, your marketplace, and your competitor set.

Conveying meaning through the story: a powerful context generator

Joseph Lepla and Lynn M. Parker, writing in *Integrated Branding: Becoming Brand-Driven Through Company-Wide Action,* make the case that a simple, compelling story is one of the most powerful of all brand-building tools.

They write, "For tens of thousands of years, human beings have been using stories to convey meaning to each other. Stories teach us about behavior. They inspire and provide insight. They are a guide to social, moral, work, and ethical actions and were used before writing to preserve the collective memories of the tribe. Human beings seem to be hard-wired to share their own experiences in story form and listen to others' tales.

"Even the modern world bases much of its communication and entertainment on stories. Movies and television are all about stories that teach behavior, from the evening news to the latest sitcom. Words and phrases from these stories become part of our everyday vocabulary. The Internet provides a new style of storytelling that is more like the traditional form than you would expect. In the new century, as ideas become more of the currency for creating value, storytelling will take on even greater importance. The structure of a story has the ability to break through the noise of daily life and create memorable impressions in customers."

Lepla and Parker go on to say that successful brand-building stories require three things:

- Ideas that fit the marketplace
- Values that resonate deeply with the existing culture
- Individuals who tell the story by the way they conduct themselves

They write, "The basic formula of a successful brand story is dramatic and even heroic. It is about how the protagonist beat the odds and became greater than he or she was previously … it's frequently about … aspirations … seizing opportunities and successfully overcoming obstacles. And the stories of strong brands are a never-ending tale. The story will continue to grow and be even more attractive to customers as long as there are new challenges for the organization to overcome."

What makes a meaningful story?

There are a number of criteria for a meaningful story:

- **Passion.** Does the story capture the heart of the brand in a way that evokes strong emotion?
- **Values.** Does the story reflect core values?
- **Audience reaction.** Once you have a story, it needs to be a shared experience with the listener. Tell the story to a variety of people inside the organization and out. Gauge their emotional reaction and analyze the questions they asked:
  - Were listeners attentive?
  - Excited?
  - Engaged?
  - Can you enhance the story on the basis of the questions they asked?

Conclude Lepla and Parker, "A story is organic and never ending; it changes over time and varies according to both who tells the story and who is listening to it. If a listener's questions were about clarification of either the facts or the reasons for doing something, the story needs to change. If the questions demonstrated an understanding of what you were trying to convey, and were further explorations into the company brand, congratulations; your story is working for you!"

Real stories. Real people.

A number of years ago, I read a wonderful recruiting piece from Carson-Newman College in Jefferson City, Tennessee. The title of the piece was *Real Stories. Real People.* Somewhere along the line I had loaned the piece to someone and was dismayed to discover that I had lost it. What intrigued me was that even though I didn't have the publication any more, I remembered the stories, and I remembered that they came from Carson-Newman. Fortunately, Sheryl Gray, director of Undergraduate Admissions at Carson-Newman, was kind enough to send me a copy of the original publication. To help reinforce the importance of stories, I would like to share a couple of the stories from that publication with you. They are short, but poignant. The first concerns a young man with an interesting approach to learning. The second is even more unique.

Scott's story

It seemed like a strange thing to do at 11 o'clock at night, but Scott was going to do it anyway. The other pre-med students were studying in the lab, but he walked right past them. Something he'd read once echoed in his mind: "You can't learn it until you teach it." Halfway through the semester, with more than 90 pages of histology notes, he had to cram for next week's test. In Carson-Newman's pre-med program, you either know it or you don't. And the college's track record was so good–what was it? Something like 90 percent get into med school. The thought made him more determined. Finally, he walked into a classroom and set his books down on the professor's desk. "You can't learn it until you teach it," he thought again. He looked towards the door to make sure it was closed tight. Then, picking up a piece of chalk, he turned to the empty desks. "Now," he said with a confident voice, "Let's review the four different kinds of tissues."

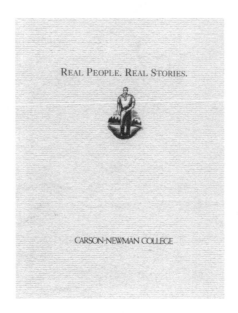

1862

It was 1862 and the few who remained at Carson-Newman looked tensely out the windows. "They're getting closer," a student whispered, "I hear musket fire!" Nothing had been the same since the Civil War began. And now the college was in the thick of it, trapped in the struggle for control of the Tennessee Valley. As the days wore on and the danger grew, Carson-Newman reluctantly closed its doors. Union troops bivouacked on campus for three long years, leaving it in ruins. When the war ended, the lands and buildings were sold at auction. But Carson-Newman's president vowed he'd buy them back again. And he rode 3,000 miles on horseback to raise the money to do it. The Civil War took its toll on colleges. Only 20 percent of those that were in existence when the war began still survive today. Carson-Newman is one of them.

The publication closed the series of stories with the following, "Stories are the stuff of life. They're part of our education, passed down from grandparents, whispered around the campfire, and traded among friends. They introduce us to one another, hold us together, and inspire us to do better. And often, they show us that everybody is pretty much the same at heart. Stories interest us because they're about people and ideas and beliefs–those living things that help us find joy in our own lives. On the preceding pages, we've told you a few stories about Carson-Newman College. They're all true, and they're true to who we are. And they may give you reasons why you'll want to start a story of your own here one day soon."

Get ink

Harry Beckwith, in *Selling the Invisible*, brings this discussion into vivid focus. He writes, "There are six peaks in Europe higher than the Matterhorn.

His question to the reader is simple: "Can you name one?"

He concludes: "Get ink."

■ ■ ■ ■

Branding Case Study
Centre College
Telling the Story

In 1921, little Centre College played No. 1 (and undefeated in five years) Harvard. The result was an odd equation: C6H0. For the uninitiated, that translates to Centre 6, Harvard 0.

This game was so big that in 1950 the Associated Press voted it "the sports upset of the first half-century." More than 75 years later, as you can see from the brochures presented below, Centre still celebrates the victory over Harvard.

Beating Harvard was an exceptional feat. But then Centre College, located in Danville, Kentucky, has a long history of being exceptional.

A defining moment....

In fact, the idea of being exceptional is at the heart (should I say "center") of Centre. Mike Norris, the Director of Communications at Centre, says the College has always considered itself to be an overachieving kind of place.

Of course, lots of colleges and universities talk about delivering an exceptional educational experience. We also know that fewer colleges actually do. Of the few that do, an even smaller number do as good a job getting the word out as does Centre.

Says Norris, "We begin with the promise of extraordinary quality." But it doesn't end there. Consider what Woodrow Wilson said in 1903, "There's a little college down in Kentucky which in 60 years has graduated more men who have acquired prominence and fame than has Princeton in her 150 years."

Big words? Of course. But keep in mind that Centre has graduated:

- 17 Fulbright winners in the last 10 years
- 13 U.S. Senators
- 11 Governors
- 7 Rhodes scholars
- 34 Peace Corps volunteers
- 6 Goldwater scholars
- 3 Truman scholars
- 2 Vice presidents

Norris goes on, "We never do anything to jeopardize our commitment to providing an exceptional educational experience. At the same time, that quality gives us a lot of confidence about who we are and what we want to say about Centre."

Centre's extraordinary marketing communication plan does not rest on big budgets. Rather, it rests on big ideas and their chosen method of communication is the story. Says Norris, "We like to put a face on marketing. We like to tell stories, and we have a number of faculty and staff on campus who are talented in this area. We like to illustrate our quality through people and their accomplishments."

By way of illustration, let me tell three Centre stories. One small. One medium. And one large.

The small story is absolutely fascinating. It concerns the man who convinced Abraham Lincoln that he had more to offer the world than being a blacksmith.

The medium-sized story is the most bizarre. It is about Dead Fred.

The large story, well, it's a big one. It is about how Centre won, then lost, and then won big with the vice presidential debate.

Let's start with the small one.

Abraham Lincoln

At 23, Abraham Lincoln had received little formal education. As he pondered his future, he was giving serious thought to becoming a blacksmith. Fortunately, Centre alum John Todd Stuart (Class of 1826) intervened and the rest is, literally in this case, history. If not for Stuart, Lincoln might not have become the 16th president of the United States. He might never have led our country through its most difficult time. Instead, he might have spent his life shoeing horses.

According to an autobiographical sketch Lincoln prepared in 1860, Lincoln's good friend, Stuart, loaned him a set of books and urged him to study law. After Lincoln was admitted to the Bar in 1837, Stuart became Lincoln's first law partner in Springfield, Illinois. They remained partners for five years.

The Kentucky natives first met in 1832 when they fought in the same battalion during the Black Hawk War (Stuart was a major and Lincoln was a captain). After their military service, both ran for the Illinois General Assembly, although only Stuart won a seat in 1832. Two years later, Lincoln joined Stuart in the state legislature.

Later, Lincoln married Stuart's cousin, Mary Todd of Lexington, Kentucky.

Though they often disagreed on issues of the day, the two remained close friends until Lincoln's death in 1865. Stuart then headed the National Lincoln Monument Association, which built a monument to the fallen president in Springfield. Stuart received his Centre degree in 1826. The law practice he established in 1828 survived until 1928.

Stuart died in November of 1885.

&&&&&

Dead Fred

The second story is about Dead Fred. I used this story in an earlier book on marketing, *Thinking Outside the Box*. The story is so good that I couldn't resist using it here as well. The story was actually written by Norris and was originally slugged, "The Adventures of Dead Fred" (or, when you don't have hard news, look for human interest).

Norris writes that "In the fall of 1993 the small Centre College communications group huddled at an off-campus retreat to try to come up with some story ideas. The problem was–though many good things were happening at the College–nothing at the moment had the potential to really grab headlines and generate major publicity.

Near the end of our session, someone came up with the idea of doing a story on an offbeat tradition that had been going at Centre for about 40 years. With nothing better in the offing, we decided to go with this idea.

We wrote a press release, timed to the next occasion when the tradition would be enacted (a home football game), and began calling print media and television stations. This was our pitch: "At Centre College we have an alum that died in 1953 and hasn't missed a home football game since. Are you interested in the story?"

The most common reactions were: 1) Long pause followed by, "What did you say?" 2) Laughter, followed by, "Tell me about it." 3) "Now let me get this straight, he died in 1953 and hasn't missed a game since?"

First, get their attention

I have to say that in 20 years of communications work, this pitch accomplished the getting-attention objective as well as any I've ever seen. Invariably the person wanted to hear the explanation. Here's how *The New York Times* recently (yes, we have recycled the story a few times) put it:

Dead Fred–in life Fred M. Vinson, the chief justice of the United States and a Truman confidant–was a Centre College alumnus who was such an avid fan of the college's football team that an unusual tradition took root after his death in 1953. "A couple of his buddies got together, and were talking about how sad it was that he couldn't go to the games anymore, so they started bringing his portrait to games," said Erik Dowden, a 21-year-old Centre senior.

There were other interesting aspects to the story of course. Fred Vinson, Centre class of 1909, had been a brilliant student, a talented three-sport athlete, and had risen to the highest levels of power in the Roosevelt and Truman administrations. During his career, he remained actively connected to Centre, visited campus regularly, and attended college athletic events at every opportunity. Thus, while whimsical, there was a rationale for the members of his fraternity brothers to begin carrying his portrait–which over the years became known as Dead Fred–to the games.

The first round

Norris began by pitching the story to Kentucky media. Heartened by their success–print stories with pictures of Dead Fred at a football game in many state newspapers, including the two largest, and several statewide TV news features–we ventured out to regional media and were successful there as well.

The story went national when CNN accepted our invitation to cover Dead Fred's appearance at our home-coming football game. They sent a full crew, which resulted in a three-minute feature that ran repeatedly over a two-week period. We then submitted a still photo that (as luck and careful planning would have it) included an umbrella featuring the word "Centre" just above the portrait to *USA Today*, where it ran prominently with an accompanying story that led the "Sports People" section.

The second round

You might think this was the end of the coverage, but it was only the beginning of round two. Using the CNN and *USA Today* features as indicators of the story's appeal, Norris pitched media that hadn't acted on the first contact. He also pitched new outlets. The result was another spate of stories that appeared in newspapers such as the *Los Angles Times, Detroit Free Press, St. Louis Post Dispatch*, *Miami Herald,* and on the national Talk America radio show.

The second round of coverage illustrated an important principle in evergreen stories like this. Coverage promotes more coverage, and a story can begin to snowball as the "story of all the publicity" becomes an additional part of the narrative. The "pack mentality" tendency of the media contributes to additional coverage as well. All in all, the Dead Fred story reached an audience of more than 10 million and provided excellent material for Centre-produced communications such as admission newsletters and the alumni magazine.

Dead Fred returns

So was that the end of Fred's 15 minutes of posthumous fame? Well, not exactly. When Norris found out early in 2000 that Centre had been selected to host the general election's single vice presidential debate, it was only a matter of time until it occurred to them that Dead Fred should attend the event. After all, Vinson served in key roles in both the Roosevelt and Truman administrations, was described by Truman as "the man I depend on most," was urged by Truman to run for president, and served for seven years as Chief Justice of the United States. (Of course, at the time we didn't appreciate how really appropriate it turned out to be, given that the Supreme Court eventually played a direct role in the 2000 election.)

The result? Dead Fred's attendance added to the already rich mix of media coverage Centre was receiving as host of the debate. The "seating ceremony" two days before the event (in which Fred, wearing a special credential, was carried in by student-members of his fraternity) was covered by CNN, C-SPAN, most Kentucky television stations, as well as stations from neighboring states, and the story appeared in newspapers from *The New York Times* to Saudi Arabia's *Arab News*.

The rest of the story

A crucial component in marketing a story like this is–like the realtor's location, location, location–details, details, details. Once you have the concept, you need to dig and uncover the fine points that flesh out the story and give it sustained interest. In this story many of the details involved the mythology that had sprung up around Dead Fred. For example:

- Has reportedly shed a tear on several occasions after a particularly heartbreaking Centre defeat
- Has been the target of kidnapping threats by other Centre fraternities, but has always been kept secure by the Phi Delts
- Occasionally travels to away games when the Centre team faces particularly strong opponents

Other details, though, related to Vinson the man:

- Vinson established a reputation for brilliance at Centre–he reportedly could recite the contents of his textbooks word for word, do large mathematical calculations in his head, and graduated with the highest grade point average ever achieved at Centre up to that time
- He starred on the baseball team at Centre and later played semi-pro baseball. A strong hitting short-stop, he once ran all the way to the end of the left field stands to catch a foul ball
- Before his appointment to the Supreme Court he held a series of high government posts, including Secretary of the Treasury

Dead Fred and the future

Concludes Norris, what does the future hold for Dead Fred? Well, there's been talk of Centre's hosting a presidential debate in 2004, and in the meantime Fred has taken to attending basketball games and can occasionally be seen at a soccer match. (After all, during his undergraduate days he was a three-sport athlete.)

&&&&&

The vice presidential debate

Our final story is a big one, the vice presidential debate held on the Centre College campus on October 5, 2000. It is about winning the opportunity to hold the debate ... losing the opportunity to hold the debate ... winning it back. And then winning big while holding the debate. It is, once again, an extraordinary story told extraordinarily well.

In Spring 1999, Centre College decided to make a run at hosting the 2000 vice presidential debate. The decision was not an easy one for the College, but Centre's new president, Dr. John Roush, saw the debate as an opportunity to affirm Centre as one of the nation's premier liberal arts colleges. He knew from his previous experience as vice president for planning and executive assistant to the president at the University of Richmond, where he helped land a presidential debate in 1992, that the debate could galvanize the College and the country.

Of course, there were detractors. Almost everyone not familiar with Centre said it couldn't be done. In their minds Centre was too small. Too far. Too inexperienced. It didn't have the resources. But Centre persisted, competing against much larger institutions, and won the opportunity to host the debate.

Then things got complicated.

Centre officials read in the newspapers that the Republican campaign had announced a new debate schedule that did not include the college in Danville, Kentucky,. Unwilling to let this extraordinary opportunity slip away, Centre mounted a "Save the Debate" public relations campaign that involved school children, a song–"We Wish You Would Come to Danville,"– campus-wide rallies, and lots of media exposure. Centre made the case not for simply holding the debate at Centre, but that small colleges like Centre–and small communities like Danville–could do extraordinary things and should not be excluded from the national political dialogue. This strategy helped build a groundswell of support among small colleges and communities nationwide that had big dreams of their own.

As a result of this campaign, 11 days after Centre was "out," the college was suddenly " in." On October 5, 2000, Centre hosted the vice presidential debate and according to almost everyone involved–including an appreciative and somewhat surprised national media–set a new standard for how a general election debate could and should be handled.

Merchandising the debate and the College

Central to Centre's success was how well it merchandised the debate and the College. For example, the College prepared a tip sheet for the press that outlined a number of good, even odd, stories, all revolving around Centre, including:

- **"If I had a hammer": The house the Veeps might build.** Centre College students will have a hammer during debate week because they intend to raise the roof on a Habitat for Humanity house. The campus and town Habitat chapters secured a grant to pay for construction of the house. Their goal: To persuade the candidates to hammer at least one nail to call public attention to homelessness and poverty.

- **PayDays for the President.** Centre College President John Roush is known for several things. Affection for the tiny black mutt, Bea, who jogs with him on campus. Relentless energy, good humor, and an addiction to PayDay candy bars. It was Roush who suggested that Centre apply to host a debate. Having been part of a prior debate as a VP at the University of Richmond (1992), he says of Centre: "When I saw the campus and met its people, I knew this college could do it."

- **The Powerhouse Palace of Culture.** Centre College's Norton Center for the Arts (actual site for the vice presidential debate) is an unusual facility for a small college and a small town. It offers a number of stories (two are underground), 85,000 square feet, and an annual subscription series that lets audiences enjoy the Boston Pops, Itzhak Perlman, Wynton Marsalis, Willie Nelson, Ray Charles, the Moscow Symphony, and the New York Opera Company. The building was designed by the Frank Lloyd Wright Foundation. The performance series is always sold out, and the center operates with a balanced budget.

- **You can look up to Lanham.** Michael Lanham was just 18-years old when he was named a Rhodes Scholar during his senior year at Centre, making him one of the youngest persons ever chosen for the prestigious academic honor. Nearly seven feet tall, he also may be among the tallest. Mostly, though, Michael is bright and affable with multiple talents in mathematics and music. At Oxford University in England, he is studying the concept of mathematical modeling as a way of understanding the spread of infectious diseases. He hopes to apply the idea to the problem of AIDS.

- **Expect the extraordinary.** In 1903, Woodrow Wilson observed: "There's a little college down in Kentucky which in 60 years has graduated more men who have acquired prominence and fame than has Princeton in her 150 years." Centre has a tradition of turning out men and women of prominence, far beyond what might be expected of a small liberal arts college. Among its former students: Two U.S. Supreme Court Justices (including John Marshall Harlan, whose 1896 dissent on segregation later gave legal footing to the Civil Rights movement), two U.S. vice presidents, the founder of *Advertising Age* magazine, the developer of the octane system for rating fuels, founder of the Hard Rock Cafe, and a 2000 Tony Award nominee.

John Glenn's cell phone

While the debate was the big story, it generated lots of small ones as well. One of my favorites is called "The Saga of John Glenn's cell phone." It involved Centre student Les Fugate. Writes Fugate, "My twin brother, Wes, and I, along with Student Congress President Jed Doty, had the enormous task of checking in all of the electronic devices that the ticketed guests brought with them to the debate hall; i.e., cameras, Palm Pilots, cell phones, and pagers. [These devices were not allowed in the hall, by order of the Secret Service.] At one point I heard my brother ask a man to check in his cell phone. The man replied, 'I've flown into space, and I know that I can take a cell phone into the debate hall.' Sure enough, it was Senator John Glenn from Ohio. Then I heard a Secret Service agent reply 'Senator, if you do not give that gentleman your cell phone, you won't get to see the debate.' All in all, the debate was one of the greatest–if not the greatest–experiences of my life. I have only one final comment: When do we apply for the Olympics?"

Merchandising the merchandise

Finally, there is the merchandising of merchandise. According to Norris, the best-selling items were stoneware mugs, teddy bears, and T-shirts.

Gauging the impact

Did the vice presidential debate and accompanying stories generate some publicity for Centre? As Norris might say, an extraordinary amount. After the debate, Centre published a fascinating brochure that tallied the national (and international) media hits for the College. More than 100 newspapers from Zurich to New York to Los Angeles to Hong Kong to Saudi Arabia ran stories about Centre and the debate. And then there was the broadcast media: CNN, ABC, CBS, NBC, C-SPAN, Fox, PBS, and NPR. The media listings–and the exposure–goes on and on.

How do alumni feel about all this exposure? Consider this: Centre is ranked No. 1 in the country for alumni giving. Each year, some 68 percent of alumni make a gift. At Harvard, only 47 percent of alumni give. Chalk up another victory for Centre.

When asked if all the hard work that went into winning the debate was worth it, Norris mentioned that it is "much easier to pitch stories to the national media now that they know who we are." He also mentioned that his transition from publications to marketing, and working with talented colleagues at Centre, has helped keep him fresh and invigorated after 21 years at the helm.

Says Norris, "The workaday stuff is critical. You need the hometowners and the Web. You need to do some advertising. This kind of regular reinforcement of your image is important. But if you want to move up, not merely hold your ground, you need exceptional reinforcement for your brand. We did that with the debate, and we have other ideas for the future."

He goes on, "It's hard to sustain exceptional reinforcement, but it does lift you to a new plateau. As I said earlier, now people have heard about us. They say, 'Oh, you're from Centre.' That makes my job much easier."

His final words, "Focus on a handful of important stories and make them memorable by putting human faces on them."

Resources

In addition to a number of interviews with Mike Norris, Director of Communications at Centre, I shamelessly used Centre's very excellent Web site as a source for this case study. For more information about the debate experience at Centre, take a glance at the article co-authored by Norris and Richard Trollinger, "The Great Debate: How a Small College Made the Most of a Big Opportunity" that appeared in the November/December 2000 issue of *Currents*.

■■■■■

Chapter 14
Differentiating Your Curriculum[21]

Sometimes, to differentiate yourself successfully, you must be willing to lasso a sacred cow. On most campuses, the biggest sacred cow of them all is the academic curriculum. Interestingly, while one college's curriculum is seldom truly different from that of its competitors, the act of differentiating your curriculum from that of your competitor offers significant branding possibilities.

Fortunately, there are four basic tools to help you differentiate your curriculum:

- Conducting a marketability audit of your curriculum
- Developing a business approach to new programs
- Identifying your tall poles
- Marketing your honors program

An earlier version of these tools was presented in my previous book, *Thinking Outside the Box*.

Tool #1: conducting a marketability audit of your curriculum

The purpose of a curriculum marketability audit, a type of portfolio analysis, is to help you more completely understand which of your programs are generating, or have the potential to generate, badly needed tuition revenue, and which programs are not doing so.

Portfolio analyses were first developed by the Boston Consulting Group (BCG).[22] Their paradigm introduced the world to the idea of rising stars and cash cows.

For our purposes, we will use a highly modified analysis that organizes your academic portfolio (your academic majors) into six categories:

- Anchors
- Problem children
- Sitting ducks
- Rising stars
- Cash cows
- Bright ideas

Before we discuss the individual categories, I want to mention that by their nature, portfolio analyses are extremely political. As a consequence, a very rigorous methodology is mandatory. At the very least, this should include:

- A comparison of your curriculum offerings with those of your competitors
- A comparison of marketing, pricing, and financial aid strategies
- A review of short- and long-term job trends in your marketplace
- A review of overall economic and demographic trends
- A survey of prospective students to ascertain their academic goals
- An evaluation of your faculty and facilities
- A review of current enrollment by:
  - Program
  - Program revenue
  - Program contribution to overhead
  - Retention rates
  - Graduation rates

The six categories

Anchors are those courses and programs that flow directly from your mission. Whether they generate enough revenue to support themselves is not a primary consideration, because while anchors represent a lot of where you came from, they also guide and offer direction for the future. They present some of your most enduring core values; the institutional qualities and characteristics you value most. If you are a Catholic school, a basic course in Catholic theology is an example of an anchor. While anchors are to be cherished, most institutions cannot afford to have more than a handful. In addition, there is a difference between a required course in theology and a major.

Problem children are programs that are in trouble. They have value, or had value in the recent past, and there is strong evidence that they are salvageable. They may lack a champion. They may need to be brought up to date. They might need a new facility, faculty, or an infusion of other resources. A business program that has fallen on hard times is a good example of a problem child. Your goal, of course, is to have as few problem children as you can, because problem children consume more resources than they generate. Problem children are also notoriously distracting.

Every campus has one or more *sitting ducks*. These are programs that many people believe should be terminated. However, they are often kept alive for political or humanitarian reasons. While I do not generally recommend closing these programs and laying off faculty, I do strongly suggest that these programs be slowly and deliberately downgraded. When faculty retire, do not rehire. Do not overly promote and thereby create a problem with students who enrolled. Reduce the sitting duck from a major to a support area. Seek to cross-train staff and transfer them to other programs.

Your fourth group of programs are your *rising stars*. Rising stars generate attention, students, and some cash. What cash they do generate, however, should be reinvested in the program. These programs are growing and are generally highly entrepreneurial. They are often centered around a strong faculty champion. Rising stars are seldom stable. Some will become longer-term cash cows. Others may become problem children. If you look around your campus, chances are the rising stars will be found in either business or information technology. On some campuses environmental science is a rising star. Former rising stars include occupational and physical therapy. At some institutions, these are now problem children. One final thought about rising stars: donors, especially corporate donors, love them.

The fifth category is *cash cows.* Cash cows generate more resources than they need to cover their costs. They are longer term. Many were former rising stars. If you have a high number of anchors, sitting ducks, and problem children, then you need a high number of cash cows. Generally cash cows require few institutional resources other than skillful management. There is a tendency, however, for cash cows to become bloated and a bit moribund. While cash cows seldom have the edge that rising stars have, they need to have enough of an edge to remain current and in tune with the marketplace.

Finally, we have *bright ideas.* Bright ideas are those programs that research, and the students in your marketplace, suggest you should consider adding to your curriculum. In an ideal world, these programs are vetted through the creation of a business plan for each potential candidate. Some ideas on how to develop bright ideas are presented in the next chapter.

Portfolio Mix

Program mix

As you might suspect, the key to a portfolio that balances mission and tuition revenue is a proper mix of anchors, sitting ducks, problem children, rising stars, cash cows, and bright ideas. As we can see from the illustration at the top of the next page, institutions with more anchors, sitting ducks, and problem children are not likely to have the cash flow to sustain themselves over the long run.

A better mix of programs is presented on the bottom of the next page. This institution's relatively modest number of anchors and sitting ducks–and even problem children–are easily sustained by a sufficient number of rising stars and cash cows. In addition, this institution has some bright ideas that might, in the future, become rising stars or even cash cows.

"Problematic" Program

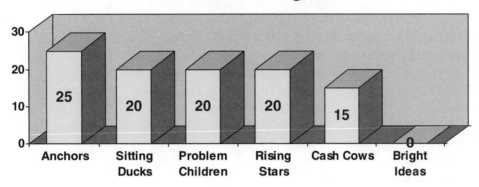

"Ideal" Program Mix

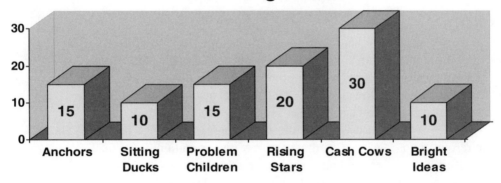

Tool #2: developing a business approach to new programs

I am no longer surprised by how few four-year colleges and universities have a strategic business approach to the creation of new programs and majors. Interestingly, this approach is much more common at two-year institutions than four-year.

Unfortunately, the failure to use such an approach to program development causes two sometimes insurmountable flaws that undermine the likelihood that these new programs will flourish. First, the rationale and impetus for new programs appears to be just faculty, rather than combined faculty and marketplace interest. As a result, ideas for new programs are seldom tested and validated externally. Usually the "research" involves discussions with some faculty, a division head or two, and maybe a dean. There is generally no real rigor, especially marketplace validation, applied to the decision.

And second, new programs are almost always under-resourced. Seldom are adequate dollars budgeted for marketing and scholarships. The champions of new programs often do not have time to manage their day-to-day activities, fight the political battles, and nurture their new programs. Ironically, it seems as if new programs are always approved so late in the academic year that there is neither dollars, because they missed the budget planning cycle, nor the time to promote them.

As one move, then, I suggest a strategic business approach to the creation of new academic programs. This approach addresses four key decision areas:

- Strategic
- Marketplace
- Economic and resource
- Marketing and promotion

Proposals for new programs must be able to weather the questions presented in the four decision areas. If they can't, they should be delayed, reworked, or even shelved.

Strategic issues:

- How will this program advance our mission, vision, and strategic plan?
- Do we have a faculty champion who will live and breathe this program?
- Does this champion have the time, talent, and political acumen to pull this off?
- Are other faculty groups and departments supportive of this new program?
- What detractors are in place? What are their concerns? Can they be brought on board?
- Will the resources for this program draw resources away from other critical areas?
- Will this program create or build on synergy with other programs?
- What other opportunities will we have to delay to fund this new program?
- What is our rationale for offering this program? Is it solely economic?
- Is this program going to be a truly high quality program or will it be marginalized because of scarce resources?
- What chances for collaboration with other organizations does this new program offer?
- Will beginning this program allow us to cut another program?
- Will this program lead graduates to higher paying jobs and thereby reduce the negative impact of cost and college debt?
- Will this program generate true excitement on campus and in the marketplace?
- In five years, will this program be a rising star or a problem child?

Marketplace issues:

- Could this be a signature program; something that attracts regional, or even national, attention?
- Is this program unique or are similar programs offered by competitors?
- If this program is not unique, can we offer it in unique ways (three-year B.A., aggressive internships, collaborations with other schools)?
- Will this program survive the Internet commoditization of programs?

- Have we tested this idea with:
  - High school influencers?
  - Prospective students (and even parents)?
  - Employers?
  - Donors?
- What absolutely solid, external data do we have that indicates this program is/will be a winner?

Economic and resource issues:

- Can we offer this program less expensively than our competitors? Will we have a price advantage?
- Will the institution provide short-term venture capital for this new program or will it have to immediately pay off?
- Have we developed a payoff schedule for this new program (when revenue surpasses real and indirect costs)? Is this schedule reasonable? Does it include reinvesting into the program to make it better?
- Do we have capacity (staff, physical plant) for this program? Do we have enough short- and long-term capacity if this program is successful?
- When we calculated the costs of this program, did we include sufficient dollars for:
  - Promotion?
  - Staffing?
  - Renovation?
  - Equipment and supplies?
  - Scholarships?
  - Contribution to overhead?
- Have we developed a model whereby revenue is shared with the sponsoring department, thereby fostering a sense of reward and innovation?
- Will special, and long-term, financial aid resources be available for this new program?
- Are there immediate fundraising opportunities for the new program?

Marketing and promotion issues:

- Is a list of prospective students available? Is this list compiled or response?
- Will we use a segmented marketing campaign to support this new program? Will it involve:
  - Direct mail?
  - Web?
  - Advertising?
  - Telemarketing?
  - Outreach?
- Have we developed an adequate, sustainable promotion strategy?
- Will this program attract media and public attention?

The purpose of these four sets of questions is to help you assess possible new programs and to help assure the success of the programs you choose. If you can't, or didn't, answer many of these questions, then your program is likely to have difficulty, and you should question your decision to proceed.

Tool # 3: Identify four or five tall poles

According to my friends in North Carolina, tall poles are those poles which rise above the rest. In a stand of timber, tall poles overarch the other trees. Sometimes these tall poles are called "centers of excellence" or "signature programs." Regardless of the name, the principle is the same: playing to your strengths.

For our purposes, tall poles are those academic programs that an institution decides to market more aggressively than other programs. In other words, the identification of tall poles is the foundation stone for a segmented recruiting strategy. Rather than pushing all programs equally, which, while being democratic, proves to be grossly inefficient, a tall pole program works on the premise that additional marketing resources should be directed at a handful of programs that show special promise (remember the *rising stars* and *bright ideas*?). Generally, these are programs that:

- Already offer substantial quality
- Are undersubscribed by prospective students
- Are high margin
- Are of high interest in the marketplace and among employees
- Have an effective champion in place
- Are of interest to the media
- Are of interest to donors

By now, you should be thinking that there is a fair degree of symmetry between the business approach model for identifying new academic programs and the identification of tall poles. This is not coincidental because both have at their core this basic tenant:

Decisions about academic programs must be more marketplace driven.

The creation of a tall pole program allows you to:

- Focus resources on those programs that offer the most immediate payoff for the institution
- Develop special segmented recruiting strategies including direct mail and Web
- Direct financial aid where it will have the most immediate impact
- Create a sense of excitement and anticipation because it is often easier to move a handful of programs ahead, where you might not have the time, talent, and money to move the whole institution

As you think about building and marketing your tall poles, remember you must be willing to:

- Allocate a disproportionate level of strategic resources to enhancing the quality of these programs, including resources for:
  - Hiring
  - Facilities
  - Scholarships and financial aid
- Develop special marketing and financial aid strategies

And most importantly, you must be willing to weather the political storms and the cries of "that's not fair" that will attempt to distract you from your vision and mission.

Is there really anything magical about having "four or five" tall poles? Well, look at it this way: you probably cannot manage more than five, and with any less the whole effort will likely not have that much impact on the institution.

—————————————————— Sidebar ——————————————————
The five card exercise

To help clients focus their dreams—and energies—I often use a simple five card exercise. In the following example we are interested in helping a college identify its signature academic programs. I hand out five index cards to each member of the strategic team. I then ask each person to think about the institution's five signature programs: Those programs that are of most value to the institution and the marketplace.

After they have each identified five programs they believe to be stellar, I ask them to remove one card from their stack; the card representing the weakest program of the five.

They now have four programs. Next, I ask them to remove another, the next weakest program. Now they have three.

During the next few minutes I ask them to remove two other cards. They are now left with what they believe, as individuals, to be their most important academic program. Often, most people in the room have named the same program. Or, as sometimes happens, a handful of programs are spread across the remaining cards. We then spend the rest of the time thinking about how we can make the programs even better by asking and answering such questions as:

- How can we attract better students?
- How can fundraising be used to raise dollars for financial aid, faculty, and facilities?
- How can we build media and public attention for the program?
- What opportunities are there for collaboration between the program and outside entities such as other schools, the private sector, and others?

Tool #4: market your honors program

Recently I completed a project for a small four-year institution on the West Coast. Historically, this church-related college had served average students; students who would need a little extra support. A year ago, they decided to pursue a higher quality student because they felt that they are more likely to be full-pay. However, they did not want to abandon the bread-and-butter students in their primary market.

The solution was the repositioning of their honors programs. They already had some success in honors programming but the new program was much more comprehensive and well-resourced. They were able to target a higher profile student, develop a customized marketing and recruiting strategy for these students and their influencers, and offer more financial aid, especially to those students who were enrolled in one of their tall-pole programs. This kind of segmentation strategy allowed them to build a brand in the minds and hearts of one audience without being in conflict with the brand it already had developed with another audience.

As you have seen, these four strategies—conducting a marketability audit of your curriculum, developing a business approach for new programs, identifying tall poles, and marketing your honors program—will help you focus and leverage your academic programming. These strategies recognize that your academic programs represent one of the most important components of your brand.

The honors brochures on the left hand page are from Miami University and Bridgewater State College. The brochures above are from the Barrett Honors College at Arizona State University and Carthage College.

■■■■■

Chapter 15
Differentiation Through Co-Branding

While driving through Lima, Ohio, a number of years ago, I stopped at a McDonald's. When I entered the store I immediately noticed a bright poster that advertised the Ronald McDonald-Ohio State University Reading Club for area primary and middle school students.

As I looked at the poster it dawned on me that it represented a marriage of the two most powerful brands in Ohio. At that time I didn't know the technical name for this marketing strategy (it's called co-branding), but I did sense the opportunity it afforded. While neither OSU nor McDonald's probably need much help with their individual branding efforts, I realized that this kind of strategy might offer other colleges and universities an important opportunity to build their brands.

Of course, we see co-branding strategies all around us:

- Amazon co-brands with Hewlett-Packard
- Every major computer maker announces that they have "Intel Inside"
- The NFL co-brands with Nike
- Nike co-brands with Tiger

But what about colleges and universities? Can they co-brand? Well, we have seen Ohio State and McDonald's. What about these real and possible co-branding arrangements:

- Western Washington University and Microsoft
- Stanford University and HP
- Wheaton College and the Billy Graham Evangelistic Association
- The University of Texas and NASA
- New York University and Goldman Sachs
- The University of Michigan and General Motors

The synergy of co-branding

In an ideal co-branding situation, the joint relationship between two separate brands creates value and opportunity that neither of the brands could achieve on their own. Usually, one or both of the partners is typically trying to gain awareness in the marketplace, often trying to leverage the partnership to increase its own stature. When the University of Washington co-brands with Boeing, it is trying to enhance its own reputation and brand.

170

Generally, organizations with less brand equity stand to gain from those with more. More established brands, on the other hand, gain from the innovative or exciting offerings of newer brands, or are seeking to "draw down" some prestige that they might not ordinarily have on their own.

Co-branding works because it creates new excitement for both of the brands involved.

Guidelines for co-branding

Before you jump into a co-branding relationship, ask yourself if the excitement that the deal will bring will build the brand or sabotage it. Sometimes a co-branding strategy isn't as advantageous as it may seem, particularly for small colleges and universities that often get overshadowed by larger partners.

As you think about a possible co-branding opportunity, consider the following questions:

- Is the co-brand logical? Wheaton (Illinois) and Billy Graham is logical. Wheaton and KISS is not
- Does the co-brand build on the strengths of both? Both Western Washington and Microsoft bring tremendous software and information technology strengths to the co-branding situation
- Does the co-brand create natural and obvious synergy? When NASA and the University of Texas partner, the resulting relationship creates legitimate opportunities for both entities
- Will the co-brand be of value to your most important target audiences? The value of a co-branding opportunity between the University of Michigan and General Motors is obvious

Finally, make sure you have a fallback position if the co-branding situation does not work out. An exit strategy agreed upon up front can save you enormous ill will.

The importance is in the follow-through

As with all brand messages, co-branding needs to be backed up by action. Merely announcing a relationship is not enough. For the co-branding relationship to be successful, the customer must benefit. Just as the individual brands achieve a synergy when linked, the benefits offered to the customer must achieve a synergy as well.

A brief co-branding example

Calhoun Community College, in Decatur, Alabama, has a co-branding relationship with Boeing. A couple of years ago, says Janet Kincherlow-Martin, Director of Public Relations, Calhoun opened the first building in a planned, three-building, $40-million technology park.

Named the Aerospace Training Center, the new facility is a 38,000-square-foot, $20 million project developed with funding from the state of Alabama as part of the incentive provided to Boeing to build its Delta IV plant in Decatur. The building and equipment are being used to train employees for the Boeing plant. According to Kincherlow-Martin, this partnership has resulted in Calhoun being able to construct and equip a state-of-the art aerospace training center, develop an associate's degree in aerospace technology, and provide trained, skilled aerospace employees not only for Boeing, but for a number of other aerospace-related companies in the north Alabama area.

■■■■■

Chapter 16
Creating a Graphic Identity Program[23]

The creation and execution of a new graphic identity, or look, can be an important part of any successful branding strategy. However, the creation of a new look can also be a time-consuming, expensive, and politically-sensitive undertaking. To help guide you through the creation of a new graphic identity program, I would like to present a three-phase approach for creating and launching a new look.

- Phase one: determine whether or not a new look is needed
- Phase two: create a new graphic identity
- Phase three: present and support the new graphic identity

Phase one: determine whether or not a new look is needed

The very first step in developing a new look involves two things. First, determining if you and your institution are ready for a new look. And second, determining whether you need a new look.

As you consider whether or not you and your institution are ready for a new look, you need to explore such issues as:

- Why do we think we need a new look?
- What marketing gains do we hope to achieve with a new look?
- Do we have the time, talent, and sometimes considerable money to develop and implement a new look?
- Is the creation of a new look the best use of our time, money, and talent at this time?
- Are we willing to fight the political battles that creating a new look will enjoin? Who (either internally or externally) is pushing for a new look? What are their motives?

If the answers to these questions support the creation of a new look, and you have empowered a graphic identity team (the internal and external stakeholders who will guide the process), then it is time to move on to determine whether or not you need a new look. You will make this determination as part of an identity audit.

The identity audit

An identity audit involves asking key audiences several questions, including:

- Who do we think we are?
- Who do external audiences think we are?
- Who do external audiences think we should be?
- Who do we want to be?

These four questions are directed at such internal audiences as students, faculty, staff, and administrators and such external audiences as alumni, donors, the education community, even community residents. Answers to these questions are gathered using focus groups, mail and telephone surveys, personal interviews, and even Web surveys.

As these data are collected, it is also important for the graphic identity development team to examine how your look is manifested in such media as:

- Internal and external publications including fact sheets, magazines, recruiting and advancement materials, announcements, etc.
- Stationery including business cards, letterhead, envelopes, forms, etc.
- Print, radio, and TV ads
- Signage and environmentals
- Web site, video, CD-ROM

In addition, you need to undertake a scan of your competitors to learn how your competitors have positioned themselves in the marketplace. You also need to identify the chief qualities and characteristics of their look.

Position and positioning

Phase one concludes with the creation of your position and positioning statements. Your position statement is a summary of your current image and look. If, as you write your position statement, you discover that your current position is satisfactory, then you may make a decision not to develop a new look, to tweak an existing look, or to do a better job policing a look that is already in place.

The positioning statement, on the other hand, is more aspirational in nature; it describes the goals of the look you hope to develop. Remember, it is the positioning statement against which you are going to measure your new look.

If you remember back to the RPI case study, you will recall that a positioning statement is a phrase that forms the foundation of your brand. As such, it must "ring true" to your primary stakeholders. The positioning statement they chose to support their brand promise was *technological creativity*.

Phase two: create a new graphic identity

It is during phase two that the actual design work for the new look occurs. This includes developing preliminary design concepts, testing initial concepts, and refining your design.

As you think about your initial design, it is important to stress that your new look must be:

- Stylistically appropriate for the institution
- Original
- Distinctive from your competitors
- Adaptable across multiple media and formats
- Long-lasting

After some initial designs are developed, they should be tested with the graphic identity development team. After this input is received, the designs will likely be refined a bit. Then, two or three designs and their rationales are tested with internal and external stakeholders.

It is very important to test these final designs as widely as possible. It is also important to recognize that consensus for one design will probably not be achieved, but you should sense general trends in the responses of your constituents to the looks you are showing.

Phase three: present and support the new graphic identity

The final four steps in the creation of a graphic identity include:

- Adopting the final identity
- Creating a comprehensive style manual
- Announcing the new identity to the campus community and to external constituents
- Supporting the new identity

Adopting the final identity

After constituent testing, a final graphic look should be settled upon. This final look should include a reconciliation with the original positioning statement and a revised rationale. The look is then presented to the graphic identity development team and to the institution's senior administrators and faculty leadership.

Sidebar

Sidebar

Criterion for evaluating a new look

- Does the look draw your attention and arouse interest?
- Is the look at least surprising, perhaps courageous?
- Is it easily linked to the institution?
- Does it evoke the anticipated emotion: tradition, excitement, innovation?
- Is it simple?
- Is it distinctive?
- Does it communicate a message?
- Will it wear over time?
- Will the image produce well in black and white?
- Will it work in various sizes?
- Will it work in multiple media: publications, t-shirts, letterhead, signage, the Web page?
- Is it compatible with other graphic devices used on campus?
- Is it consistent with the key elements advanced in your mission, vision, and positioning statements?

Creating a comprehensive graphic identity manual

The next step is the creation of a comprehensive identity manual. The key word here is *comprehensive*. A solid, well-conceived and executed identity manual should address major questions and usage options. One of my favorite identity manuals (see below), was developed by Loyola University New Orleans. Of course, with the advent of the Web, manuals are much more likely to be virtual than printed.

Announcing the new identity to the campus community and to external constituents

Chances are, most of your internal audiences and probably a fair number of external ones are aware that there is a new look coming. Even so, the announcement of the new look should be celebratory in nature. It has been a long process, and many people have been involved. For this reason, it is important to show the flag.

As you can see from the graphic below, Dickinson College, working with Neustadt Creative, developed a Web page for its new logo (see below) that included a rationale for the new logo, color samples that allow you to see the new logo in different colors, and against different backgrounds, a schedule for launching the new look, and some logo games.

The Dickinson site also included a series of FAQs about the new look.

Supporting the new identity

The final step is to set in place the mechanisms that will support that new identity. This includes everything from helping people learn to use the look on the one hand to enforcing the look on the other. Supporting the new identity also involves communicating a timeline for the complete rollout. Of course, this is part of a larger brand stewardship effort.

A comment about costs

As noted earlier, there is almost no way to estimate how much the creation and rollout of a new graphic identity system will cost. At a CASE conference I once asked marketing professionals who were attending a session I was holding on branding to give me some ballparks. Once we worked beyond the predictable "that depends," I was consistently hearing numbers in the $75,000 to $125,000 range for the initial identity audit and design.

176

The cost for the "splash" rollout that might include a Web page and/or a well-executed graphic identity manual might cost another $35,000 to $50,000. The actual placing of the new look on stationery, signage, and vehicles, is directly impacted by two variables: the size of the campus and how quickly you want to establish the new look. It is much more expensive for larger campuses that want quick rollouts. Smaller campuses who can take longer to roll-out a new look will get by less expensively.

To sum: If you don't have at least $100,000 to spend on the look and initial rollout, I would seriously consider refining your current look.

Elements of a graphic identity program

A college or university that is considering updating or changing its look must remember the very significant costs that will be incurred as it develops, launches, and maintains a graphic identity system.

On most campuses, the graphic identity systems should embrace:

1. Stationery
    a. Business cards
    b. Letterhead (all sizes)
    c. Envelopes (all sizes)
    d. Mailing labels
    e. Checks, invoices and statements

2. Publications
    a. Recruiting
        1. Search piece
        2. Viewbook
        3. Financial aid brochure
        4. Campus map
        5. Secondary pieces
    b. Fundraising
        1. Annual fund
        2. Capital campaign
    c. Academic
        1. Catalog
        2. Academic viewbook
3. Marketing
    a. News releases
    b. Kiosks
    c. Advertising
    d. Web site

4. Athletics
    a. Uniforms
    b. Sport equipment
    c. Scoreboard identification
    d. Floor and field markings

5. Transportation
    a. Parking decals
    b. Vehicle identification

6. Architecture
    a. Signage
    b. Perimeter marking
    c. Nameplates
    d. Office identification

7. Special events
    a. Exhibits
    b. Lecturns
    c. Bunting and banners

8. Bookstore
    a. Apparel
    b. Mugs
    c. Insignia items

9. Specialty
    a. Diplomas
    b. Certificates
    c. Affinity cards
    d. Lapel pins

Licensing and trademarks

The selling of licensed and trademarked college and university insignia clothing and other items is a hundred million dollar a year business. If you have a great look and a great name, take the time to trademark it. Schools like Notre Dame and Ohio State can make thousands, even hundreds of thousands of dollars a year in licensing fees. In addition, a name and look that is trademarked is also a name and look that is protected.

■■■■■

Section Four
Brand Research

Like a lantern on a dark path, research can clarify direction and offer guidance on the brand-building journey. The following two chapters are designed to provide an overview of brand research. Chapter 17 will lay a general research foundation, while Chapter 18 will focus more completely on brand-related research.

■■■■■

Chapter 17
Using Research to Build Your Brand

The adroit use of research can play a major role in the building of a successful brand. First, at the outset, research can help you answer the three critical brand questions:

- Who are your most important target audiences?
- What is your target geography?
- What is the brand promise your target audiences are most interested in?[24]

Second, research can be used at all four essential stages of brand development. First, research should be used to help you define your brand promises by exploring the needs and expectations of your target audiences as well as the hopes and dreams of your institution.

Research can also be used to help you more effectively communicate your promise. Research to discover the communication habits of your most important target audiences, or to refine the brand benefits they seek, for example, can be extremely valuable.

Research can also be used to help you live the brand promise. Research directed at internal audiences might reveal that your rank-and-file employees do not understand how your brand promise impacts them and their job.

And finally, research can be used to help you strengthen your brand promise. You might discover, for example, that your prospective students are consistently frustrated by how long it takes to receive financial aid information. Using research in this fashion allows you to address problems and strengthen your brand promise.

Research overview

Before we move on, I want to spend a couple of minutes outlining a basic research strategy so that you are a more savvy producer of your own market research and a more judicious consumer of the research of others. Individuals desiring a more comprehensive understanding of research are encouraged to take a look at several of the research books presented in the bibliography.

What is research?

As I wrote this chapter, I realized that I was using the terms *market research*, *brand research*, *audience research*, and *communication research* almost interchangeably. The reality is that these four terms are largely synonymous when you consider that the basic definition of market research is the systematic design, collection, analysis, and reporting of data and findings relevant to a specific marketing situation an institution faces. It is what you plan to do with the research that differentiates the various kinds of research, not so much the research tools themselves.

In short, research involves finding specific answers to specific questions–information that, in our discussion, is used to develop and refine the brand promise, help you communicate your promise, assist in delivering your promise, and finally, aiding you in strengthening your promise.

Not data but information

It is not difficult to generate research data. The odds are high that you have volumes of data sitting on a shelf somewhere in your office. But more than just data, successful research must generate information upon which you can act. It must provide answers to real questions. It must clarify options and provide clear direction. And it must set out options in order of priority. In other words, it is not the collection of data that matters most, but its interpretation and application.

Confidentiality and anonymity

As you prepare to develop a research study, it is important that you understand the definitions of and differences between confidentiality and anonymity. *Confidentiality* means that you will not release these data or findings to outside parties. This sounds simple in theory but it is usually quite difficult in practice. Erik Larson, writing in *The Naked Consumer: How Our Private Lives Become Public Commodities,* suggests that the law of data dynamics indicates that data migrates, and that it often ends up in places distantly removed from the study. In our era of e-mail and photocopying, it is very difficult to keep studies confidential.

The second term is *anonymity*. Anonymity means that you will not attempt to match the name of the respondent to their individual survey responses. Anonymity is especially important if you are going to ask respondents questions dealing with such sensitive issues as household income, giving patterns, perceptions of campus leaders, and other similar topics.

Like confidentiality, preserving anonymity can also be a challenge. This is especially true for surveys of prospective students, donors, and alumni when there is incredible pressure to immediately use the findings to enhance the "sell." For example, I am aware of more than one college that undertook a supposedly anonymous survey of prospective students and then used the data collected on the individual surveys to customize their telemarketing efforts. This approach is unethical, potentially illegal, and just plain dangerous.

Be very careful about promising confidentiality and anonymity. If promised, those responsible for the survey– including the institution itself–are honor bound to deliver.

Components of a research study

While a thoughtful methodology is important for any research study, it is even more important for brand-related research for an obvious reason: if you make a mistake, you may do irreparable harm to your overall brand; harm that may take years to undo. A faulty sample or a misinterpretation of a confusing question can have disastrous and very public results. For this reason, research designed to support your brand strategy must be extremely well-planned and executed. To help guide you through the completion of a study, I suggest a protocol that embraces the following eight sequential steps:

- Develop the research agenda
- Identify the target audience
- Develop the initial research methodology
- Write the research instrument
- Draw the sample
- Execute the study
- Input and analyze data
- Present the results

Step 1: develop the research agenda

The first step in developing a research project is to develop the research agenda. This typically involves answering questions such as:

- What are our brand's strengths and weaknesses?
- Why do we think that our brand is in trouble?
- What branding opportunities are there in the marketplace?
- What elements of our brand–and our competitors' brands–do our target audiences value most?
- How can we more effectively communicate our brand promise?

The purpose of the research agenda is to help you focus your instrument, and study, on the truly most important issues so that it doesn't balloon as it is developed. In addition, the research agenda forces you to think through, from the earliest stages of the study, how you plan to use the research.

Step 2: identify the target audience

The next step involves clarifying the target audiences that matter most. In this era of political correctness, when including everyone in everything seems to be in vogue, effort must be undertaken to limit the number of target audiences to a scant handful. Remember, the key here is strategic focus.

We have covered this topic a number of times, so there is little need to expound here except for the reminder that you must define your target audiences as carefully and completely as possible. This includes reviewing such variables as:

- Where they live
- Age
- Predisposition, attitude, or awareness of you
- Current relationship with you
- Values, attitudes, and lifestyles

Step 3: develop the initial research methodology

Now that the research agenda and list of target audiences are beginning to take shape, you must decide which research methodology is most practical for the branding study you envision. Keeping in mind the information on different methodologies presented in **Appendix C,** it is likely that a comprehensive study involving more than one population may, in fact, include a number of different methodologies.

To help guide your overall research project, you might want to create a *Research Strategy Grid* that links the important components of each study. As you can see from the example below, such a grid is a useful way to keep things organized.

Research Strategy Grid					
Research Question	Audience	Methodology	Population Size	Validity Sought	Sample Size
How do prospective students perceive your brand?	Prospective engineering students	Web survey	2,000	95 percent	322
How do alumni feel about your new brand promise?	Alumni	Mail survey	12,000	95 percent	375

In the above table, the first column presents the key research question. The second column defines the target audience. The third column indicates the chosen methodology. At this point, some judgment comes into play as you weigh several factors including:

- Audience size
- Audience importance or status
- Amount of money available for research
- Level of validity sought
- Time frame for completion of the survey
- Geographic distribution of the audience
- Survey length
- Survey complexity
- Sensitivity of survey questions

In the example on the previous page, I would suggest a Web survey for the study of prospective engineering students because of their geographic distribution, because the survey will be relatively short, and because I want a high response rate. I would choose a mail survey for alumni because of the size of the sample, its geographic distribution, and because the intended alumni survey is long, complex, and covers several sensitive issues. I also know that alumni are often more responsive to mail surveys than other target audiences because of their emotional attachment to the institution.

The fourth column gives the population size. You must know the size of the population before you can establish the sample size. Next, establish the level of reliability that you want. At this point you must ask yourself:

- How important is this particular audience?
- How important are these data?
- What major decisions will we make as a result?

Because of the direct relationship between cost and reliability, use these questions to guide your thinking about the level of validity you should seek.

The final column, sample size, comes from computing the reliability level sought and the size of the population on a standard sociometric chart such as the one found later in this chapter.

Guidelines for choosing a research strategy

Consider three rules as you choose your research strategy. First, there is a relationship between the significance of the decision to be made and the amount of time and money you should spend on research to support it. In other words, decisions that will have far-reaching implications, such as those involving your brand, warrant more research.

Second, as the complexity of the project increases, balance quantitative research methods (surveys) with qualitative research methods (interviews and focus groups). This will improve the overall quality and validity of the final data.

Finally, remember that a good research methodology protects not only the subject and the data, but the credibility of the researcher.

Focus groups

Even though **Appendix C** includes an overview of different research methodologies, it is important at this point to spend just a little time discussing focus groups. Believe it or not, there is a great deal of debate about the value of focus groups. Research purists, at least those with a strong quantitative bent, feel that focus groups are usually more misleading than they are insightful. Others laud focus groups and use them with great conviction.

The fact is, focus groups can gather valuable information when used properly. For example, they can be used to gather initial information and insights early in the study; particularly at the instrument-development stage. Focus groups are also an ideal way to test brand promises and concepts, taglines, vivid descriptors, publications, and even advertising.

As you think about focus groups, it is important to keep in mind one very important fact: no matter how many groups you do, the data are not statistically significant. Focus groups should never be used as the sole source of data when major, expensive, and often very public brand-related decisions are to be made.

——————————— Sidebar ———————————

Enhancing the effectiveness of focus groups

To make your focus groups as successful as possible, consider the following suggestions:

- Moderator guide. Always use a moderator guide so that you stay focused on the most important issues.

- Length. About 60-75 minutes per session. Can be adjusted so a session can be completed during the dinner hour or a class period.

- Number of participants. Ten to 12 per session. It is extremely difficult to control the discussion with more than 12, and the quality of the results will suffer.

- Screening participants. Where possible, screen participants so they are as similar as possible. The participants should closely match the profile of the target audience.

- Location. Almost any room will do as long as it is comfortable. Because the sessions are usually recorded, the room should be fairly quiet. Ideally, chairs and tables should be movable.

- In-depth examination of a single publication or Web site. If participants will examine a publication or Web site, they should receive a copy of the publication or the URL ahead of time so they can review it before the session begins.
    - Remember, it takes time to scrutinize a publication, so you will only be able to discuss one or two during the session.

- Mounting samples. If you are interested in comparing different visuals, mount each one securely on identical, numbered mat boards.

- Displaying samples. If you want to compare samples, have enough tables or easels so all are easily seen at the same time.

- Refreshments. When available, it is appropriate to serve soda or coffee. However, avoid messy finger foods such as pizza at sessions where people will handle samples.

Step 4: write the research instrument

For many people, writing the survey instrument is the most difficult part of the research process. Although experience is always helpful, these guidelines will help you get off to a quick start.

First, don't forget the research agenda. What do you hope to learn? What brand decisions will you make as a result? Your survey must focus on answering these key questions. Often the most important questions are asked in different ways in more than one place in the instrument.

Second, keep the methodology in mind. Telephone surveys are generally shorter and less complex. Mail surveys, because the recipients will read them, can be longer and cover more complex, even sensitive, issues. Web surveys provide almost instant results and can include visuals for recipients to consider, evaluate, or compare.

Mail surveys can also include publication, ad, video, or Web images that might be reviewed and evaluated. Focus groups and personal interviews are usually more conversational in nature, and plenty of time must be given for responses. Focus groups and personal interviews tend to cover fewer topics, but cover each topic more thoroughly.

Third, remember to move from general questions to specific questions, from safe questions to sensitive ones. As in any good interview, save the most difficult questions for later; open with those that are easy to answer and that gain the respondents' trust and establish a sense of momentum.

Finally, keep the instrument as short as possible. Nobody likes wading through endless questions. As you write the instrument, focus on what's important and not what's merely interesting.

———————————Sidebar———————————
Questionnaire guidelines

As you develop your questionnaires, remember:
- Seek only information that is not available elsewhere
- Test directions, such as skip patterns, to make sure they are clear and simple
- Use examples to illustrate any questions that may be confusing
- Place personal or sensitive questions later in the survey
- Ask important questions more than once and in more than one way
- Do not put the most important questions only at the end of the survey
- Clarity is essential. All items must mean the same thing to all respondents. Terms like "several," "most," and "usually" have no precise meaning, so avoid them
- Vary the types of questions
- Do not talk down to respondents
- Do not assume too much knowledge on their part
- Avoid hypothetical questions; you will get hypothetical answers
- Avoid negative questions; respondents often misread them. For instance, people may overlook the negative word, then give an answer opposite to their real opinion
- Avoid questions that contain stereotypes, slang, or emotionally loaded words or phrases
- Avoid technical terms, abbreviations, jargon, and "big words" that some respondents may not understand
- Avoid items that require people to respond to two separate ideas with a single answer
- Avoid biased or leading questions. If you hint at the type of answer you prefer, respondents may tell you what you want to hear
- Avoid questions that may embarrass respondents or place them on the defense
- People are less likely to complete long surveys than short ones, so use as few questions as possible

There is as much art as science to writing good research questions. Two helpful sources are Ken Metzler's *Creative Interviewing* and Stanley Payne's *The Art of Asking Questions.*

Software considerations

Because there is nothing more frustrating than having a box of 372 surveys that your software cannot analyze, it is very important to understand the statistical software you will be using to analyze the data even as you develop the instrument. If you are not familiar with statistical software, take the time to review an early draft of the instrument with the people who will be doing the analysis so they can evaluate the suitability of your question formats.

Before you rush out and buy some software, the odds are high that are someone in the department of psychology, sociology, or education at your institution already has statistical software that you can borrow.

Step 5: Draw the sample

To be statistically valid and projectionable, it is important to draw the sample correctly. In essence, this means that everyone in the population has an equal chance to be chosen for the study. This helps assure reliability. Assume, for example, that you are developing a survey to determine how 610,000 community residents perceive your institution and that your goal is a reliability level of 95 percent. To achieve this validity level, using the chart on the next page, you will need a sample of 384.

If the population is homogeneous, you can use a basic random sample. This is sometimes called "*n*th name sampling" because you choose every *n*th name from the larger population. To obtain a basic random sample, you need to divide your population of 610,000 by 384 and then draw every 1,588th name from a randomly generated list.

Don't forget that you should never choose the first 384 people on the list. Most lists are organized alphabetically, geographically, or chronologically, and taking the sample from the first part of the list would mean that the names are not randomly selected. Fortunately, more sophisticated database software packages often include provisions for randomly generating lists, so it should not be difficult to develop a truly random sample.

If the population is heterogeneous, use a stratified random sample. This means you actually break the larger population into subpopulations and then sample each subpopulation separately. For example, you might break the larger group of 2,000 potential donors into three segments according to the size of the gift they are able to give, their age, or some other variable.

Size of Population	Sample Size for Reliability				
	+/-1%	+/-2%	+/-3%	+/-4%	+/-5%
1,000	**	**	**	375	278
2,000	**	**	696	462	322
3,000	**	1,334	787	500	341
4,000	**	1,500	842	522	350
5,000	**	1,622	879	536	357
10,000	4,899	1,936	964	566	370
20,000	6,489	2,144	1,013	583	377
50,000	8,057	2,291	1,045	593	381
100,000	8,763	2,345	1,056	597	383
500,000	9,423	2,390	1,065	600	384

Often, I use a stratified random sample as part of alumni research. For example, let's suppose that you are a large university located in Columbus with 360,000 living alumni. If you treat this as a homogeneous sample, you will need approximately 383 in your sample to achieve a validity level of 95 percent. However, you also know that the average age of the alumni population is 43 and that the age range is from 19 to 102. After some thought, you decide to break the larger population into six subpopulations:

- Alumni who graduated one year ago
- Alumni who graduated more than one but less than five years ago
- Alumni who graduated more than five but less than 10 years ago
- Alumni who graduated more than 10 but less than 20 years ago
- Alumni who graduated more than 20 but less than 40 years ago
- Alumni who graduated more than 40 years ago

While the exact breakdown of these age groups is somewhat arbitrary, samples drawn from these six subpopulations will, overall, be much more representative of the larger population of alumni. The next step, of course, is to ascertain the size of each subpopulation and then draw the required sample. The resulting sample sizes are represented in the table presented on the next page.

A stratified random sample would require you to treat each subpopulation as a separate study. In other words, you would have to draw a specific number of names randomly from each of the six pools. The level of reliability you seek, of course, would determine the number of names.

If, for example, you are completing a survey of prospective students, you might want to divide your larger sample into several smaller ones to categorize students by ethnicity, household income, distance from the institution, or some other characteristic or quality you feel is important.

Of course, it is possible to stratify every large population into smaller subsets. However, you must always balance the need to stratify with expediency and economy. Stratified studies are more complicated, take longer, and cost more.

Alumni Pool	Age Range	Size of Subpopulation	Sample Size for 95 Percent Reliability
Pool 1	One year out	1,800	322
Pool 2	Two to five years out	9,300	357
Pool 3	Six to 10 years out	12,300	370
Pool 4	11 to 20 years out	19,000	370
Pool 5	21 to 40 years out	22,000	377
Pool 6	More than 40 years out	18,200	377
These are fictitious data			

What's so special about a 95 percent reliability level?

The preceding pages have referred to reliability levels of 95 percent a number of times. However, it is important to keep in mind that reliability levels can vary dramatically. The goal is to balance cost and reliability. You will note, for example, that sample sizes–and costs–increase significantly as you move toward higher reliability. Consider a population of 4,000. A reliability level of 95 percent requires a sample of 350. At the same time, reliability levels of 97 percent and 98 percent require samples of 842 and 1,500, respectively. These marginal increases in reliability require great increases in sample size and overall project cost. So what's so special about 95 percent? Well, it represents a good balance between high reliability and moderate cost. You can spend more for more reliability, but the reality is that the additional cost is generally not worth it. Often, it is more important to heighten response rates than to use a larger sample.

Response rates

At this stage in the project you must also begin to think about probable response rates. This is especially true for mail surveys because responses have dropped dramatically over the past few years. Response rate is less of an issue for telephone surveys because you generally keep calling until you have an adequate number of respondents.

When you assign levels of reliability to a study, you assume a response rate of at least 50 percent for each sample. If the response rate is less, you have what is called non-response bias; more people in the sample didn't respond than did.

There are three basic strategies for dealing with non-response bias. First, oversample your population. For example, if your study calls for a sample of 370, you should consider surveying twice or even three times that many. This oversampling will help boost response rates.

Second, include incentives with your survey. Mail surveys often include incentives such as cash, the opportunity to win a larger sum of cash or a prize through a drawing, or a small gift such as a calendar, booklet, or coupon.

A third strategy to reduce non-response bias is to use ART, an acronym that reminds you to:

- Announce the study with a postcard or e-mail
- Remind participants to complete the survey (use another postcard or perhaps a second survey)
- Thank respondents for their help

ART is especially suited for mail surveys and Web surveys, though the basic strategy, with a little tweaking, works for all kinds of research.

Keeping records

After you have drawn the sample it is very important to record the specifics of the sample. This will be invaluable when you write the methodology section of the final report and should you decide to replicate the study in the future. At the very least, this summary should include:

- Size of the population
- Size of the sample
- Degree of validity that was sought
- Source of the names
- How the names were chosen
- How the sample was drawn (random, stratified random, etc.)
- Subpopulations that were oversampled

Later, you will also want to add the response rate for each study, especially the mail survey.

Step 6: execute the study

After you have chosen the research methodology and drawn the sample, it is time to execute the study. Because each methodology has slightly different protocols, it is sometimes helpful to have a faculty member who understands research review your methodology beforehand. This is especially important if you are relatively inexperienced.

Step 7: input and analyze data

As surveys are returned or interviews finished, check them for validity and completeness. It is also helpful to number each survey before you enter it into the computer so that you can later verify randomly selected surveys against the data to ensure the accuracy of the data entry.

Analysis of quantitative data

Inputting the data from close-ended questions is usually just a matter of correctly inputting the responses. Handling data from open-ended questions is more problematic. All responses must first be read, categorized, and then coded. Finally, they must be entered. In many respects, this process converts open-ended data to close-ended data so that you can analyze it with the other close-ended responses.

In most cases, analysis is relatively straightforward and includes descriptive statistics such as percentages (frequency counts) and statistics that highlight central tendencies and the shape of distributions such as mean, median, mode, and standard deviation. In a few cases, you might want to use more sophisticated techniques such as analysis of variance (ANOVA) or regression analysis.

As you move into this kind of analysis, you are also moving from being a serious amateur to a becoming a statistics professional.

Analysis of qualitative data

Analysis of qualitative research is usually not very sophisticated. It typically involves preserving and categorizing comments drawn from in-depth interviews and focus groups and, within context, using these comments to support or illustrate quantitative data. The merging of qualitative and quantitative data is often highly insightful.

However, handling qualitative data warrants at least one word of caution. It is very important that you preserve the anonymity of the respondent when presenting qualitative data if anonymity was promised as part of the data collection. In some instances it is easy to determine who said something based on the particular words and phrases he or she may use. Even if you don't use names of respondents, people may be able to figure who said what. It is very important to sanitize some comments to protect the anonymity of the source. Of course, you must take care not to change the meaning of the response.

Step 8: present the results

Presenting the findings actually involves two steps: writing a detailed final report and deciding which parts of it you want to present.

The written report

The written report is the document of record. If your research and its conclusions are to be accepted, they must be well-written. At the very least, the report should include the following sections/topics:

- Introduction
- Goals and purpose of research
- Brief overview of the methodology; a more detailed methodology should be in the appendix of the final report
- Descriptive snapshot of who completed the study
- Analysis of all data

- Executive summary
  - Review of key data including graphs
  - Relevant cross-tabulations
  - Implications
  - Strategies for implementation
  - Suggested areas for further research
  - Conclusion

- Appendices
  - Detailed methodology
  - Sample of instruments
  - Hard copy of all analysis

The tone of the report is important. It must be authoritative yet not overly technical. The report should include a clear table of contents so readers can focus on the parts of most importance to them. The methodology section should include information on survey design and pretesting, the timeline for the study's execution, response rates, and a description of the statistical software and analyses used.

As you write the report, avoid the tendency to focus only on the negative findings. In fact, it is often useful to stress positive findings early in the report to increase support for the research. The presentation of your research is also extremely critical. The integrity of your study, and your reputation, may rest on the quality of this presentation

The report itself should be expertly prepared, well-illustrated, carefully proofed, crisply reproduced on high-quality paper, and presented in a three-ring binder so individual pages can be removed and photocopied.

Present the findings

In addition to a written report, you will probably be asked to present the data to a group or two. This is a very important opportunity to enhance not only the credibility of the research, but of yourself as well. When developing the presentation, remember three cardinal rules.

- First, by emphasizing everything, you actually emphasize nothing. Be judicious in deciding how much of your data to present. Remember, you must focus on the truly important
- Second, people can absorb only so much information and most have trouble dealing with endless columns of numbers
- Third, take the time to present the most salient bits of data in high-quality graphs

Do the research yourself or go outside?

As you think about research, you are probably wondering whether you want to conduct the research yourself or seek outside help. The guidelines on the next page should help your thinking.

Staying inside

Undertaking research yourself may save you money. Additionally, your familiarity with your institution is a bonus. Of course, you are also aware of in-house research resources upon which you can depend. And the odds are high that there are already some existing budgets for such items as postage, stationery, and clerical support that you can tap into. For these reasons, conducting the research internally might be a good idea.

Going outside

While there are benefits for staying inside, there are also benefits for turning to outside help. Going outside will save you time. This is especially true when you are conducting multiple studies or when your internal resources are tight. Also, outside companies often have more expertise across all types of research methods and can often correctly match the research question with the audience and the type of study to be undertaken. In addition, an experienced outside source likely has samples of questionnaires which you can modify and customize.

In addition, an outside researcher has no stake in the findings–has no hidden agenda–and is not trying to use data to prove something. This impartiality and objectivity is especially important if you are examining a sensitive or political issue. Finally, go outside when you need perspective on the findings. Good research is much more than simply collecting data, it is using data to provide direction in improving programs and strategies. One of the biggest reasons colleges and universities go to a company that specializes in higher education research is that they realize the importance of data interpretation and application. It is one thing to collect data, but quite another to know what to do with it.

Now that we have laid a research foundation, let's explore the application of research that more directly relates to brand development and evaluation.

■■■■■

Chapter 18
Brand Research Strategies[25]

The previous chapter and following appendices look at basic research methods. In this chapter, we will build on that foundation and focus on research strategies that will help you build a stronger brand. Note that we will be touching on promise testing only tangentially. That topic was already thoroughly addressed in Chapter 8.

As we think about the probable roles of research in the branding process we can conclude that it plays different roles depending on whether research is being use to help make, communicate, live, or strengthen your brand.

At the first stage, making a brand promise, research is perceptual, comparative, and investigative. It is used to determine how you and your brand are perceived by key audiences. It is also used to determine how these audiences compare you and your brand with competitors. Research at this stage is also investigative because it is used to explore the met and unmet needs of your target audiences. Finally, research can be used to test potential brand promises.

At the second stage in the branding process, communicating your promise, research can help you determine the media habits and expectations of your target audiences. It can also be used to help you "trial balloon" different brand communication concepts and strategies.

At the third stage in the branding process, living your promise, research can be used to help you determine the efficacy of your brand stewardship programs by querying stakeholders about their role, their concerns, and obstacles they encounter in living the brand.

Finally, research can be used to help you strengthen your brand by asking internal and external audiences, "How'd we do?" In other words, go back to your most important target audiences and literally ask them if you delivered on your promise.

Using research to help you make a brand promise

This chapter will be organized in two broad sections. First, we will explore, in greater depth, how to use research as part of the brand audit. In other words, how to use research to help you examine your:

- Institution
- External target audiences
- Competitors and marketplace

After discussing the brand audit in greater depth, we will then explore some brand research tools that build on the research methods presented in the previous chapter.

As you review the basic research strategies, you will likely note that most are used early in the brand development process, most often when creating the initial brand promise. In this manner they are investigative. A number of them, however, can also be used to help you strengthen your brand promise. At this point in the branding process they are evaluative.

Before we begin, an organizational note is in order. For the sake of simplicity, I chose to put internal audiences in the institutional audit and external audiences in the target audience audit. Of course, this blurs some lines. For example, are alumni internal or external? In many respects it does not matter how you categorize your audiences as long as you focus on gathering pertinent data from the audiences you value most and that value you most.

Finally, where appropriate, I added brief words of caution and ideas about situations where a specific research method might work best.

SECTION ONE: THE ROLE OF RESEARCH IN THE BRAND AUDIT

Using research to complete an institutional audit

The institutional audit has two goals. First, to begin establishing support for the creation or refinement of a brand promise among internal stakeholders. Second, to gather insight into what that promise might be. If you have been involved in a strategic planning or visioning process, then you are familiar with the mechanics of an institutional audit. At their most basic, audits involve asking faculty, staff, administrators, students, donors, and others how they view themselves and their institution. Not surprisingly, there are two essential questions for a successful institutional audit:

- Who do we think we are?
- Who do we want to become?

Questions and dialogue about goals, dreams, and even frustrations are the bedrock of a successful institutional audit. To obtain these insights, you will want to hold interviews, focus groups, and conduct quantifiable and defendable research with key stakeholders including senior faculty, staff, and administrators.

As part of the audit, you will also want to review your foundational documents: your mission, vision, and strategic plan.

Other areas of investigation might include evaluations of:

- Campus climate and sensitivity to branding and marketing issues
- Existing planning documents
- Existing market research, especially nonmatriculant and withdrawing students research
- Recruiting and fundraising programs and messages
- Recruiting communication flow/funnel
- Media plans
- Public and community relations plans
- Internal communication strategies
- Web strategies
- Your facilities and physical plant
- Internal communication strategies

As you design your institutional audit, remember that you must have a process that is as open and non-threatening as possible. In addition, the process must not only encourage– but actually solicit–different, sometimes even unpopular, views. Finally, the institutional audit should educate people about the whole branding process that is being undertaken so that stakeholders will have a greater understanding of what's ahead.

Words of caution: Many audits use only focus groups to gather insights. However, because focus groups are non-quantitative, they are seldom defendable and are unlikely to clarify issues that depend on clear, concise data. For this reason, it is recommended that you use both focus groups and quantitative studies as part of the institutional audit. Ideally, you might use focus groups to gather initial impressions and insights and then test these your conclusions in a more empirical fashion through the use of quantitative research.

Second, be wary of the alphas. While the input of the president, senior administrators, and senior faculty is absolutely critical to the planning process, sometimes there is a strong temptation to follow their lead to an alarming degree. Harry Beckwith, author of *Selling the Invisible*, reminds us that too many organizations run on the Alpha Principle. He notes, "Ideas do not follow the good thinking in an organization; ideas follow the power. The alphas dictate what the group does and thinks. But are alphas better at decision-making? Not necessarily. Alphas are just better at getting and keeping power."

Third, I suggest you undertake the external assessment first (see next section). Beginning with an inward look encourages a tendency for institutions to solidify positions based on historic paradigms and ways of doing things. In other words, looking inward first may distort your view of the marketplace and cause you to either overlook opportunities or to continue on a course of action that is increasingly outmoded.

Which research methods work best: Individual interviews, focus groups, quantitative studies including telephone, mail, and Web surveys, and document review.

Using research to complete the external target audience audit

Determining how you are perceived and positioned by key external target audiences is a fundamental requirement for the creation of a successful brand. Even as we remember the critical need to focus and limit your number of target audiences, recognize that a target audience audit may include an examination of:

- Prospective undergraduate or graduate students (this broad category is often broken into segments by major program, ethnic group, age, full- or part-time, affluence, or other variables)
- High school influencers including counselors, club advisors, and coaches
- Community and/or business leaders
- Donors (current, prospective, or former)
- Local and regional media

As part of the external target audience audit, you want to learn:

- How these audiences perceive you
- How these audiences hear about you
- How these audiences have positioned you in their minds
- Their feelings and attitudes toward you
- Which of your brand benefits they value most
- How much equity (hopefully, but not always, positive) your brand has to them
- What your identity (look, logo, and letterhead) "says" to these target audiences

In addition to focusing on issues related to brand awareness and brand relevance, we can also explore such issues as the media habits, information needs, and the service/program needs and expectations of your target audience.

Enhancing the effectiveness of your target audience audit

To make your external target audience audit as effective as possible you should remember to:

- Limit the number of audiences to those who are critically important to your current brand or the brand you aspire to hold
- Use statistically valid research so your data and conclusions are defendable
- Create forums that allow you to capture anecdotal data that will give life and meaning to your quantifiable findings

Which research methods work best: Individual interviews, focus groups, and heavy quantitative research because you will be creating an important baseline against which you will measure future progress.

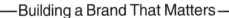
Finding the sweet spot

Branding expert David Aaker, writing in *Brand Equity*, believes that making an effective brand promise and the relationship that results begins with a thorough understanding of your target audiences both as a larger group and as individuals. He writes, "You cannot develop deep relationships without a rich and insightful understanding of the customer. You need to find the customer's sweet spot, that part of his or her life that represents significant involvement and commitment and/or expresses who they are–their self-concept."

He goes on, "The key to finding the sweet spot is to learn from customers as individuals rather than about customers as groups and how the brand linked to the customer's self-concept and behavior patterns. Finally, look at customers' values and beliefs, activities and interests, and possessions."

Using research to complete the marketplace and competitor audit

Because an effective brand cannot be built in isolation, the brand audit concludes with an examination of your marketplace and your competitors. A comprehensive marketplace and competitor audit seeks to answers such question as:

- How are you and your brand are perceived, compared, and valued in the marketplace?
- What demographic, economic, and societal forces are impacting your marketplace?
- Are there unique, sufficient, and sustainable populations that are not being served?
- What brand promises are already owned by your competitors?
- Is there a promise your external audiences believe you should make?
- What promises are "unclaimed" by your competitors?
- What do your audiences think of your competitors?
- What promises are your competitors making in the marketplace?
- Are your competitors communicating their promise more effectively than you are?
- In what ways are your competitors (and their brand promise) vulnerable?
- Are there opportunities for sponsorships and collaborations?
- What linkage and exchange relationship possibilities exist with key publics?

Gathering competitor and marketplace data will involve a balance of primary research (asking people) and secondary research (reviewing the marketing and promotional material of your competitors).

Words of caution: Many of the concerns outlined in the institutional audit portion of this chapter apply here as well. The only other caution is a reminder to keep focused. Often a comment or bit of research (particularly from an alpha) can drag you off strategy. This is especially problematic when a potential donor says, essentially, "if you build it, I'll pay for it." The problem is that the building is sometimes not in line with your long-term strategy. For example, a college that is almost wholly engineering in focus recently completed the construction of a performing arts center (the third such center in a 25-mile radius). Now the academic dean is looking at expanding the college's majors to include, of all things, drama because he feels compelled to support the performing arts center.

Which research methods work best: Individual interviews, focus groups, and heavy quantitative research because you will be creating an important baseline against which you will measure future progress.

SECTION TWO: BRAND RESEARCH TOOLS

The following section will explore some basic and advanced brand research tools including:

- Words and phrases
- Promise testing
- Gap analysis
- Brand mapping (or competitive positioning)
- Pre- and post-testing
- Perception differential
- Factor analysis
- Preference regression

Brand research tool: words and phrases

The first and least sophisticated brand research tool is called *words and phrases*. At its most rudimentary, this involves asking a sample of your target audience the following question:

What words and phrases do you use to describe XXYYZZ University?

Designed to gather top-of-mind perceptions, this can be posed as an open-ended question on a telephone survey or personal interview or a close-ended question–with a range of options for scoring–on a mail, Web, or telephone survey.

Recently, for example, we asked a sample of college-bound prospective students to describe a major university in the Southeast. The client was interested in top-of-mind impressions so the students were not prompted. Because this was a telephone survey, the survey respondents had a list of the words and phrases most often mentioned in focus groups and in other surveys we had undertaken. We knew the likelihood was high that the words and phrases used by students were likely to be found on our prepared list. We also had space on the survey to record responses we had not anticipated.

After the survey was completed, we discovered that the top seven words and phrases used *most often* by students who completed the survey were the following:

- Hot
- Not well-known
- Athletics
- Far away
- Party school
- Big
- Football

These data were very helpful, but what made it even more insightful was how this list of words and phrases compared to the words and phrases chosen by senior administrators to describe brand. The senior administrators used words like:

- Academic quality
- Research university
- Economic asset

The fact that there was such a discrepancy between how the university described itself and how prospective students described it indicated that they had a major disconnect on their hands. The administrators and faculty had one perception of the university and the students had another. In other words, the institution had a brand that was badly mis-aligned.

Words of caution: While *words and phrases* can be enormously revealing, the strategy does have a major flaw: ambiguous definitions of the words and phrases that are being evaluated. For example, one college was pleased to learn that students described it as "challenging." They were less pleased to learn that students were not describing academic quality, but the parking situation.

In a similar vein, it is important to make sure that you understand how target audiences are defining the words and phrases. We know, for example, that faculty and students often have very different and sometimes conflicting definitions of academic quality. Faculty are thinking about quality of the faculty, facilities, and curriculum. Students are thinking about access, speed, and parking. Recognizing this, it is always important to walk the definition back to the target audience to make sure that your understanding is complete and whole.

Which research methods work best: Use focus groups to gather the words and phrases used by your target audiences and then "test" these initial conclusions quantitatively using either a telephone, Web, or mail survey.

Best uses for this brand research tool: Early in the brand development process, typically at the promise creation stage.

Brand research tool: promise testing

Sometimes called benefit testing, promise testing involves testing potential brand promises with your target audiences. It generally works like this: after you have completed your institutional, external target audiences, and marketplace and competitor audits, the data you have gathered is assessed and evaluated. As part of this assessment, some likely brand promises are synthesized. Promise testing involves asking your most important target audiences to evaluate five or six different promises on four criteria. First, is the promise important to them? Second, is the promise believable? Third, is the promise interesting? And fourth, is it unique? As part of this research you might also ask your target audiences if they:

- Understand the primary benefits or attributes of the brand promise
- Have ideas on how the brand promise can be communicated
- Have insights into how the brand promise might be distilled into a tagline

To help you more completely understand the importance of promise testing, consider the following example. Suppose, after completing your brand audit, you have isolated several brand benefits that were consistently mentioned in your research. The benefits were:

- Quality faculty
- Faculty who teach
- Future oriented
- An educational experience that leads to jobs

After considering these benefits, you developed four brand promises:

- A real education for the real world
- Partners working together
- The future is yours
- Great ideas begin here

To test your four brand promises, you set up focus groups of prospective students, donors, and alumni. You ask each group to think about the brand promises. Again, the focus is important, believable, interesting, and unique.

During the focus groups you discover that all three groups think the first brand promise is too much of a cliché. However, the groups do like the idea of "partner" that is presented in the second brand promise. At the same time, they are ambivalent about "working together." They also respond positively to the idea of "futures" presented in the third brand promise. Finally, the focus groups respond positively to the notion of "ideas."

After reviewing the focus group findings you finalize the new brand promise:

Bright people working together.

This brand promise is then refined into a tagline: Partners.

Words of caution: It is very important to use a segmented research strategy that allows you to accommodate the needs and expectations of different target audiences. It is also useful to gather insights into how different audiences feel your potential brand promise might be conveyed and projected.

Also, don't forget to test brand benefits as part of the promise test. Testing brand benefits can often offer significant insights into how your audiences perceive and value your brand promise.

Which research methods work best: Promise testing usually begins with focus groups. After the initial brand promises are refined, they are often empirically tested using quantitative research methods.

Best uses for this brand research tool: Like much of the research we have already discussed, promise testing logically occurs as part of the brand promise creation stage. Promise testing may also occur at the final stage: strengthening your brand as you seek to refine your brand promise to an even greater degree.

Brand research tool: Gap analysis

One of my favorite research tools is a basic gap analysis. Essentially, a gap analysis involves asking respondents two questions. First, what qualities do they value most about a specific type of educational experience? Second, how do they perceive the institution is delivering on that quality or characteristic?

Let's look at an example. Suppose we asked prospective engineering students to rate 36 key college-choice variables on a five-point scale. We then graphed the six qualities they valued most:

- Quality of faculty
- Quality of academic advising
- Quality of facilities
- Quality of career counseling
- Job placement record

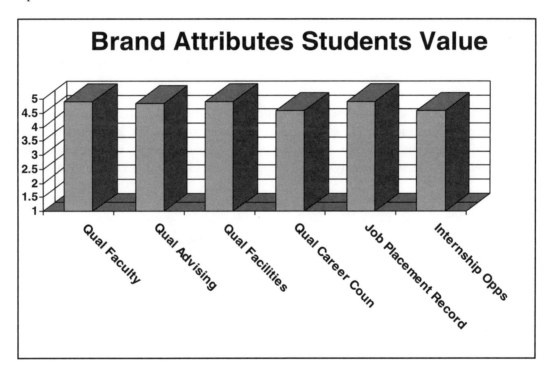

At the same time, we asked students to "rate" the college on these same variables.

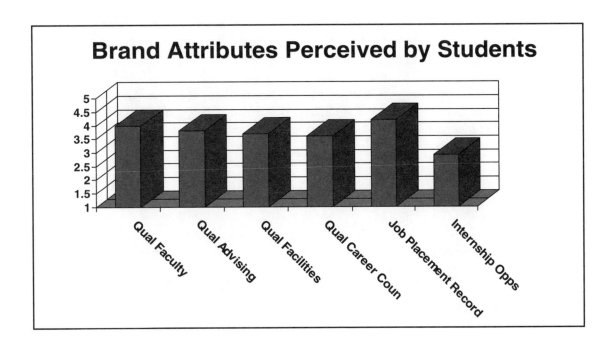

The difference between how much students valued something and how they rated the school's delivery of the variable is called the performance/perception gap. Generally, the larger the gap on highly-valued qualities and characteristics, the more problematic for the college or university. When the gap is large, the target audience does not believe that the institution is credible, or relevant, in something they value.

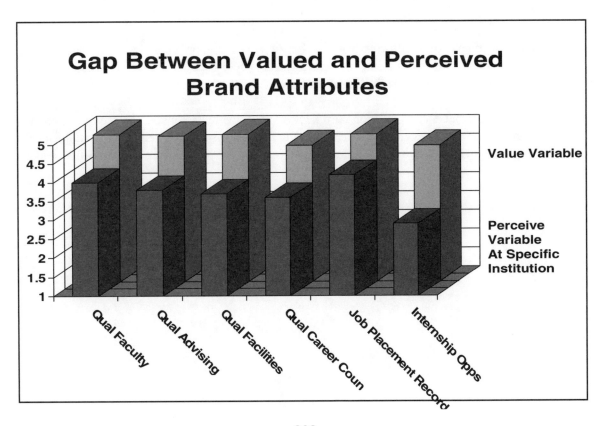

As you might imagine, there are two ways to interpret gap data. Some institutions may, in fact, have a basic flaw–their programs and facilities may be tired or out of step with the marketplace–and they need to respond strategically. This is a <u>performance gap</u>.

However, gaps are not always performance related. For example, a college or university might have an attribute that students value but the students are not aware of it. This is a <u>perception gap</u>. These institutions might have quality faculty and great advising, but they were not communicating this information to prospective students. Perception gaps can typically be addressed through more effective communication.

Of course, if you have a gap problem, it is better when the gap is related to perception, or in this case, mis-perception, rather than performance. The key to differentiating between the two is the quality of the external research and the analysis.

Which research methods work best: Because a gap analysis is heavily quantifiable, it is dependent on statistically valid mail, telephone, or Web surveys.

Best uses for this brand research tool: The gap analysis can be used at the initial stages of brand promise development and at a later stage when you work to strengthen your brand promise.

Brand research tool: brand mapping (or competitive positioning)

A slightly more sophisticated form of branding research is called brand mapping. With brand mapping we do two things. First, much like the gap analysis, we ask the target audience to describe the benefits of an ideal college or university. Second, we ask the target audience to position our client and its competitors on the brand map.

As you can see in the graph on the following page, we began by plotting, on a brand map, the benefits our target audience, prospective engineering students, see as ideal. These benefits are weighted and they merge at a point on the brand map that represents the "ideal" college.

Next, we asked our target audience to position our client on the same map. As you can see in the example on the following page, School F comes closest to the ideal. Our client is positioned well away from the ideal. This map also reveals that our client is closely positioned to School B in the minds of these prospective students.

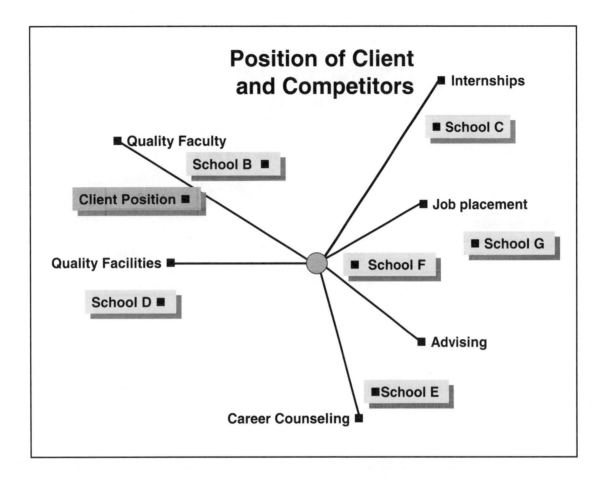

Words of caution: Brand mapping is a very powerful tool and care must be taken not to focus solely on its perception and awareness dimensions. For example, I have seen faculty try to make the case that a school has been mis-branded because of faulty communication when, in fact, target audiences simply believed that the brand promise is tired.

Which research methods work best: Again, brand mapping requires quantitative data obtained through telephone, mail, or Web surveys.

Best uses for this brand research tool: Like much of the research we have discussed so far, perceptual mapping is extremely helpful at the brand creation stage. It is also helpful, however, when you see options for strengthening your brand.

Brand research tool: pre- and post-testing

By definition, perceptual research and branding research are designed to gather data on how you are perceived or branded by a key audience. In an ideal world, research is done before undertaking any branding activities. While the initial research may provide a preliminary measure, it is important to repeat key studies to determine progress and to refine programs and strategies. This is the idea behind a pre- and post-test scenario. A pre-test determines where you are and establishes the initial benchmark. At this point, a strategy is developed to move you in a specific direction. Later, after the strategy has been implemented for a given period of time, a post-test (post-strategy, that is) is undertaken to evaluate your progress.

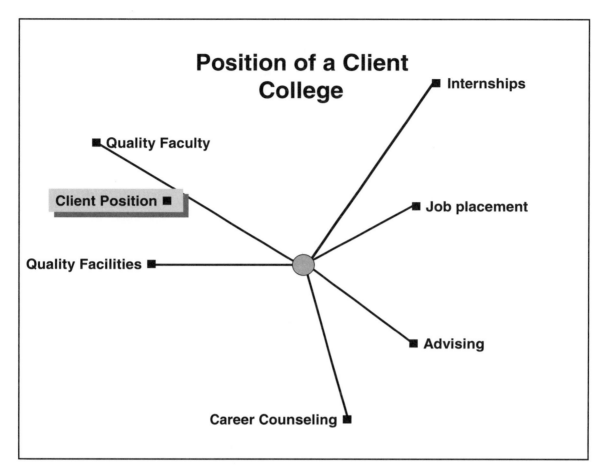

A couple of years ago we undertook an image study (this is the pre-test) and discovered that 43 percent of community residents had branded a college "high cost." Using these data, we helped the college develop a communication campaign that stressed value (the relationship between cost and benefits). Two years later, we repeated the original study (this is called the post-test) and discovered that only 27 percent of community residents described them as "high cost." Based on the pre- and post-test data, we knew that their value-based communication campaign was successful.

A pre- and post-test scenario can be used for any of the brand mapping tools presented in this chapter. However, it is very important when undertaking pre- and post-tests to use the same methodology directed at a similar sample from the same population. Of course, the same questions are also used.

Remember, data gathered at the pre- and post-stages are longitudinal in nature. This shows direction. Without a post-test, it would be impossible to measure the overall effectiveness of your brand communication strategies with any degree of precision. While a pre-test offers a data snapshot, pre- and post-tests are the beginnings of a data movie.

Words of caution: An effective, and defendable pre- and post-strategy requires that the target audience, sample, research method, and questions be consistent for both groups. Any variation can lead to false conclusions.

Which research methods work best: Because statistical validity and representativeness is critical, the data must be quantitative and gathered via telephone, mail, or Web surveys.

Best uses for this brand research tool: By definition, pre- and post-research must be completed at the initial assessment stage and again at the evaluative stage after the branding activities have been implemented.

Brand research tool: perception differential

One of my favorite branding research tools is called perception differential. This is not so much a data-gathering technique as an insightful way to present data. As you can see from the example below, a perception differential is actually a graphic representation of how multiple audiences respond to the same image or branding question or questions.

In this illustration, data from studies of five different audiences is presented on one graph. Each audience was asked the following questions:

On a five-point scale, with one being poor and five being excellent, how would you rate XXYYZZ University on the following attributes:

	Poor				Excellent
Academic quality	1	2	3	4	5
Academic reputation	1	2	3	4	5
Overall friendliness	1	2	3	4	5
Concern about cost	1	2	3	4	5
Concern about grad debt	1	2	3	4	5
Likely to recommend	1	2	3	4	5

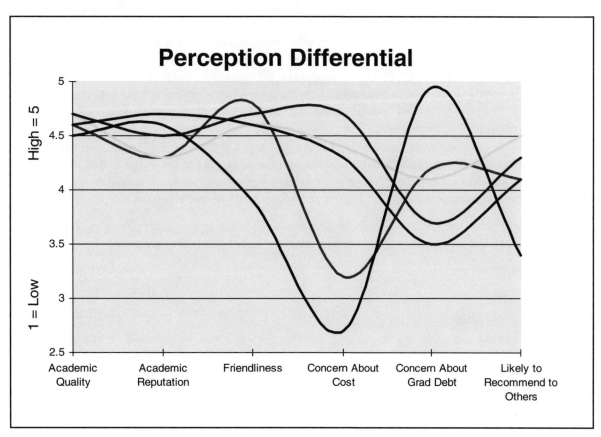

As you can see in the example on the previous page, each line represents the perceptions of a different audience. Perhaps the most important insight to be gained from this type of presentation is not how individual audiences perceive you, but how each audience has a different perception of you. For added impact when presenting this kind of data, it is possible with PowerPoint and other presentation software to add each data set independently during the actual presentation. This heightens the differences held by each and is a powerful way to keep the audience involved in the presentation.

Words of caution: Take care that this research does not disintegrate into a "whose opinion matters most" contest. Ideally, it is used to show that institutions often have multiple perceptions and that many of these perceptions contribute to mis-aligned brands.

Which research methods work best: Again, quantitative research is strongly suggested.

Best uses for this brand research tool: Early in the branding process to help set the stage for a more unified and consistent brand and brand communication strategy.

Brand research tool: factor analysis

Factor analysis is a bit more sophisticated. At its most basic, it is a data-reduction technique that involves removing the redundancy from a set of correlated variables and representing the variables with a smaller set of "derived" variables, or factors. By reducing the variables to a manageable number, we can focus on the groups of characteristics that are most important in determining differences in perceptions between institutions. Once a factor analysis has been completed for a set of variables, a brand map of the results may be developed. In its simplest terms, the resulting map answers the question, "Who do we look like?"

In the example on the facing page, a client institution and five competitors were mapped on two sets of factors. The x-axis factors include issues of reputation (quality, reputation, technology, adult focus, career orientation) and the y-axis factors include issues of access (cost, personal attention, location, and safety). Following the factor analysis, the institutions were placed in their relative positions with regard to these qualities.

From the graph on the next page, we can see that institutions A and B are very similar and are perceived as being the most accessible. Institutions D and E are also similar and have a good trade-off between access and reputation. Institution F has no peers and is perceived as having excellent reputational qualities.

Words of caution: Factor analysis requires rock-solid data with large, representative samples. In addition, because the analysis is fairly high order, it sometimes takes a bit of explaining to colleagues before its significance is understood.

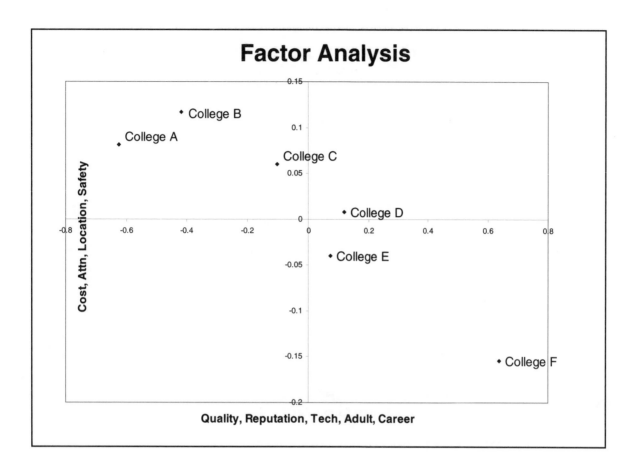

Brand research tool: preference regression

The next brand research tool is called preference-regression analysis. Rather than a new perceptual-mapping technique, preference regression is another way to assess and graph brand and competitive-positioning data.

In the example on the next page, preference regression is used show the relationship between the respondents' *preferences* for a set of institutions and their *perceptions* of the institutions with respect to reputation and accessibility. In other words, we can tell which perceptions influence preferences. In the case of the analysis presented below, we can go beyond, "What do they think of us?" to "Do they like us?"

Using the positioning data from the factor analysis presented earlier, an ideal vector is estimated using regression analysis (based on reputation and accessibility) to show which institutions are most preferred by this target audience. This vector shows institutional preference and has direction.

In the following illustration, we examine the perpendicular position of a given institution on the ideal vector. Those institutions whose perpendicular positions are closest to the positive right end are more preferred. We can also surmise from the direction and slope of the vector that issues of quality, reputation, technology, adult focus, and career orientation are more important to this audience than issues of access (cost, personal attention, location, safety). The groupings of characteristics were determined by factor analysis as described previously.

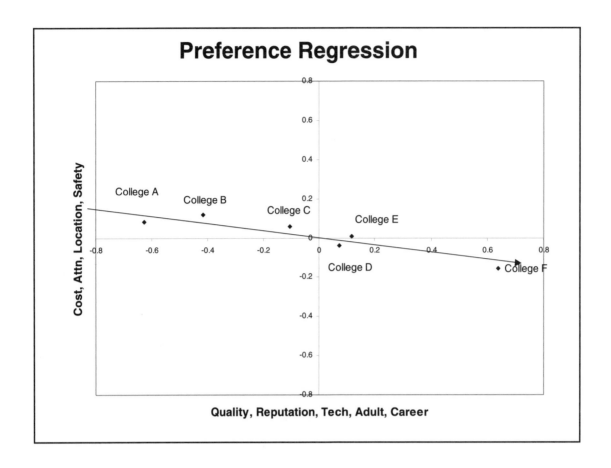

Quadrant analysis

Quadrant analysis, though a bit more aggressive than previous mapping tools, is still a relatively simple analytical tool for graphically representing an institution's strengths and weaknesses.

A type of gap analysis, quadrant analysis involves comparing the *desirability* ratings of key qualities or characteristics to the *quality* ratings of an individual institution. Quadrant analysis shows the major and minor strengths and weaknesses for a single institution at a time. Importantly, this analysis can be undertaken for a particular institution as well as its competitors, thereby garnering key competitive-positioning information.

This involves actually asking two questions:

- How desirable is a certain characteristic or quality?
- How does an institution "rate" on those qualities or characteristics?

As you can see from the graph, students are asked to rate an institution on a specific characteristic such as reputation. At the same time, these students are asked to indicate how important reputation is to them. Quadrant analysis will help you focus your attention on qualities and characteristics that students value on the one hand but also don't think you do particularly well on the other.

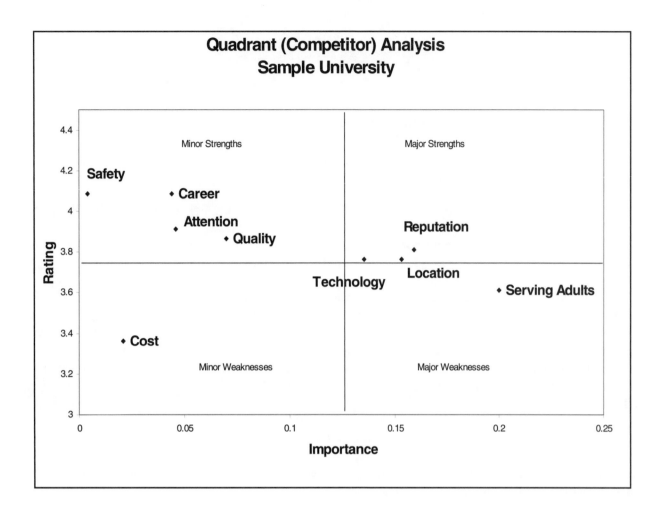

Some research reminders

We need to conclude our discussion of brand research tools with a handful of important reminders. First, remember that good research is faculty-proof. In other words, if the brand questions and answers are likely to have political overtones–and almost everything does these days–then use a sound, defensible methodology.

Second, good brand studies include both qualitative and quantitative methodologies. Don't be afraid to use focus groups or some personal interviews to help you develop your survey instruments.

Third, if you are going to be gathering research to create a baseline, the research should include a solid quantitative methodology.

Fourth, don't forget to illustrate your data with insightful graphs. No one enjoys wading through columns of numbers. Illustrate key findings in ways that are both meaningful and compelling.

And finally, remember that without data, it is only an opinion. The creation, communication, living, and strengthening of any brand promise requires solid, defendable data.

■■■■■

Conclusion

Historically, brand-building efforts in higher education had as their goal the creation of awareness. The primary vehicle was the mark or logo. This brand management approach was image-based and was most often directed by junior- or mid-level public relations and marketing directors. Its focus was the look, letterhead, and logo. Its goals were image consistency and saturation. Issues of relevance were seldom entertained.

The brand leadership strategy outlined in this book has a much more ambitious goal: the creation and positioning in the minds of key audiences of a valued promise. In other words, the building of brand equity. Of course, this involves brand image; after all, building awareness is critical. But it also seeks relevance. At its core, a brand leadership strategy seeks to ask and answer the question: what promise can we offer our prospective students, donors, and others that is of such value that they will support it with their tuition and donated dollars? Furthermore, what brand promise can we make that faculty and staff will support and even allow to guide their actions?

Where brand management is tactical in nature, brand leadership is strategic. Where the brand management strategy was directed by a mid-level administrator, the brand leadership strategy is directed by senior administrators, perhaps even the president. And where brand management is short-term, brand leadership is long-term, perhaps as enduring as the institution itself.

We now know that the four steps to the creation of a blockbuster brand–making a promise that matters, communicating your promise, living your promise, and strengthening your promise–represent a radical departure from most previous approaches to brand-building.

We also know that creating a strong brand is not easy. It will require careful analysis on the one hand and thoughtful introspection on the other. It will require discussion and debate. Most of all, it will require commitment and focus. But the reward is there. Perhaps more than any other tool in the marketer's tool kit, the creation of a strong brand offers true opportunity in today's competitive marketplace.

A number of years ago Warren Buffett once said that he invests in companies with strong brand identities because a great brand, he believes, creates high barriers to entry for competition and acts like a "moat" protecting the business from encroachment by competitors.

You can put that kind of moat around your campus.

■■■■

■■■■■

Appendices

∎∎∎∎

Appendix A
Brand IQ Test - Answers

1. The best definition of a good brand is:
    a. An easily identifiable logo
    b. A great tagline
    c. <u>Being perceived as the only solution to a problem someone has</u>
    d. Why your college is the best in its class

    Ultimately, the goal of branding is to position yourself as the only possible solution to the student's concern about where he or she wants to go to college or the donor's need to give funds. Branding is all about meeting needs, including the professional needs of faculty and staff.

2. A brand is focused around:
    a. Your logo
    b. Your look
    c. Your mission
    d. <u>A valued promise you make to your target audiences</u>

    Branding is about making and keeping promises with your customers. Nothing more and absolutely nothing less.

3. Your brand strategy should be led by:
    a. The people in your bookstore
    b. <u>Your president</u>
    c. Your athletic department
    d. Your graphic design department

    Great brands are not built by committees. Branding involves leadership and vision. Anything less and it's just promotion.

4. Branding and advertising are:
    a. Synonyms
    b. Antonyms
    c. <u>Distant but related cousins</u>
    d. Two different approaches to the same problem

    Advertising (and the rest of the promotion tool bag) focuses on building awareness of the brand. But you need to build brand relevance first.

5. Branding is:
    a. 100 percent emotional
    b. 100 percent irrational
    c. <u>50 percent rational and 50 percent emotional</u>
    d. 100 percent rational

    Branding is a 50/50 proposition.

6. The truest test of a brand is:
    a. People remember it
    b. People like it
    c. <u>People will seek it out, support it, and pay more for it</u>
    d. None of the above

    Harvard can charge as much as Harvard does because it is a great brand. Many families would gladly pay even more for the opportunity to attend Harvard because Harvard is arguably the greatest and most valuable educational brand in the world.

7. The value of branding is proven when:
    a. Your endowment take a downturn
    b. The marketplace becomes even more competitive
    c. You decide to open a branch campus
    d. <u>All of the above</u>

    When the economy takes a downturn, it is the non-branded or commodity four-year schools that suffer most. When the marketplace becomes even more competitive, it is the branded schools that rise above the fray. And when you decide to open a branch campus (we might call these brand extensions), it is the branded campus that will do best.

8. A brand must appear:
    a. On your letterhead
    b. On your Web site
    c. On your printed material
    d. <u>In every aspect of your institution</u>

    Branding is about everything you do. It is about making promises and keeping them. It is about anticipating customer needs. It is about being the only solution to a problem the customer has. Branding occurs at the switchboard, in the bursar's office, in the classroom, in the midst of a capital campaign. Branding occurs among prospective students, current students, donors, alumni, and among faculty and staff.

9. Branding is:
    a. A fad that will likely pass
    b. <u>Long-term and enduring</u>
    c. Something you only do in a crisis
    d. Something that will go away as the Web becomes the dominant marketing tool

Branding focuses on where your core values meet the most important needs of your most important target audiences. As such, it is long-term and enduring.

10. The creation of an effective brand:
    a. Is tactical, chances are your public relations office can handle it
    b. Is tactical, if your public relations office can't handle it then you should hire a good consultant
    c. <u>Is strategic, it begins with your mission and is proven in the marketplace</u>
    d. Is strategic, it begins with the quality of your academic programming

Part of branding is tactical, but only a minor part. Instead, branding begins with strategy and involves fulfilling your mission each day in the marketplace.

■ ■ ■ ■

Appendix B
90 Days to a Better Brand

The March 2001 issue of *Promo* magazine contained a fascinating article, *90 Days to a Better Brand*. While some of the insights do not apply to higher education, a surprising number do. I excerpted the suggestions that apply most to colleges and universities.

Day 1. Take a good look at your brand. Some of it might seem flabby and in need of a makeover. But maybe there's a bit of equity that's being overlooked. Many brands underestimate their own power and resonance with the customer base.

Day 2. Define the brand. It sounds fundamental, but is your brand really defined? How do customers see it? What can they tell you about the benefits your brand delivers and the values it stands for? What sets it apart from the competition? If the answers are not clear, refine your message to more clearly position yourself.

Day 4: Find the unique selling proposition. The USP (unique selling proposition), or point of difference, is what sets your brand apart from competitors. Be sure it is sharply defined, unique, and effectively communicated to consumers at all touch points. Analyze your positioning relative to others in the market, and explore opportunities to more clearly differentiate your brand from competitors.

Day 6: Get the consumer's perspective. Pretend you're the consumer. How would you purchase your brand? Actually go through the purchase process from start to finish. Next, explore how to register a complaint. What type of satisfaction would your consumers receive? This exercise should prove rewarding, and might be surprising. If you identify problems, take actions to correct them and then repeat the process.

Day 7: Make sure promises are fulfilled. Building customer loyalty means always delivering on promises. Build the USP around benefits that are credible and realistic. Don't make product or service claims unless you're certain you can keep them, and constantly monitor quality to ensure consumer expectations are met in all areas.

Day 8: Monitor vital signs. High brand equity is high customer equity. Keys to building customer equity are brand awareness, image of quality, strong emotional associations, and high customer loyalty. Measure those variables. Monitor them to identify shifts. Compare brand metrics to those of your competitors. Branding requires a never-ending cycle of setting objectives and strategies, building and implementing programs, measuring key metrics, and repeating the process.

Day 9: Examine customer segments. You can't please all of the people all of the time–at least not in the same way. Conduct category segmentation studies to understand different consumer groups. Who are they? What do they like? What do they do? And how can you reach them? What's growing, fading, standing still?

Attack opportunity segments with funds redirected from fading segments. Quantify the relative value of key consumer groups. Which segments drive the bulk of your sales? Which segments are most profitable? Once you've identified your best customers, find ways to extend and reinforce the brand relationship. Not only will this help build sales, it will help insulate your best customers from competitive offers.

Day 13: Review customer touch points. Examine each of your consumer contacts as an opportunity to influence and shape attitudes about the brand. Are you using each touch point to deliver a singular marketing message, reinforce the brand, and deepen relationships? Develop touch point integration: track customer interactions over time and use this information to better meet their needs.

Day 14: Schedule a synergy day. Plan a full-day meeting, preferably off-site, to bring together all brand agencies (general advertising, promotion, direct, public relations) and internal resource groups to share plans and programs. Collectively discuss the role each group plays in supporting and building brand equity.

Day 15: Bench press more. Ask your media buyer for a list of value-add events from the networks and magazines in which you advertise. If there aren't any, look for new media. If there still aren't any, look for a new media buyer.

Day 16: Evaluate the Internet strategy. The Web is lightning quick. To keep up, you must constantly reconfirm that your Internet marketing efforts are Grade A. Start with the essence of the home page (navigability, load time, content, interactivity level). Then consider adding chat rooms, bulletin boards, and links to relevant and complementary sites. (Also, mainstream high-speed Internet access is coming. Are you ready?)

Day 18: Call field staffers. Few people understand the brand's challenges and opportunities as well as the field sales force. They hear what clients and consumers are planning next. Chances are they'd love to tell you what they know.

Day 20: Target your weak areas. Simple research will tell you the current status of your brand in consumers' minds, and will illuminate areas where you need work. Do consumers know you? Are they getting the right brand message? Have they tried you? Find out.

Day 22: Lay down the law with agencies. Make sure brand-building is a key objective for all plans and programs developed by your agencies. In fact, put it into their evaluation criteria. If you don't insist on it, you can't expect it to happen.

Day 25: Reach out for strategic partners. In an era of global brands and increased consolidation, even the world's largest companies can't compete alone. The right partnership–Kraft and Nickelodeon, Disney and McDonald's–is gold. You can leverage the equity, capabilities, resources, properties, distribution, and other assets of non-competing companies. Consider product, service, promotional, and logistics agreements, as well as event marketing and spokesperson deals. Carefully select partners that are consistent with your positioning.

Day 26: Make your best customers happy. Make sure your high-value customers are satisfied. Don't wait until something goes wrong to begin a dialogue with them. Once you've identified the best customers, find ways to extend and reinforce the relationship. This helps build sales and insulates your best customers from competitive offers.

Day 27: Evaluate convergence marketing. Your online brand experience is no less real to consumers than the offline experience. Online branding must have a look and message consistent with other communications, and it must deliver on the brand promise. The media is new, not the marketing principles. Don't cut corners.

Day 29: Check on the customer relationship. Do you speak to all your customers the same way? Create customized messaging, offers, and even special products wherever possible. Develop one-to-one media to deliver the personalization.

Day 30: Push partners in the right direction. Don't allow marketing partners to sail away without clear direction. Create an ongoing relationship with them that allows for easy communication of objectives, goals, and results.

Day 31: Mine segments. Many brands suffer from obsolete assumptions about demographic and ethnic segments. At a minimum, you should know where you (and your competitors) stand with the African-American, Hispanic-American, and Asian- American communities. Various lifestyle segments may also represent profitable markets for products. Be sure your plans capitalize on the realities of today's market and prepare yourself for the large and diverse consumer segments of the future.

Day 32: Understand cultural segments. Not only will marketers need to understand how Cuban-Americans in Florida differ from Mexican-Americans in California, but they'll need to know what the brand "means" to each group. Conduct long-term attitude and usage research as well as short-term, one-on-one interviews and focus groups. Explore attitudes, priorities, perceptions, usage history, and unique usage practices.

Day 37: Shadow a customer. Office cubicles and PowerPoint presentations don't cut it. To truly understand how the brand operates in the marketplace, go check out the marketplace. Take a trip to visit consumers. Go to stores. Sit and watch your product on the shelf. Speak with store employees and consumers directly. You'll never receive the same impact or understanding from second-hand information.

Day 38: Start to buy, not sell, share. Increase profits by reducing the marketing budget? Bad idea if you plan to be in business for a while. When promotion and advertising budgets are cut to shore up short-term profits, you're selling off expensively won share points. Admit it.

Day 40: Make creative stand out. Today's consumers are bombarded with more brand messages than ever before. To stand out in the crowd, the creative needs to be more attention-grabbing and memorable than ever. Challenge conventional approaches and corporate "dumbing-down" of communications. Give staff members time to go the extra mile, but demand they get it right.

Day 42: Explore licensing. A well-known brand with strong emotional appeal to consumers can make the most of that asset with selective licensing. For example, toy versions of the brand icon or products could place your logo in living rooms across the country. Licensed apparel allows consumers to make a lifestyle statement and spreads your message among their friends–likely to be target consumers. Choose items for fit with the brand and potential to extend your message's reach.

Day 51: Keep your hands off the talent. Let the marketing team do what they're paid to do. Once you've established where you are and where you want to go, let the creative minds and hands do their jobs. The best way to put your imprint on marketing materials is often by keeping your hands off.

Day 56: Reorganize focus groups. Stale focus groups are a waste of time and marketing dollars. Breathe new life into the effort by rewriting questions, finding new demographic groups to poll, and adding excitement to the environment. Leave the labs and take the chats into new rooms or even outdoors. Subtle changes prove catalysts for solid results.

Day 59: Fine an online partner. You don't have to be Pepsi and Yahoo! to execute stellar online-offline integration. Research where your target audience is surfing and get in touch with the sites. Dot-coms, now more than ever, are wide open to partnerships that ship before signing on the dotted line.

Day 60: Evaluate suppliers. Contact promotional suppliers and explore what's happening in their R&D labs. Never-before-seen products and services are right around the corner. Be the first brand to use them in promotions. If something strikes your fancy, negotiate an exclusivity contract to prohibit another brand (read: competitor) from using it for a specified period.

Day 61: Create an experience. There are reasons why experiential marketing is flourishing. Develop promotions that are relevant, intriguing, and entertaining. Reach out to customers through multiple touchpoints and channels, and engage them in a way they'll never forget.

Day 62: Assess your customer service. How easily can an unhappy customer reach you to resolve a complaint? Understand and quantify the relative value of key segments in the customer base. Which segments drive the bulk of your sales? Make sure customer service departments are tuned into this group.

Day 64: Reassess the competition. Savvy marketers regularly track competitors' promotions. Investigate every channel, from in-store to online to direct mail. Understand their strengths and weaknesses, and use them to your advantage.

Day 66: Talk to legal. Marketing laws are rewritten all the time, especially when it comes to the Internet. Keep promotions in check by staying in constant touch with the legal department. Learn what changes are on the horizon and how they may impact your plans.

Day 71: Go beyond the ad buy. Push your media outlets to offer more than air time. Try a sponsorship, a watch-and-win game, or a chat room on the channel's home page. Household cable boxes now run into the triple digits–your audience is out there if you take the time to look.

Day 72: Run a cause effort. It's well-documented that consumers will adjust purchase decisions based on a charity tie-in. But cutting a check isn't enough. Create a community program that shows you really are committed. Get the workforce involved and you may see more smiles around the office, too.

Day 74: Go beyond signage at events. Consumers are almost oblivious to event signage these days. Find other ways to let the populace know you're a part of the festivities. One-to-one activities are effective, as are giveaways and post-event direct-mail programs. Remember to use on-site surveying and follow-up telephone polling to confirm your initiatives are working.

Day 75: Don't rely on the past. Yes, the brand has been running that fourth-quarter ad since time immemorial, and you don't want to rock the boat. But it never hurts to investigate other options. Maybe its time for a whole new boat.

Day 79: Use your home page as a test lap. Internet promotions are so cost-effective they can be used simply to compile consumer information for future sales-generating campaigns. Consumers will generally trade information for the right incentive; make sure the offer matches the request.

Day 80: Talk to your neighbors. They're bound to be more relaxed and candid than a formal focus group. Even if they're not trendsetters, they know what they like and dislike.

Day 82: Read the complaint letters. Disgruntled consumers are quick to point out a company's shortcomings. And some of their gripes are valid. Give them an objective read before filing them away.

Day 83: Stretch. Who else might like your brand? What other ways might your current customers use it? What other brand in a completely different category shares your audience? What if ketchup were green? (of course, now it is).

Day 84: Get paranoid. The equity you hold in your brand is your property. You have invested large sums of money to build that equity. Encourage every employee to be on the lookout for possible brand encroachments by competitors. The legal team can often stop problems before they reach a large audience.

Day 86: Avoid overextension. To be strong, brands must be meaningful to consumers. For many, a product or line extension can cloud a brand's identity and confuse customers. Choose extensions wisely and sparingly.

Day 87: Leverage real people. Look within your company for folks regular people can relate to. Using employees in marketing campaigns or leveraging customer testimonials are proven winners.

Day 88: Look at the results. Be honest with yourself. At the end of the day, your efforts need to build the business. Examine the measurable results–sales, new distribution channels, increased market share, and new audiences–and respond appropriately.

Day 89: Recruit some zealots. By developing a brand promise and keeping it, marketers can transform core audiences into brand zealots, people who are positively evangelical about their product or service. Why? Because people will embrace honesty and a promise kept.

Day 90: Look in the mirror again. Once you look at results and decide if you truly made good on your original promise to customers, you'll find yourself back at the assessment stage, where the process begins all over again. Hey, nobody said this was going to be easy.

■■■■■

Appendix C
Basic Research Methodologies

Focus groups

Focus groups are designed to focus discussions around a specific topic so peoples' attitudes, perceptions, and language can be captured and analyzed. This makes focus groups ideal for exploring opinions and attitudes held by students, donors, parents, and others.

Typically, focus groups involve 10 to 12 people, are about 60 minutes in length, and are directed by a moderator. Potential respondents are selected and screened so they are relatively homogeneous, thereby minimizing both conflicts among group members on issues not relevant to the study and wide-ranging differences in perceptions, experiences, and verbal skills. During the discussion, the moderator follows a guide, a pre-established list of questions and topics to address during the session. Sessions are usually audiotaped. The tape transcriptions and the moderator's notes are the raw information to be analyzed and presented in the final report.

Mail surveys

Mail surveys are widely used in research for examining dispersed populations such as alumni, community residents, or, if you use campus mail, students or faculty. As you write and pre-test the survey instrument, draw a representative sample of the population, or audience, to be investigated. In some cases, a pre-survey postcard should be sent to notify your sample that it will be part of an important research project. The survey goes out with a cover letter that explains the need for research. Depending on the audience, these surveys may include some sort of incentive to increase response.

After a short period, you may send a follow-up letter to people who have not returned the survey. This helps increase response. As the surveys come in, you or your researcher will review them for completeness and validity. The actual analysis involves frequency counts (percentages) of how each question was answered and cross-tabulations (comparisons of how different groups answered the same question). In some cases, more sophisticated statistical analyses may be applied.

Web surveys

Web surveys are essentially mail or telephone surveys delivered over the Internet. For a Web survey, sometimes called an e-mail survey or Internet survey, to be successful, they are generally preceded by an e-mail to the respondent. In most cases this e-mail points them to the Web link. E-mails are also used to thank respondents for completing the survey.

For the most part, Web surveys tend to be shorter than mail surveys and less intrusive than telephone surveys. They are able to show visual images so Web surveys are ideal for testing ad, Web, and publication concepts. Finally, Web surveys depend on having a good e-mail distribution list. In addition, they almost always benefit from an incentive.

Telephone surveys

Telephone surveys are actually a combination of in-depth interviews and mail surveys. Their methodology is largely similar to that of mail surveys, except the interview is conducted over the phone. Because the interviewer reads all the questions, telephone surveys tend to be less sophisticated and shorter than mail surveys. In addition, telephone surveys can often encounter difficulty in handling sensitive issues.

In-depth interviews

Lasting 30 to 45 minutes, in-depth, or one-on-one, interviews are designed to elicit information and opinions from people who are unable or unwilling to be approached through other research techniques. Like other forms of research, in-depth interviews follow an interview guide, a series of questions that serve to direct the discussion. Most in-depth interviews are conversational in nature.

■■■■■

Appendix D
Research Terms and Definitions

A necessary vocabulary

Like any specialized endeavor, market research has its own vocabulary. To help give you a better grasp of market research and its intricacies, it is important to understand some key terms.

Primary research and secondary research

Essentially, there are two sources of research data: primary and secondary. Primary research uses data that originates with your specific study. Secondary research uses existing data from an already completed study that may be applicable to you.

Suppose, for example, you want to know why alumni give to your institution. If you conduct a survey, you are engaged in primary research. On the other hand, if you use data from a study completed by a colleague at another institution, you are using secondary research.

The difference is important for several reasons. First, because primary research involves designing an original study, it is more expensive and time consuming. Secondary research is usually less expensive or even free and is usually available quickly.

The second major difference involves the quality, suitability, and integrity of the data. A well-designed primary research study should offer high-quality data. With secondary data, you are inferring conclusions from someone else's research, so you must take extra care to ascertain the data's relevance, examine the impartiality of the study's sponsor, and ensure that the correct methodology was followed.

Quantitative research and qualitative research

Just as there are two broad sources of research, there are two broad types of research: quantitative and qualitative.

Quantitative research uses a statistically valid and randomly generated sample to represent a larger population. Validity is important because you want to project data obtained from a relatively small sample to the larger population. Quantitative research requires a carefully designed methodology. For this reason, it is usually fairly expensive and may take some time. Mail surveys and telephone surveys are two forms of quantitative research.

Qualitative research, on the other hand, is not statistically valid, and data cannot be projected to larger populations with any degree of certainty. Because qualitative research uses a much less strict methodology, it can usually be conducted more quickly and at lower cost. Focus groups and in-depth interviews are two forms of qualitative research.

The key difference between quantitative and qualitative research is how you wish to use the data. Qualitative research is descriptive, but it is not projectionable. In other words, you cannot project the findings from a focus group of six students to predict how other students might react to your new viewbook. However, with a well-done quantitative study, you can project the findings to a larger population with a high degree of reliability. If 73 percent of your sample responded a certain way to a question, you can be reasonably sure that roughly 73 percent of the larger population would respond in the same manner.

Populations and samples

A population is the group of people to be studied. A population might be faculty, staff, donors, alumni, current students, prospective students, parents, or community residents.

A sample is a small subset of that population. In statistical or projectionable studies, the sample must be of a certain size, representative of the larger population, and randomly generated to be considered valid.

Sampling is important for three reasons. First, it is much less expensive to survey a sample of 370 than a population of 10,000. Second, correctly drawn samples are highly representative. Third, it takes less time to survey a sample than an entire population.

Reliability

Reliability, often called confidence or validity, is usually expressed as a percentage. A study that is reliable at the 95 percent level has a range of error of five percent. If 68 percent of respondents say yes to a particular question, the assumption for the population as a whole could range from 63 percent (68 percent minus five percent) to 73 percent (68 percent plus five percent). The greater the reliability, the more valid the findings.

However, as in many things, there is a tradeoff. Although many factors affect reliability, one of the most important is sample size. The more reliability you want, the greater the sample must be.

■■■■■

Appendix E
Options to Lower Research Costs

For some institutions, the biggest obstacle to market research is its cost. To help reduce the cost of obtaining good research data, I offer the following strategies and resources.

Check secondary sources

Before you begin a primary research project, see if secondary research is available from an association or consortium to which you belong such as CASE, NAICU, NACAC, AACRAO, AMA, CIC, AGB, NASFRE, NAIS, and others. The Web can also be an excellent source of secondary data.

Develop a central research registry

It is not unusual for more than one office at a college to initiate research projects. This can mean duplicated studies or portions of studies, missed opportunities to piggyback, and wasted dollars and time. To avoid this problem, consider developing a central, on-campus research registry that keeps track of who is doing what study.

Involve faculty experts

For a sophisticated study, seek guidance from faculty experts in statistics or research design. Their input and direction may save you time and money. Take care, however, that the topic of study will have no impact on any faculty involved. For example, you would not want a psychology professor to participate in the evaluation of publications produced by his or her spouse working in campus public relations.

Scale down the study's size

Some colleges and universities insist on trying to survey an entire population when a representative sample would be satisfactory. Instead of trying to see how all 18 of your constituent publics perceive you, rank these publics and seek information from the most important five or six.

Use sound methodology

A solid, balanced research methodology will increase the integrity and vitality of your research data. Don't cut corners and be forced to redo the study.

Standardize your instruments

Writing the survey instrument is one of the most expensive components of a research project. If possible, standardize your instruments to get all possible life out of them. This is extremely important if you are trying to create longitudinal data and plan to test, at a later date, the effectiveness of your integrated marketing communication strategies. Choose a less expensive type of research.

There is an enormous difference in the costs of doing 370 mail surveys and 370 phone surveys. With minor modifications, less expensive strategies may gain the same information. However, if response rates are important, sometimes the more expensive research will, over the long run, be more economical as well.

When possible, use close-ended questions

Questions that ask respondents to choose from an established series of answers (yes or no; very good, good, or not very good; and the like) are much easier and cheaper to tabulate.

Pre-test your instruments

A solid pre-test can uncover questions that need rewording or are confusing. Revising your survey will increase its validity.

Develop a research cycle

As discussed earlier in the book, a research cycle involves doing smaller studies each year rather than one massive study every three years. Not only will you have more control over the research, you will also be able to focus on current problems and opportunities. In addition, you will be able to monitor your market continually, probably pay less for the research, and assimilate data more easily.

Balance what you need to know with what would be interesting to know

One quick way to cut your costs is to reduce the size of the survey. I have seen three-page surveys burgeon to eight or more pages after everyone in the administration has a chance to add a few favorite questions. When looking over the questions, ask yourself, "How can I realistically use these data to improve my marketing and communication efforts?"

■■■■

Bibliography

1. Aaker, David A. and Alexander L. Biel. *Brand Equity & Advertising: Advertising's Role in Building Strong Brands*. Hillsdale, NJ: Lawrence Erlbaum Associates, Publishers, 1993.

2. Aaker, David A. and Erich Joachimsthaler. *Brand Leadership*. New York: The Free Press, 2000.

3. Aaker, David A. *Building Strong Brands*. New York: The Free Press, 1995.

4. Aaker, David A. *Managing Brand Equity: Capitalizing on the Value of a Brand Name*. New York: The Free Press, 1991.

5. Aaker, David A. "Measuring Brand Equity Across Products and Markets." *California Management Review,* 1996.

6. Alreck, Pamela L. and Robert B. Settle. *The Survey Research Handbook: Guidelines and Strategies for Conducting a Survey*. Toronto: Irwin Professional Publishing, 1994.

7. Beckwith, Harry. *Selling the Invisible: A Field Guide to Modern Marketing*. New York: Warner Books, 1997.

8. Bedbury, Scott and Stephen Fenichell. *A New Brand World: Eight Principles for Achieving Brand Leadership in the Twenty-First Century*. New York: Time Warner, 2000.

9. Beemer, C. Britt. *It Takes a Prophet to Make a Profit*. New York: Simon and Schuster, 2001.

10. Bentley, Diana. "Stand by Your Brand." *Hemispheres*, October 1998.

11. Bhide, Amar. "Hustle as Strategy." *The Harvard Business Review*, September-October 1986.

12. Blakenship, A.B., George Breen, and Alan Dutka. *State-of-the-Art Marketing Research*. Chicago: American Marketing Association, 1998.

13. Bradburn, Norman M. *Polls and Surveys: Understanding What They Tell Us*. San Francisco: Jossey-Bass, 1996.

14. Breen, Peter. "One Short Month to Brand Ruin." *Promo*, March 2001.

15. Buchholz, Andreas. *What Makes Winning Brands Different?* New York: Wiley and Sons, 2000.

16. Burge, Randy. "Rensselaer Builds Marketing Bridge to World," *Marketing News*, August 30, 1999.

17. Chapman, Randall G. *Brandmaps: The Competitive Marketing Strategy Game*. New Jersey: Prentice-Hall, Inc., 1997.

18. Charmasson, Henri. *The Name's The Thing: Creating the Perfect Name for Your Company or Product*. New York: AMACOM, 1991.

19. Collins, James. *Built to Last: Successful Habits of Visionary Companies*. New York: HarperCollins, 1997.

20. Crainer, Stewart. *The Real Power of Brands: Making Brands Work for Competitive Advantage*. London, England: Pitman Publishing, 1995.

21. Crispell, Diane. "What's in a Brand?" *American Demographics,* May 1993.

22. Cross, Richard and Janet Smith. *Customer Bonding: Pathway To Lasting Customer Loyalty*. Lincolnwood, IL.: NTC Business Books, 1995.

23. Czerniawski, Richard D. and Michael W. Maloney. *Creating Brand Loyalty: The Management of Power Positioning and Really Great Advertising*. New York: AMACOM, 1999.

24. Delano, Frank. *The Omnipowerful Brand: America's No. 1 Brand Specialist Shares His Secrets for Catapulting Your Brand into Marketing Stardom*. New York: AMACOM, 1998.

25. Dolan, Kerry A. "Ghost Cars, Ghost Brand." *Forbes*, April 30, 2001.

26. Dotz, Warren and Jim Morton. *What a Character: 20th Century American Advertising Icons*. San Francisco, CA: Chronicle Books, 1996.

27. Duncan, Tom and Sandra Moriarty. *Driving Brand Value: Using Integrated Marketing to Manage Profitable Stakeholder Relationships*. New York: McGraw-Hill, 1997.

28. Farquhar, Peter. *Branding: Building Your Company's Best Asset*. New York: McGraw-Hill, 1998.

29. Fedler, Laura Koss. "Branding Culture: Nonprofits Turn to Marketing to Improve Image and Bring in the Bucks." *Marketing News*, January 5, 1998.

30. Finn, Chester E. *American Outlook*. New York: Hudson Institute, 1998.

31. Fombrun, Charles J. *Reputation: Realizing Value from the Corporate Image*. Boston: Harvard Business School Press, 1996.

32. Frank, Robert H. and Philip J. Cook. *The Winner Take All Society: Why the Few at the Top Get So Much More Than the Rest*. New York: Penguin, 1996.

33. Frankel, Rob in Roy Forbes, "Branding: The Last Word." *I-Advertising*, February 2000.

34. Gelbert, Doug. *So Who The Heck Was Oscar Meyer? The Real People Behind Those Brand Names*. New York: Barricade Books, Inc., 1996.

35. Gladwell, Malcolm. *The Tipping Point: How Little Things Can Make a Big Difference*. Boston: Little, Brown and Company, 2000.

36. Godin, Seth. *Permission Marketing: Turning Strangers into Friends, and Friends into Customers*. New York: Simon and Schuster, 1999.

37. Griffith, Carolyn. "Aaker Urges Universities to Get on the Brand Wagon." *Lawlor Review*, Fall 1997.

38. Griffith, Carolyn. "Shaping a Brand in the Higher Education Marketplace." *Lawlor Review*, Fall 1997.

39. Hallberg, Garth. *All Consumers Are Not Created Equal: The Differential Marketing Strategy for Brand Loyalty and Profits*. New York: John Wiley & Sons, Inc., 1995.

40. Harari, Oren. *Leapfrogging the Competition: Five Steps to Becoming a Market Leader*. California: Prima Publishing, 1999.

41. Heilemann, Anne. "The Benefits of Branding: Leverage Your Institution's Brand Eqiuity During a Comprehensive Campaign." *Currents*, January 2001.

42. Hersch, Richard H. *Intentions and Perceptions: A National Survey of Public Attitudes Toward Liberal Arts Education*. New York: Hobart and William Smith Colleges, 1996.

43. Hesel, Richard. "Winner Take-All Culture Permeates Attitudes About College Admission." *StudentPoll*, Art & Science Group, ND.

44. Hutchinson, Kevin and Patrick Opatz. "Building Trust Through Strategic Planning." *Planning for Higher Education*, Winter 1998-99.

45. Keller, Kevin Lane. "The Brand Report Card." *Harvard Business Review*, January-February 2000.

46. Keller, Kevin Lane. "Managing Brands for the Long Run: Brand Reinforcement and Revitalization Strategies." *California Management Review*, Spring 1999.

47. Keller, Kevin Lane. *Strategic Brand Management*. New York: Prentice-Hall Inc., 1998.

48. Khermouch, Gerry. "The Best Global Brands." *Business Week*, August 6, 2001.

49. Kotler, Philip and Karen Fox. *Strategic Marketing for Education Institutions*. New Jersey: Prentice-Hall, 1995.

50. Kuchinsakas, Susan. "The End of Marketing: An Interview with Regis McKenna." *Business 2.0*, Web site: http:/www.business2.com, November 2000.

51. Larson, Erik. *The Naked Consumer: How Our Private Lives Become Public Commodities*. New York: Henry Holt, 1992.

52. Lawlor, John. "Brand Identity." *Currents*, October 1998.

53. Lepla, F. Joseph and Lynn M. Parker. *Integrated Branding: Becoming Brand-Driven Through Company-Wide Action*. New York: Quorum Books, 1999.

54. Leuthesser, Lance et al. "Brand Equity: The Halo Effect Measure." *European Journal of Marketing*, 1995.

55. Light, Larry. "Brand Erosion: A Waste of Assets." *Business Marketing*, August 1993.

56. Light, Larry. *Building Brand Relationships: The Trustmaker's Road to Enduring Profitable Growth*. New York: The Coalition For Brand Equity, 1993.

57. Light, Larry and Richard Morgan. *The Fourth Wave: Brand Loyalty Marketing*. New York: Coalition for Brand Equity, 1994.

58. Lloyd, Martin. "Five Ideas about Branding, Online Response to Roy Forbes, I-Advertising." InternetAdvertising.org, February 14, 2000.

59. Lucas, James R. *Fatal Illusions: Shredding a Dozen Unrealities That Can Keep Your Organization from Success*. New York: AMACOM, 1997.

60. Masiter, David H., et al. *The Trusted Advisor*. New York: The Free Press, 2000.

61. Marconi, Joe. *The Brand Marketing Book: Creating, Managing, and Extending the Value of Your Brand*. Chicago: NTC Business Books, 1999.

62. Marconi, Joe. *Image Marketing: Using Public Perceptions to Attain Business Objectives*. Chicago: NTC Business Books, 1996.

63. Martin, David N. *Romancing the Brand*. New York: AMACOM, 1989.

64. McCulloch, Lane. "Branding Campaign Basics." Workz.com., November 2000.

65. McKenna, Regis. *Real Time: Preparing for the Age of the Never Satisfied Customer*. Cambridge: Harvard Business School Press, 1999.

66. Metzler, Ken. *Creative Interviewing: The Writer's Guide to Gathering Information by Asking Questions*. Chicago: Allyn and Bacon, 1996.

67. Ogilvy, David. *Confessions of an Advertising Man*. New York: Atheneum, 1980.

68. Payne, Stanley. *The Art of Asking Questions*. Princeton: Princeton University Press, 1980.

69. Randazzo, Sal. *Mythmaking on Madison Avenue: How Advertisers Apply the Power of Myth and Symbolism to Create Leadership Brands*. Salem: Probus Publishing, 1993.

70. Rhodes, David. "Building a Successful Experience Brand." Boston Consulting Group Web site, (BGC.com), December 2000.

71. Ries, Al and Jack Trout. *Positioning: The Battle for Your Mind*. New York: McGraw-Hill, 1981.

72. Ries, Laura and Al Ries. *The 22 Immutable Laws of Branding: How to Build a Product or Service into a World-Class Brand*. New York: HarperCollins, 1998.

73. Ries, Laura and Al Ries. *The 11 Immutable Laws of Internet Branding*. New York: Harper Collins, 2000.

74. Schultz, Don and Jeffrey Walters. *Measuring Brand Communication ROI*. New York: Association of National Advertisers, 1997.

75. Senge, Peter et al. *The Dance of Change: The Challenges of Sustaining Momentum in Learning Organizations*. New York: Doubleday, 1999.

76. Sevier, Robert A. "Brand as Relevance." *White Paper # 8*, Cedar Rapids, IA: Stamats Communications, 2000.

77. Sevier, Robert A. "A Branding Primer." *White Paper # 10*, Cedar Rapids, IA: Stamats Communications, 2001.

78. Sevier, Robert A. "A Review of Perceptual-Mapping Techniques as the Essential First Component of a Larger Institutional Image-Enhancement Strategy." *CASE International Journal of Educational Advancement,* Summer 2000.

79. Sevier, Robert A. "Shifts and Nudges Revisited: Important Lessons from Old and New Approaches to Marketing Colleges and Universities." *Admissions Marketing Report*, January 2001.

80. Sevier, Robert A. *Strategic Planning in Higher Education: Theory and Practice*. Washington, D.C.: CASE Books, 2000.

81. Sevier, Robert A. *Thinking Outside the Box*. Iowa: Strategy Publishing, 2001.

82. Silverstein, Michael. "Creating a Flawless Brand Experience." Boston Consulting Group Web site, (BGC.com), December 2000.

83. Simonson, Alex and Bernd H. Schmitt. *Marketing Esthetics: The Strategic Management of Brands, Identity and Image*. Free Press, 1997.

84. Stalk, George. "Experience Your Brand." Boston Consulting Group Web (BGC.com), December 2000.

85. Travis, Daryl. *Emotional Branding*. California: Prima Publishing, 2000.

86. Trout, Jack. *Differentiate or Die*. New York: John Wiley & Sons, 2000.

87. Trout, Jack. *The New Positioning: The Latest on the World's #1 Business Strategy*. New York: McGraw-Hill, Inc., 1996.

88. VandenBerg, Patricia. "Singular Sensation: Developing and Rolling Out a Unified Brand Identity for the University of Massachusetts." *Currents*, March 2000.

89. Webber, Alan M. "What Great Brands Do." *Fast Company* Web, November 2000.

90. Weilbacher, William M. *Brand Marketing: Building Winning Brand Strategies That Deliver Value and Customer Satisfaction.* Chicago: NTC Business Books, 1993.

91. Wiechmann, Jack G. and James R. Gregory. *Leveraging the Corporate Brand.* Chicago: NTC Business Books, 1997.

92. Wilemon, William H. "Your Message Here." AGB *Trusteeship*, May/June 2000.

93. Winkler, Agnieszka M. "The Six Myths of Branding." *Brandweek*, September 20, 1999.

94. Woodruff, Jan. "Marketing Darwinism: Successful Brand Evolution in a Product-Driven Culture (A Brand –New Way of Thinking)." *American Marketing Association Proceedings*, Baltimore, Maryland, November 2000.

95. Zievis, Mary Lou. "Beauty Is Only Skin Deep. It's What's Inside That Makes a Brand." *FSM*, September/October 2000.

96. ____. *Harvard Business Review on Brand Management.* Cambridge: Harvard Business School Press, 1999.

97. ____. "Two Business-Building Principles From Warren Buffett." *Leadership* Newsletter, November 1999.

98. ____. "90 Days to a Better Brand." *Promo* Magazine, March 2001.

■■■■■

End Notes

[1]This branding IQ test was modeled after a similar test developed by Rob Frankel. I modified the questions and answers to reflect the higher education marketplace.

[2]An earlier version of this chapter appeared in *Thinking Outside the Box*, published in 2001 by Strategy Publishing.

[3]Adopted from C. Britt Beemer's, *It Takes a Prophet to Make a Profit.*

[4]See Diane Bentley, "Stand by Your Brand."

[5]See Morrisbeecher.com.

[6]See robfrankel.com.

[7]ibid.

[8]Interview by Joe Mansuerto, *Leadership* Newsletter, November 1999.

[9]I am embarrassed to admit that I do not have the citation for this information. I know it came from the *Journal of Marketing* but I am at a loss as to what issue or when.

[10]This graphic was adapted from a graphic developed by SMART as depicted on their Web site: s-m-a-r-t.com.

[11]Ongoing branding forum at I-Marketing.com; Martin Lloyd can be reached at martin@domino.com.

[12]Originally I had called this step "keep your promise" but during dinner one cold December night a good friend stressed that for the brand to be successful, it had to be "lived" by the organization.

[13]See my book, *Strategic Planning in Higher Education: Theory and Practice.*

[14]I touched on this issue repeatedly in my earlier book, *Thinking Outside the Box.*

[15]David Rhodes, Boston Consulting Group Web site, (BGC.com).

[16]As you look over these three sets of questions you will notice a bit of overlap. It is less important which question is asked as part of which audit as long as all important questions are asked.

[17]Sharp-eyed readers will recognize that some of this material on the creation of a communication plan was covered in an earlier book, *Creating an Effective Integrated Marketing Communication Plan.* While some of the nuances have been adjusted to reflect the branding emphasis, the basic planning steps are largely the same.

[18]This section is drawn from my previous book, *Thinking Outside the Box.*

[19]These kinds of questions are the focus of the final brand characteristic: strengthening your brand promise.

[20]The title of this chapter is inspired by a book with the same by Jack Trout. However, this phrase has been well-presented in marketing and branding for a number of years.

[21]This material was presented in my earlier book, *Thinking Outside the Box.*

[22]For more information on portfolio analyses you might want to take a look at Carl Stern's *Perspectives on Strategy from the Boston Consulting Group* (New York: Wiley and Son, 1997).

[23]This chapter is addresses the creation of a graphic look. It is important to note that a graphic look is not the same thing as a brand. While brands do include a look, they are much more comprehensive in nature.

[24]Clearly the third essential question is closely related to the four essential steps in the brand promise.

[25]A portion of this chapter was previously published in the *CASE International Journal of Educational Advancement,* Summer 2000.

■■■■■

Also Available from Strategy Publishing

Thinking Outside the Box: *Some (fairly) Radical Thoughts*
on How Colleges and Universities Should Think, Act, and
Communicate in a Very Busy Marketplace.

Thinking Outside the Box stresses action and results. It begins with the need for the creation of a coherent go-to-market <u>strategy</u> based on a careful assessment of the problems and opportunities that are before you and on the creation of a vision that focuses rather than diffuses time, talent, and resources.

Thinking Outside the Box then builds the case for strategic <u>action</u> that galvanizes and inspires. Strategies for overcoming complacency as well as six audacious moves that will significantly impact how you market your institution are included in the book.

Thinking Outside the Box concludes with a series of proven ideas to help you <u>communicate</u> more aggressively in a marketplace that is easily distracted and overwhelmed with messages.

Available from Strategy Publishing at
www.strategypublishing.com

About the Author

Dr. Robert A. Sevier is a Senior Vice President at Stamats. With nearly 50 years of experience in the higher education marketplace, Stamats is one of America's most experienced higher education research, planning, marketing communication, and consulting companies.

Each year, Sevier directs more than 100 research studies and helps nearly a dozen colleges with their marketing and strategic plans. He has also written more than 60 articles for *Currents*, *The Journal of College Admissions*, *Trusteeship*, *Communication World*, *Admission Strategist*, and *College and University Journal*, and conducted more than 400 seminars, workshops, and presentations for the AAU, CASE, NAICU, NACAC, ACT, AACRAO, CIC, CCCU, AAU, NACCAP, the AMA, NCMPR, and the College Board. His work has also been reproduced extensively in ERIC and he writes a monthly column on marketing and planning for *University Business*.

In 1998, Sevier authored *Integrated Marketing for Colleges, Universities, and Schools*. Published by CASE, it is the most comprehensive book on educational marketing available. In 1999, he co-edited another book for CASE, *Integrated Marketing Communication*. His third book, *Strategic Planning in Higher Education: Theory and Practice*, also for CASE, was published late Fall 2000. Finally, Sevier published *Thinking Outside the Box: Some (fairly) Radical Thoughts on How Colleges and Universities Should Think, Act, and Communicate in a Very Busy Marketplace* in 2001. This book is available from Strategy Publishing (strategypublishing.com).

Prior to Stamats, Sevier worked in the public and media relations offices of the Oregon Health Sciences University in Portland and Denison University in Ohio. Sevier also taught at Mount Vernon Nazarene College and The Ohio State University.

Sevier earned a Ph.D. from The Ohio State University in 1986 in Policy Analysis and Higher Education Administration. His dissertation, titled, "Freshmen at Competitive Liberal Arts Colleges: A Survey of Factors Influencing Institutional Choice," involved a nationwide study of how college-bound high school students choose a college. He also holds an M.S. degree in Journalism/Public Relations from the University of Oregon (1979).

Bob can be reached at (800) 553-8878 or bob.sevier@stamats.com.

July 2002

About Stamats

Stamats is a full-service higher education research, planning, marketing communications, and consulting company serving college and university presidents, boards, and senior administrators nationwide.

Stamats' services and products are organized into two broad categories: consulting services and creative services.

Consulting services include:

- Market research including image and perception, and competitive positioning studies
- Audits including brand, recruiting, and academic program marketability
- Planning including strategic, brand, integrated marketing, and recruiting
- Staff development
- Consulting

Creative services include:

- Publications including print materials for student recruiting and fundraising
- Interactive media including the Internet/Web, CD-ROM, and DVD
- Traditional media including print, radio, and outdoor advertising

Stamats has a variety of resources available on its Web site including the Great Stamats Tagline Repository, downloadable copies of White Paper series, a gallery of work completed for clients, and a list of awards and recognitions. You can contact Bob Sevier at (800) 553-8878 or bob.sevier@stamats.com. The Stamats URL is www.stamats.com.

Every year, more than 100 colleges and universities nationwide rely upon Stamats' research, planning, consulting, and communications services to help them keep their promises.

STAMATS
Promises kept.